WILD-FOWLERS AND POACHERS

A SPICY YARN

'WHEN THE LONG TALE, RENEW'D WHEN LAST THEY MET,
IS SPLIC'D ANEW, AND IS UNFINISH'D YET.'

Crabbe

WILD-FOWLERS AND POACHERS

FIFTY YEARS ON THE EAST COAST

BY

ARTHUR HENRY PATTERSON

REVISED EDITION

EDITED AND INTRODUCED
BY
TONY JACKSON

Ashford Press Publishing
Southampton
1988

Published by Ashford Press Publishing 1988
1 Church Road
Shedfield
Hampshire SO3 2HW

First published in 1929

Re-published in 1988

British Library Cataloguing-in-Publication Data

Patterson, Arthur Henry
Wildfowlers and poachers.
1. Fowling — England — Norfolk — History
I. Title II. Jackson, Tony
799.2'44'09426 SK331

ISBN 1-85253-021-9

CONTENTS

LIST OF PLATES

LIST OF ILLUSTRATIONS IN THE TEXT

INTRODUCTION

TONY JACKSON

EVERY era, however parochial it may seem to bystanders at the time, should have its chronicler, its Samuel Pepys, to record the incidents, the trivia and the commonplace which are the skeletal frame of history. Wildfowling has never wanted for descriptive writers, from Colonel Peter Hawker to Stanley Duncan, Jimmy Wentworth Day and latterly Tim Sedgwick and Peter Whitaker. Yet, curiously enough, the latter part of the 19th century, that strangely evocative period of the gentlemen gunners, the longshoremen and the bird collectors, has been largely neglected, with one notable exception – the works of Arthur Henry Patterson.

Now valuable collectors' items in their own right, A.H. Patterson's books, devoted solely to eastern Norfolk, are pure magic and deserve a much wider audience. With a brilliant, facile pen Patterson lovingly drew the men and women of Breydon from the 1870s to the early years of the century. He moved among and was accepted as one of them, observing their idiosyncracies and speech with an attentive ear and able to convey, through his writing, that wonderful lilting Norfolk dialect which, to my mind, is perhaps the most sonorous of all rural accents.

Patterson was born in 1857 and died on October 28, 1935. Thus his life span embraced the days of the great bird collectors, men such as "Squire" Booth, and he was to observe the true foundations of wildfowling as we know it today. Peter Hawker, who had shot through the early years of the 19th century, is often referrred to as the Father of wildfowling and, in the sense that he wrote the first major work on the subject, then so he was. Yet, in a sense, Hawker was an aberration living out of his time. Longshore fowling was in those distant days a livelihood, a very tough one to boot, and was seldom looked upon as a sport or recreation.

It was not till the latter part of the century when communications and leisure had expanded, that the gentlemen gunners became an established part of the shooting scene. Suddenly a whole new vista opened up before them. Imagine vast acreages of foreshore, virtually unshot and available at no cost, other than the hire of guides. Wildfowl still proliferated in vast numbers, bird protection laws were embryonic or could not be applied so that, for a brief period, amateur fowlers enjoyed a Utopian existence and knew few restraints, other than weather or physical hardship.

In his early days Patterson was himself a keen gunner, ever ready to pick up a gun and try for flighting duck, geese or a handful of waders yet, as he admits, time mellowed his ardour and he was at last content to watch, observe and record the wildlife of his beloved Breydon without the desire to lift a gun. Yet he was never a hypocrite on this score; not for him to condemn the gunners working hard for their livelihood, even though he may have pitied the muddy, bedraggled corpses lying in the bottom of the returning punt or hawked round the bird dealers for a few shillings.

Today, with the benefit of that easy virtue, hindsight, we can raise our hands in horror and condemn the bird collectors for their greedy, irresponsible selfishness. Yet one must understand the era and appreciate that ornithology was still in its infancy. Bird numbers appeared inexhaustable and knowledge, for the serious bird enthusiast, could only be acquired by handling the actual creature – or so it seemed at the time.

The great bird collections were assembled during this period, not the least of which was the Booth collection which is still on display at the Booth Museum, Dyke Road in Brighton. There one can see case after case of beautifully mounted birds, each one taken in Britain and, with the exception of a small additional collection, every bird was shot by Edward Booth. Several references are made to the "Squire" in this book, for the East Coast was a source of much of his material and one senses the eagerness with which every specimen was sought and notes the generosity which rewarded fruitful information.

Much of the amusement to be derived from "Wild-fowlers and Poachers" lies in the vivid description of the ceaseless warfare between the gunners collecting rare birds to sell on to collectors and the "Watcher", the first warden appointed when the Close Seasons Acts came into force. Little Pintail Thomas, for instance, was a constant thorn in his flesh, roving the marshes for avocets or spoonbills and returning from each foray apparently empty-handed. Then the little rascal would collect Mrs Pintail from the Bowling Green inn, row her upstream for "a blow" and back again under the eye of the Watcher. But on the return journey the insides of her petticoats would be laden with Pintail's feathered spoils!

The charm of this delightful book lies in A.H. Patterson's unique ability to convey to the reader the period atmosphere, the smell of the salt flats, the vast, vaulting skies of the east coast, the clouds of wildfowl and the bustling self-absorbed village community of the late Victorian period. For him each of the rough, self-reliant fishermen-fowlers, relying on their nets and guns for their meagre livelihood, was a character well worthy of John Knowlittle's pen.

Much beloved and respected by the simple folk amongst whom he lived and moved, Patterson was widely known as "John Knowlittle", though he used his own name as an author. From his earliest days an enthusiastic naturalist whose whole existence was wrapped up in studying the fauna of East Anglia, he had a brief spell as a head keeper in a north country zoo in 1884 and a short period in Dublin Zoo. But his real love was the Broads and in this, and his other books, he has left us with a penetrating and faithful picture of life on the East Coast and the changes that occured within his lifetime.

An obituary notice published in the Eastern Evening News, October 28, 1925 is worth recounting in full as it sums up the man and the affection in which he was held.

"He was always a lively and entertaining companion, with a sense of humour that served him well in his difficult early life, and ensured for him a hearty welcome wherever and whenever, he was with friends. The life he loved was that he spent alone, or with a congenial companion, in his houseboat beside the wildfowl-frequented Breydon mudflats, or in cruising in the 'Yarwhelp' on the rivers and broads. There he was as much at home as was the eel-catcher or smelt-fisher in his ark. Yet there was nothing of the recluse about him, for he was always making friends. Many of them will miss him much, as I shall, who think of him passing as if he has just sailed westward in his punt into golden sunset of the Broadland he loved."

"Wild-fowlers and Poachers" is a vivid pen-portrait of an era long past which deserves a wide and appreciative audience. I am delighted to know that Ashford Press Publishing have had the foresight to appreciate its pure, unadulterated magic. This was the ninth of Patterson's books on the Broads and Breydon and will, I hope, set the pattern for a revival of his fascinating works.

Tony Jackson
Chobham
Surrey
January 87

PREFACE

AT the age of seventy-one one has outlived the heroes of his youth and is apt to look back through the years with a touch of sadness as he recalls faces once so familiar that will not be seen again ; and when conjuring up old exploits upon salt tides and oozy flats in company with the rude, stalwart fellows who wrested a precarious livelihood from the Old Breydon Estuary, one feels lonely and derelict. It is possible to-day, on occasion, to walk upon the Breydon walls to Burgh Castle without seeing a solitary eel-fisher or gunner. The Breydon men of past years have no legitimate successors. Drainage of the vast area of marshlands, the growing up of the flats, and the decadence of bird and fish life have made of these men a now extinct race. The passing of the Wild Birds' Protection Acts forbids a resurrection. Of all the many professional punt-gunners I knew in my early manhood, at the moment of writing but one aged man survives.

I have elsewhere described the 'great broad-water' under seasonal changes of winter and summer, and under alteration of many years. The conversion of the swamps behind Yarmouth into fertile grazing marshes has been set forth in *Wild Life on a Norfolk Estuary* ; the contrast of Breydon a hundred years ago, with its condition to-day, has been hinted at before. In brief, the tidal basin was less affected by the sea, because of the sand-bar across the harbour mouth which dammed the incoming tide, and which also bridled the freshets from up-river. The mudflats were then some feet lower than to-day, and large portions of them were never bared of water. The lengthy groin, known as the Dickey-works, at the 'Berney Arms' end of Breydon, aided the change which was due to the alteration of the sand-bar. The waters of the Yare and Waveney were focused sharply into the main channel, automatically dredging it ; but what was to the benefit of shipping had a disastrous effect on the mudflats, which were no longer cleared of silt. Bygone generations of eel-men were rarely prevented from using eel-bab or eel-spear, and wild-fowlers could get about nearly all over the place without touching bottom. So fresh were Breydon waters then, and so long fresh that until the middle of the nineteenth century the common reed grew in luxuriant fringes and patches, in whose wide gaps and recesses the fowlers pushed their scows and punts and hid for flight-time, when fowl passed over Fritton Lake to the well-weeded flats or marshes to feed. The growing-up of the flats has tended to the destruction of the 'wigeon-grass', the *Zostera marina,* and year by year its area has been reduced until where acres of it grew so thickly as to be known as 'The Garden', great bald patches of mud show up at low water. A similar process has been going on in the Essex estuaries, and there, as here, the lessening of wildfowl has been partly due to this.

What the *Lincolnshire Magazine* in 1801 called 'a vast and deep fen, affording little or no benefit to the nation, except the production of great quantities of fish and fowl' is now a basin roughly four miles in length, east and west; it is a mile in width at its widest part; its irregularly running walls are a good five miles in length on either side. The great use of this tidal receptacle is to form a spending-basin for the tides to spread in, and so to give relief to the rivers. To reduce its area would mean a greater susceptibility to flooding the marshes and low-lying Norwich, and might do a vast amount of damage. The question has often been put to me, 'What can we do with Breydon?' My invariable answer has been, 'Let it alone'.

To-day the South Wall is a delightful promenade for the lover of salt tides and a great green level outlook, not to mention solitude; it is the more interesting when, in summer days, the tide is coming in with a fleet of barges and white-sailed yachts floating upon its bosom. The way is hedged in along the top of the wall by grass and spreading goosefoot, which may occasionally need a careful stride. Various thistles, hawkweeds, salt-marsh plantains, with pepperwort and sea-southernwood, not to mention lichens and mosses, variegate the pathway of greenery with sprightly colouring.

A tramp along these walls, soon after sunrise on a bright May morning, offers a very pleasant recreation, particularly if the tide be flowing in with scarce a ruffle on its surface. Parcels of black-headed gulls, with here and there some late-staying, pearly-backed common gulls, lightly rise and dip above the green water, watching for every likely bit of floating edible; whilst the greater black-backed gulls patrol the flats with tilted heads and necks upraised to greet the joyous morning. Whimbrel titter as they trot about the muds; curlews yelp; little dunlins and plovers race to and fro, seeking the choicest salt-worms and for stranded shrimps. Herons stand leg-deep and statuesquely, with yellow eyes searching in the shallows for passing eel and slithering flounder. Rooks pass to and from marsh to nesting-trees, and back again constantly. Maybe you will hear the clear, plaintive note of the grey plover, and by a careful glance through the sunlight observe it flying in from the eastward. Bird answers to bird; and you find yourself calling up another nature-lover, Robert Burns, as you catch sight of a flock of long-billed birds, and quote his pleasing rhyme:

Ye curlews calling through a clud.

In early autumn you might find a livelier crowd, when the terns are working southward from their nesting-quarters at Blakeney and Scolt Head. You may catch sight of them, dipping and splashing, as they strike at the herring-syle—baby herrings—that flash with silvery brightness at the surface of the water, and are seized by unerring bill as they play with every little bit of bent or twig floating upstream; and never will you see the tern go completely under water. Young dunlins in grey, and dunlins black-breasted, trot with ringed plovers about the moist flats, examining each 'low' for gammarus and mud-screw. Young grey herons now fish in the drains, independently of their smarter parents, though, maybe, hardly so successfully. Quite a riot of water-loving birds patrol the channel, and many a strange call-note puzzles the uninitiated ear. As you ramble, the sea-southernwood diffuses a pungent odour as you crush through it; the tall reeds in the ditches behind you, and the flowering rushes nod their tufts and plumes at you; whilst light-hearted butterflies dance gaily around you as you sweep through the long, lush grasses. Michaelmas daisies on the rond below are breaking into flower and turning up a blue eye here and there at you.

Then comes the winter of our discontent. In wildest snow-time the well-wrapped stroller finds a ramble bracing; but a weakling had better stay at home. There comes with it an anxious time for the birds; and some demoralization when the ice shuts in the waters with a relentless grip. The autumnal hordes of gulls, which came southward for the herring fishing, are mostly gone; flocks of mostly immature wigeon and mallard glide across the fretted waters wherever a wake in the ice occurs, eager to splash among the waving *Zostera* for a hurried meal. And once in a while long skeins of geese pass over in well-trimmed ranks toward the marshes; or, as the case may be, making seaward. Hooded crows prowl around, eagerly searching for wounded knot or carrion. The rambler who would add much to his pleasure had need sling a pair of binoculars across his shoulder before he slams his gate. To view Breydon when the storm is high and its waters are boiling is most exhilarating and stirs one like a tempestuous sea-breeze.

For a number of years past I have been jotting down stories of the Breydon men's adventures and exploits, not forgetting the manner of life lived by these unique outdoor men, their prowess, their hardihood, and their shortcomings. The stories herein related, with the exception of perhaps two or three, have been corroborated, 'that in the mouth of two or three witnesses every word may be established'.

I have to express my indebtedness to Messrs. Arthur Bellin, William Brand, and John Quinton, contemporaries of mine—who, like myself, followed Breydon as far back as the 'seventies—for several spicy conversations and characteristic stories.

With regard to the setting of this story of the Breydon Men, it may be well to state that the old 'Bowling Green' pub, empty and forlorn, still stands, for how long it is impossible to say. Its romantic surroundings have vanished; the 'Staff of Life' and the 'Lord Nelson' have also disappeared. Beckett's workshop has been supplanted by ugly red- and white-bricked cottages; 'Pintail' Thomas's 'pork-and-gull shop on the Hill' is now a smarter shop; Flaxman's smithy remains, but is so altered by brickwork and cement facings as to be almost unrecognizable. Gun-punt building has ceased; and to use a commonplace of the old gunners and fishermen, 'Breydon is about done for'.

And then the Birds. Migrants and strangers still visit the Estuary, and during the more important months of the year they are carefully guarded by a Watcher. From year to year their numbers fluctuate, but those of the whimbrel and the ringed plover rarely; and long may we listen, in the words of Robert Burns, to

A gentle curlew bidding kind good-night.

ARTHUR HENRY PATTERSON

BELLIN'S SPANIEL

CHAPTER I

THE 'BOWLING GREEN' PUB

MY first acquaintance with the once-famous 'Bowling Green' pub, and my introduction to the unique rabble of odd characters who loitered and gossiped away their idle hours upon the excellent green, or lolled in contemplation upon the boundary parapet that shut in the grassy level from the often turbulent waters of the Estuary entrance, dates back to the hard winter of 1870, when, on one fog-steeped November afternoon, I accompanied a newsboy chum to deliver the weekly local newspaper into the hands of bluff John Bessey, the then landlord of the inn. The rubicund face of John, with its fringing of snowy beard, and his keen blue eyes, are as fresh to my mental vision as on the day when I first saw him hanging a bucket of lively eels upon the scales, with two or three sturdy eel-babbers watching the balance keenly, as they awaited their turn to sell him their previous night's catches. Bessey came of a race of typical East Anglians, who had wrested from the Estuary an arduous livelihood with punt-gun and eel-pick and draw-net. He was the last of his line to follow Breydon. He was as exact with his ale-measures as he was with his beam-scale; and in his dual role of publican and eel merchant found much for his sinewy hands to do—for men who notably were droughty vessels, and whose guns and punts and weapons of offence that, from old age and rough usage, were in need of skilful tinkering.

That winter of 1870–1 was a memorable one to me; it was famous in the fowlers' annals for its severity—its snows and its frosts, and for the inches of its ice that covered the mudflats and drains. Against this hard covering the salt tides waged warfare, and dragged downstream a medley of big slabs and jagged floes, that broke in the drains or creeks, and surged away noisily and stubbornly to the sea. One calls to mind the tinkling of the sledge-bells in the snow-covered streets and on iron-bound roads; the pitiful condition of the redwings and fieldfares that fluttered and moped in garden and roadway, and at which we boys flung our caps; one remembers also that an otter from the Broadlands was overtaken and killed upon the frozen surface of Breydon; the shooting of five swans at a single discharge of Old Thacker's punt-gun; and a race between a man and a pony on the ice that covered the flooded marshes. Those were stirring and memorable events to an impressionable boy like myself.

To return to that gloomy November afternoon. The creaking of the tavern signboard added to the witchery of the gathering shadows. To the fishers and fowlers answering its beck it seemed to be voicing—eerily—a welcome to every open-air ruffian into that haven of warmth and refreshment, and emphasizing the fact that inside was shelter from the adverse elements, added to the comforts of a home—a refuge, indeed, where for the nonce the nagging of impecunious wives might be forgotten. There was, too, a club-like air about the place, where men of kindred occupations and tastes could discuss, over mugs and pewters, their mutual rivalries and reminiscences. Here they could emulate or flatter to their hearts' content; could bicker or jest, and jink their glasses in bibulous amity; and by closing time in right mellow good-fellowship.

My heedful boyish mind was instantly impressed by the sawdust-smothered floor—it smelt *so* like a circus! Dotted about were dust-filled spittoons; there were stuffed birds on the shelves behind the counter, in an odd setting of barrels and bottles. Rows of well-scoured pewters hung upon hooks fixed in the shelf edges, with blue-tinted mugs at intervals. But the birds held me. I had never before been so close to godwit or whimbrel, to sea-swallow or bittern: these names the landlord gave me, in answer to my eager queries. There were two smart grey plovers—'Full-eyed plovers' he named them, with their black and white chequered backs and tails, and their velvety black under-parts. 'Shot in May-time,' said he. I found afterwards that 'Pintail' and Jack Gibbs, 'Gaby' and other gunmen were much taken by this species, and each boasted a case of birds hung upon the walls as the pride of their cottages. The patrons of the house not seldom talked and gossiped Breydon birds when a stranger, dropping in, turned his eye up at the cases and asked questions about the plovers and the sheld-duck; then it was that you would note 'the developing provincialisms and humours . . . like an old tale'. Ah! those yarns and stories, too many of which are irretrievably lost to us, told in that old tap-room by these Breydonian knights of the ramrod and the pickshaft! . . .

The centre of comfort was the old iron stove, with its glowing red body, whose blackleaded chimney-pipe poked a way out through the wall. One noticed the slops of spilt ale displayed in rings and 'swidges' between the mugs and tankards on the counter, with here and there a muddy elbow perilously near to them. Still more impressive was the human aspect—the lounging smokers on the worn settles, some arguing guns and prowess with rough unmusical voices ; others as silent and meditative, yet alert to pick up advantageous gossip, with lips focused into pouting rings, like touched sea-anemones, into which short clay pipes had been thrust. The faces of the men, lined and hardened by storm and sun, were full of character, indexing a sturdy, contentious self-reliance. The smokers spat at intervals with queer precision, now into the ugly spittoons, as often into the glowing stove, which latter exercise, accompanied by a lengthening of the neck, appeared to be as often due to the emphasizing of an opinion, as to an overflow of nicotine juices. When knowing them better I found their conversation crude, incisive, picturesque, and almost invariably savouring of the wild-life pursuits that at first had allured them and then enslaved them. 'Once a water-dog, always a water-dog.' Their jests were coarse, their laughter hearty and gross, their expletives, whether used in good-fellowship or in anger, were usually apt, but discomposing, maybe, to a stranger to water-side provincialisms.

To-day the men and their vocations have vanished. The rambler upon the walls of Breydon now rarely sees more than a boat or two with a crew of two men each plying their nets for smelts ; a solitary fellow in a worn-out boat throwing out an eel-line, or dropping in a few eel-pots, hoping to find a stone or so of eels in them on the following morning. In spring the Bird Watcher creeps around with his punt, or aims a pair of worn binoculars at passing yachting folk ; and when I wander upon the grass-topped walls, or ramble upon the marshlands—the habitat of a lost and departed brotherhood —I feel as lonely and bereaved as old Job upon his scrap-heap. Sometimes as I loiter at Stone-corner, or perch myself upon a marsh-rail, I recall those rugged faces vividly to mind ; those muddy, tanned slops and oily boots ; I seem still to inhale the acrid grey fog of tobacco smoke, the reek of moist, warm clothing, and the stale odour of sundry liquors. The old pub still stands, naked, empty, and decadent ; the elm-trees are gone ; the bowling-green covered with tons of tarry road material. Hungry spiders only people the tap-room which was these men's parlour, club-room—call it sanctuary, if you will —where warmth loosened their tongues as it thawed their often frozen clothing. The poet Crabbe must have known and associated with their like in the bar-parlour of the ancient 'Anchor' at Aldeburgh:

It may not be thought out of place if I quote some lines written of one night's lonely vigil in my punt, as we lay moored beside the Watcher's house-boat in the middle of Breydon, when so dense a fog came on that I could not see the nose of my little boat.

'By a quarter to twelve I had turned Stake six, and gone up the Ship Drain, and moored to Jary's house-boat. He was not there, and so in the midst of 2,000 acres of mud and water —both in turn—I lashed to, put up my fixtures by feeling, and turned in for the night.

'As I peered over the waters in the silence I thought I saw the ghosts of Breydon, of many an old sporting "pal", long-since vanished from tidal waters. Passed me ghostly punt and smelt-boat, with noiseless oar-dip, carrying shadowy guns and nets. Hallo! "Snicker", and a hail to "Short 'un" Page; but the dead went mutely by. Passed by "Pintail" Thomas in search of phantom avocets and spoonbills; and Fielding Harmer, the Breydon authority of his generation, fading like his contemporaries—"Salt-fish" Jex, Billy Sampson, "Limpenny Joe", giant eel-men in their day—with "Silky" Watson peering over the rail adown his flint-lock fowling gun at spirit wigeon, the cool breezes of the Styx a-fluttering his long grey ringlets; whilst the spectre of gaunt "Cadger" Brown, off on some phantom poaching expedition, was silhouetted on the estuary wall. As we grow older how more real the past becomes to us. . . . These were Men once, "going away with long duck-guns, with water-tight boots . . . (seeking) teal, sheldrakes, whistlers, black ducks, ospreys . . . such (men) as they who sit in parlours never dream of.

'. . . I had been the only living soul on Breydon the whole night, and felt like Fenimore Cooper's *Last of the Mohicans* weeping over his lost prairies, his dead tribe, and the extirpation of his buffaloes.'

The green attached to the tavern was one of some half dozen dotted about on the outskirts of the town, that provided amusement and recreation for the townsfolk, who, perforce, spent most of their holidays and idling times within the boundaries of the town. Old guide-books and 'tours' of the town spoke of the 'Bowling Green', early in the seventeenth century, as a favourite resort, when Church dignitaries, sporting folk, and river-side dwellers resorted there to enjoy their old-time pleasures. Onc Deacon Davies, as far back as 1689, remarked that 'after dinner Mr. Crow sat with me, and with him I went to the Green to see Mr. Milbourn play bowls.' Sylas Neville, a local 'Mr. Pepys', scribbled a great deal about the townsmen's recreations, himself went shooting on Breydon, when writing in 1771, making an entry of one special event, He also says, 'I went with Walker to the Bowling Green on the Quay'. In all probability he might have told us of sailing-matches, of wrestling bouts and boxing, of cock-fights, and of flower-covered rustic bowers for those who sat and drank and flirted.

There was but one house of amusement—the old theatre; there were no reckers, piers, beach-gardens, charabancs, or motors. The railways did not run excursions before the 'forties; and a coach journey to Norwich was somewhat of an undertaking. In 1725 the coach set out in the morning at nine, 'and making no dinner by the way'. It is recorded that the 'Green' was 'a great resort for the Tory Party, where the leaders made open-air harangues, and the working and independent electors indulged in beer'. And hereat one might enjoy lively views of many sailing-craft, as well as the finest sunsets in East Anglia. In an ancient 'Norfolk Tour' occurs the following: 'The Bowling Green is pleasantly situated upon the east bank of the river, and the assembly-room being open two nights in every week during the bathing season, agreeable entertainment can seldom be wanting'—an excellent testimonial to the then cleaner condition of the confluent waters.

In the 'seventies and 'eighties the 'Bowling Green' pub was yet well-peopled and prospering; the most noted of the wild-fowlers were still in the prime of life, or in its earliest decadence. Thc well-trampled green, which extended from the house-front to the water-side parapet, flourishing for all the shuffling of heavy feet; the tall elms ran around three sides of the square, leaving the water view free and unshaded. In summer evenings there gathered a crowd of idlers—local tradesfolk, gunners, fisherfolk—when the tides were unfavourable; and others for whom the water-side had attraction. On the long seats provided they sat and gossiped, watching the players; boy waiters with white aprons trotted about with refreshments. Idlers had but to turn, or saunter to the parapet, and lounging thereon, watch the white-sailed yachts and laden wherries sail by, and out into the sunset that tinted their pathway with golden rippling. It was always entertaining to sidle up to a group of gossipers—gunners, eel-men,

A NORFOLK WHERRY
'FORGES ITS WAY UP-CHANNEL'

river-poachers, yachtsmen, yarning of past adventures and discussing anticipated new ones, of possibly great deeds and still-remembered misdeeds. Their boats and catches and guns and birds were favourite topics ; and many a delightful bit of observation recounted upon the ways and doings of strange and beautiful birds that came to the mudflats and marshes.

Here and there a shrimper, laying-to at the staithe, might be mending his nets ; another giving a touch of paint to his small ship ; yet another would be cutting new tholes for his boat out of bits of sound, hard wood. By the quay-side punt and shrimp-boat tugged at painter and hawser, as if eager to be off and join the small fleet of eel-catchers and smelters gliding upstream to their fishing quarters. In coarse weather, when north-westerly winds fretted the waters, the restive craft were rowed round the corner into the sheltered Bure, to be moored in safer quarters.

On either side the 'Bowling Green' premises stood rough boat-sheds, boat-builders' workshops, and warehouses ; there were rollered slopes for hauling up the punts, and landing-stages. In late years all these have been swept away. Opposite, on the Cobholm side, there still stand boat- and yacht-sheds, but whose tenants are of an entirely different order.

Nearly two thousand tides had frolicked upstream from the sea, and as many ebbs had drawn them back to it, between my first glimpse of the old pub and when I first flung my painter over a mooring stump near the 'Bowling Green' staithe ; tired enough was I, after having rowed my first punt down from Oulton Broad, to hear the water-man's hail from the quayside : '*Here you go, then.*' It seemed to me a kind of password into the homogeneity of the Breydon brotherhood —who were no crowd of saints nor wholly impossible sinners ; landsmen bunched the whole crowd together. I am bound to confess that a few odd fellows well deserved the name given to them of 'Breydon Pirates', and owned to the title without blush or protest. In most of them there ran a streak of the blood of the old Saxon and Danish sea-rovers—in the professional yachtsmen and wherrymen in particular of those old days ; and almost to a man the Breydon folk had shared in every occupation incidental to riverway and ocean, as smacksmen, herring-drifters, coasters, and before the mast on wider seas.

The wherryman has been for generations an outstanding figure on our inland waters ; his graceful vessel, unique in its beautiful lines, adds to the picturesqueness of Broadland, its 'crossin' o' Breydon' to the charm of an Estuary sunset, even dignity to the ruffled waters as it forges its way up-channel on the breeze-swept tide. The wherryman in the past century was the dominating figure of Breydon. In the chronicles of the port it is stated that, in 1875, there were no less than 112 sailing wherries, with a carrying power of 1,963 tons, 'being an increase of 93 tons for the year' ; this meant many crews of two men ; sometimes the boy assisted the father, and here and there was a helpmate in the 'Lady of the Barge'. Wherry-building has ceased to-day ; and but thirty sailing wherries are afloat. Here and there old hulks have been scuttled in weak places to protect the river banks. The handy little river tug of to-day heads its team of ugly iron lighters Norwich-wards, each of them able to carry several times the tonnage of the 30-ton and 40-ton craft of the past. These move to and fro without daring to stay at suspicious quarters or rest at the river-side pubs ; which removes incentives to lapses from grace.

It has been admitted that honest intentions in the past were not always carried out ; and many a sack of coal or grain never reached its destination ; and was not there a glaring case, not so long ago, where erring wherrymen, with a craft of 30-tons capacity, were found guilty of charging a Corporation for 40-ton loads of road material?

One prefers to think of the wherryman in our memories of Broadland beauty, in which he and his vessel have so largely figured; and one heaves a sigh to know that steam afloat and petrol on the roads will eventually see him drop out. He lived a precarious existence, for storm and calm were ever against him, and freightage rates were often crippling. His pleasures were few; he was rarely long ashore; indeed, many of the fraternity lived in the little cabin, with here and there one with a wife and little family sharing it.

In the 'seventies and 'eighties, it was a pleasure to lean on the 'Bowling Green' parapet, with a gossiping fowler or landsman at either elbow, to watch the fleets of graceful craft, laden with merchandise, sail by into Breydon, as a rippling tide and a cool south-easterly breeze bowled them away into the golden sunset and the empurpling distance. The silent skipper was content with the glorious prospect as he stood in the cockpit, with buttocks planted against the tiller, lolling with elbows on the cabin-top, smoking his old 'du-dee', whilst a curl of bluey coal smoke coiled away from the red square chimney and evaporated ere it reached the mudflats. Maybe, the missus, who at a pinch could help at helm and handle the sheet, was busy with tea-time preparations down below; the big kettle steamed brownly, for these good folks used 'biled tea', to save a 'copply' teapot, whilst on the gridiron kippers or bloaters or 'blacks', dripped fat into the fire that spurted into little flames fitfully. Often when the breeze was spirited, a lively competitive impulse entered into rival skippers, and impromptu races ensued, when the best sailors forged ahead, or the light craft beat the heavily laden, and left it behind with the stragglers. In long black and white lines the saddle-back gulls preened their feathers after the eventide foraging; curlews called to curlews that flew overhead and on migration, or chortled to their fellows that still probed soft ooze for red mud-worm, or juvenile clam and cockle; whilst slatey-hued herons loped upon their long green legs, and, with every sense alert, sought heedless little flounders and slithery eels in the shallows.

On a moonlight night some of the wherries would sail on until the breeze died away, and then would moor beside a rond or river's bank until morning. Sailing was not always ideal, for gusty storm and floating ice meant hours of idleness; once in a decade, perhaps for weeks, they lay ice-bound. Breydon and river were busy highways in those good old days.

Certain of the wherrymen indulged in a little sport once

in a while : a gun hung in the cabin, always loaded, in readiness for a shot at a fowl paddling about on the river, or for a pot-shot at a hare on the marshes ; some of them boasted a light open boat that could be towed behind. Maybe, one here and there had a cast- or draw-net, which was handy for a bit of illicit fishing ; a few liggers were easily hidden away in a convenient locker. On occasion the river bailiff discovered a ton or so of poached freshwater fish hidden in the wherry hold, under a sail, or it may be under a heap of ice ; for wherryman and fish-poacher, if not chummy, were often on terms of tolerance. Sometimes a wherryman was genuinely surprised to find such a cargo smuggled on board.

The 'Lady of the Barge' had a way of her own : two wherrymen lay with their empty craft by the quay-side near the North River refuse-pits, then inelegantly known as the 'muck-holes' ; the more refined knew them as 'Spice Islands'. Town refuse and night-soil were dumped into big square pits, where is now situated the Yacht Station. From thence some of the older wherries frequently went laden up-river, for the benefit of the marsh-dwelling farmers. Alas ! local modern sanitary methods have scarcely improved upon the old-time system.

The said brace of wherrymen were revelling over-long in the tap-room of the 'White Swan', under the shadow of the North-west Tower—which continued idleness their penurious spouses greatly resented. Finding their drunken mates incapable of loading or sailing, or even walking the plank, they repaired to the 'Islands', and themselves barrowed the cargo into the wherry-hold ; caught the flood tide, hoisted sail, and proceeded upstream. At Stokesby they delivered the goods—which they did with some protest and considerable satisfaction. Their practical joke was much relished by riverside dwellers.

Among their women-kind were several who were not a little strong-minded. One business-like home ruler, Mrs. Thomas, was not to be trifled with by the interesting little Pintail : her look was demand, her word was law, and if Master Johnny felt rebellious, so long as she could shepherd him away from the 'Bowling Green' or the 'Lord Nelson', he was more or less amenable. On more than one occasion she had been seen to help push off his punt from the quay-side and order him to get to business, waiting a while to see that he did not within due time return. I may admit that these forceful resources were incidental to certain knowledge, on her part, of some rare bird or other seen or talked of—which it was her desire to prove by an early production of the creature in his possession. My old friend Thomas was not the only hen-hustled wild-fowler.

Several of the old generation of Breydoners had died since that afternoon which found me a new-comer to the old ' Bowling Green ' ; others had passed the meridian of their manhood, but still pursued wigeon and mallard in their season, still prowled around after rare bird visitors, and spread their nets for smelt and mullet. Here and there a son who had inherited his sire's ancient punt and gun, his eel-picks and his tarry old ark, as well as his predatory instincts, literally had stepped into the old man's water-boots. The older stagers had no alternative but to keep afloat or retire to the workhouse ; or, if a lucky chance favoured one or another, he took his ' little sticks ' into Yarmouth's most beneficent institution, the Fishermen's Hospital, to spend the remainder of his days basking and gossiping in the sunshine, placidly burning his 'bacca, until the Great Scythe-wielder levelled him, as the reaper mows his ripened corn.

Bessey, the tavern-keeper, had grown greyer, but still pulled at the beer-pumps, still tinkered at the defective weapons, still weighed the buckets of eels brought in by muddy hands, weighing the receptacles against the total, after the eels had been shot into the pontoon lying in the shadow of the railway bridge. Various coins were placed into extended palms, to be grumbled over if the catches realized a penny a pound less than yesterday's, as they meandered off to a favourite pub for consolation, thence to wander home to a typical breakfast of fried flounders, or a stew of undersized eels made savoury by onions and potatoes, the Breydon man's favourite dish. It may be that the eels were those that had died in the eel-trunk ; therefore not to be sent to Billingsgate, but fresh enough for the catcher's table.

In the old days there were plenty of eels in rivers and Breydon, and plenty of eel-men that went after them. Prices ruled high or low as the market figures fluctuated. Sixpence a pound for big eels, half that per pound for small ones ; it was all right if a stone or more came to the ' bab ', or were gripped by the eel-pick ; but bad times heavily punctuated the pursuit, as when storm and frost affected the waters, or droughts parched the earth, when the earthworms tunnelled far beneath the vibration of ' wriggling-iron ' and spade-work,

THE FAMOUS 'BOWLIN' GREEN' STAITHE

From a Water-colour drawing by the late C. H. Harrison (1879)

and spoiled their fishing. How they lived then—some of them—was only known to themselves and women-kind; as for themselves, a gossip and smoke on the Green was by no means a hardship to most of them.

'Hullo, Sharper!' said W. B., as he rowed past a quaint old eel-catcher in Breydon Channel, 'what luck?'

'Nothin', bor, nothin' much,' replied Sharper, accidentally dropping his stump of black clay pipe on the bottom boards as he turned. 'Nothin', only a few little titty-totty ones, d—— 'em.'

'Then, why the deuce do you waste your time going after 'em?'

Sharper, looking at his shattered pipe, shook his tousled head, as he lifted and swung the lead sinker with its bunch of threaded worms into the boat. 'Theer's another darned titty-totty little 'un!'

'All right, Sharper,' said my friend. 'You're like them angling fellows: the bad fisherman always brags about his catches, and the monster fish he just lost; sly, lucky old dogs merely grumble, and say nothing.' I think that is so. But 'titty-totty little eels' was the regular excuse to save trouble, or to get rid of another eel-catcher whose roving around had not yet brought him to the spot where good eels were running and biting.

Charlie Higham, Breydoner, in the finer months drifted in his house-boat upstream, and moored her at some spot conveniently near a broad for his eel-catching. A jovial wherryman bowling along towards him one early morning bawled out, 'Charlie, boy, kin yew let us have a pound or tew o' eels for a fry?'

'Neery a one!' shouted back the old fellow. 'Duin' orful bad; I'm only gettin' a few little titty-totty warmin not wuth a haulin' out.'

On returning a day or two after with his wherry he asked the same again of Charlie.

'No, bor, no! Nothin' duin'; got only a few little titty-totty b——s.'

So it went on, till one day the persevering wherryman came by again, and on putting the usual question received the same unsatisfactory answer.

'I'm right down glad on it, Charlie!' came the wherryman's voice across the stream; 'and I'm awful sorry, for I jist now run'd into yar big old eel-trunk, and busted her up!'

'Oh, my blissed father!' groaned the old fellow, 'and

theer go eight stone o' good eels!'

Most of the fowlers and fishers had a strong objection to being overlooked, and when doing fairly well had a decided dislike to being questioned; they had, too, certain unwritten laws, that they must not be ousted from their 'place' or 'turn'. Gunners and eel-men resented too near an approach of passers-by. It was against their policy for an eel-catcher to use an eel-pick upon the flats or among the *Zostera* when babbing time had come along, for the disturbing forces of such a procedure disquieted the feeding eels and dispersed them.

The 'Bowling Green' premises were so shut off from the public highway and traffic, yet so easy of access, that for generations it was the favourite resort, not only of those who found their livelihood on the estuary forefronting it, but of those who made friendship or profit an excuse for frequent visitation. Certain fish-poachers found the staithe, and the adjoining boat-sheds, handy places for the fishes they had netted; to shooters and bird-collectors it was also convenient for departure or return. The crabbers' carts from Cromer and Sheringham, before the railways were accessible, came hither for peds of fresh flounders from the nets of the Breydoners. Amateur gunners whose boats were in safe quarters were much in evidence; the police, however hot the day or cold the night, rarely visited the place—it was 'off their beat'. Our especial lady friend—good Mrs. Thomas—passed with impunity to and fro, sometimes with forbidden birds suspended about her, under cover of her skirt: who would dare—even a 'self-appointed' amateur watcher—who would dare to search a lady?

Old 'Ducker' Chambers, the first Bird Watcher appointed, was then in the autumn of his life: a man of large build, bluff and boisterous, and not over officious. He had come back to Cobholm Island from Breydon on the Saturday evening for a night ashore, a rather regular habit of his that was only too well known to the sporting fraternity, and was not seldom taken advantage of. His favourite hotel was the 'Bravo Tavern', where he gossiped and recuperated, and kept his ears open, until certain repeated 'measures' had been emptied, when two or three somewhat interested chums would stand treats for other pints; these were administered with skilful flattery, until he began to hiccough, and then to snore. I never saw the process myself, but it was said that ten pints was his capacity; some of the crowd vowed the limit was a much greater count. On this particular Sunday morning he remained late in bed, sleeping off the effects of his previous night's exploit, when 'Jiggy' Hall, a young punt-gunner, and esteemed an excellent fowler, who had cajoled him on the previous night at the tavern into that happy state of somnolency, slipped out to his boat and to Breydon, and made a great haul of migrant waders, and had rowed back to his boat-shed before Chambers had come back to his boat hard by, to return to his watching. This was by no means the last exploit that was to the disadvantage of Chambers.

Lord! what sunsets—before that ugly iron bridge straddled across the Breydon entrance—glorified the brown sloppy mudflats, and the heavens that looked down upon them, as the big red ball of the sun dipped behind fleecy clouds, that became golden as the moments fled; and the night-cloud of purple became edged with silver as it slowly lowered behind it, its upper half tinting the rippling surface of the waters with flaming crimson. The gaunt herons lifted their grey heads as in wonder at the glory of the riotous colouring, and the greater black-backed gulls—free of domestic duties for the year—squawked contentment as they halted in their quest of shore-crabs to peer at the wondrous show. Even the fustian-clad Breydon men, lounging on the parapet, phlegmatically gazing at the vision, accustomed as they were to it, felt in their hearts the beauty of it all, and made laconic remark on the short-lived splendour.

'Fine sunset!' said Snicker Larn, nudging his little mate.

'Not 'arf bad!' replied Short'un Page, and let the nearly burnt-out match fall from his fingers with a much more definite remark.

But some time before this setting of the sun one would have observed the eel-catchers paddling upstream on the tide; a boatload or so of netters pushing out with designs upon the smelts; and half a dozen wherries following in each other's wake, steering outward into the golden west, making for the lower reaches of the Yare or Waveney before night came on. Snicker and his little chum had boarded their smelt-boat, and were just setting out, when Cadger Brown came racing past them in his dilapidated punt; then suddenly pulled up and waited until they were abreast, whereupon the astute poacher threw into a smelt-ped a fine young marsh hare, with a peremptory demand that they take care of it (with a wink) until he came back from the 'Bowling Green'. He needed a drink badly; the 'cops' were on his track. The two smelters knew exactly what to do: they hid the hare under the net, and awaited him. . . .

Cadger drew up at the staithe, and slung ashore his ped of fresh-culled watercress that he had gathered in the afternoon upon the marshes for the morrow's sale. He had also used his gun on the Mautby marshes when coming downstream, and bagged the hare. The keeper had observed Brown; the poacher had 'twigged' the keeper; and a race downstream and along the river-bank had ensued. While he was mopping down the punt at the staithe, the keeper put in an appearance, a local policeman, whom he had hailed on the North Quay, being with him.

'I want that there hare!' demanded Velveteens, as he shot out the watercress on the quay from Brown's basket, but finding no hare.

'*Me* got a hare?' said the ready-witted Brown, assuming an air of great surprise. 'Wal, bor, yew hev made the mistake of yer life, and upset my vegetable shop into the bargain, and don't you forget it.'

'Then, Master Brown, we'll overhaul the punt,' responded the constable, who by no means nimbly descended into it.

'You shove yer foot through the punt's bottom, and you'll hev to make it good, Mr. Knowsuffin'!'

No hare was to be found, and the two investigators reluctantly took their departure, Brown following close behind them to the tavern for another much-needed refresher; after which he returned to the staithe, where the rather impatient smelters speedily came and delivered up the hare.

'He'll be all snug there,' remarked Brown, covering the hare in his basket. 'It ain't the fust old Sally as hev bin so nicely tucked up under a wreath o' watercress!' . . .

Little Stork Thacker was the only idler hanging about the staithe at the moment, save for myself. He had been watching the little episode of the hare and the poacher, and had seen the last of the bowlers off the Green. We sat together on the bench beside the low boundary wall, and began to compare impressions. The sun had set behind its curtain of cloud, leaving behind it fast empurpling cloudlets high in the heavens, that had looked to me so much like a little flock of golden sheep a few moments before. Thacker made remark about Brown being a 'reg'lar cute old rascal, what you don't often catch nappin'.' He drew out his burnt old briar pipe, gauged it with his little finger, and finding it empty, rapped it cunningly on the seat back. Such stealthy hints are usually worth the taking from such interesting characters Having refilled his pipe, with a bit of 'bacca to spare, he lit up, puffed for a bit with vigour in silence, and presently waxed reminiscent. Said he :

'The time *was*, young Patt'son, when a pretty good livin' could be arnt amon' the ducks and eels—up yinder' (pointing Breydonwards). 'Things ain't so spry nowadays, an' if it worn't for takin' them gentlemen gunners afloat we might as well be dade. My brother Billy—Baker Stork, you know—don't grumble like I do ; he's got his week's arnin's safe, outer the dough-trow, and bakin' hot dinners, reg'lar enough, afore he even step aboard the punt. My father—Old Stork, they called him—wor a noted gunner, and they looked up to him as a sorter boss. Law ! how he could roar when he liked, and 'specially at my brother Billy, for he fared to went his spleen on *him* when things went wrong. Father arn't plenty, one way and the tother. I fust fired Father's gun when I was twelve ; it wor an old flint gun, what fired half a pound o' shot ; but the bloomin' old pan *would* colleck the damp in bad weather, an' had to be rubbed with a dry cinder, allers kep' ready in Father's pocket. Rain an' snow was the werry dowse. We made our own flints for the gun ; Father'd chip off a lump off one o' them big chunks on the North Wall, pickin' a big flint-stone with plenty o' fire in it. This he'd knock, werry clever like, into proper sizes, with a iron nut on a stick—sizes what fitted the cock, five or six flints out of a chunk—good as any from the flint rappers at Brandon. Flint-locks was the dowse, what misfired sometimes when the fowl in a frost was axin' you to shoot 'em, a'most. But that old gun did its job proper when it liked—shot close an' sharp.'

'You had some queer old guns afloat,' I interjected.

'Yes, bor, we *hed*. Theer's some nice old crocks about *now*, I'll allow ; and a nice old warmin of a 11-bore you hed, what you tied to the post, behind the cimitery, double-charged, and pulled a hunderd-yard string, for fear of a bust up, testin' on her ! She might ha' bin wuss, for she only chucked one screw out of the trigger-guard. Father's old punt-gun worn't the only flint 'un in use in them days—when I first went 'longer Father. Short'un Page's old man hed a flint-lock carryin' three-quarters o' shot—not quite a pound ; and she *was* a killer, too. Some gent what took a fancy to her tried to persuade his father that she orter be *moralized*, hevin' sich a lovely barrel.'

'You really mean *modernized*,' I laughed—'made into a plug- or a screw-breech—a cap gun.'

'Same thing, more or less,' assented Stork. 'Flints was

goin' outer fashion. But Short'un's old man, arter all, got Hicklin', who done up guns, to conwert her into a crack-patch, and he made a werry good job on it. *She would kill*, I'll take my solum oath on it. I remember Pintail Thomas's father gettin' mucked up with his punt-gun—and Pintail had some old crocks hisself, first to last. Why, Pintail hed one old warmin what was that sick and weak she'd hang behind for him to pull the trigger tew or t'ree times sometimes afore she'd let go. So he allers carried a bit o' iron to 'splode the cap with when she hesitated.'

'By the way,' I asked, 'what got Johnny Thomas the name of "Pintail" for him—pintail ducks?'

'Pintail ain't ezackly right; if it is, you orter call it *Pintle, it sound easier*. You hev tew pintles on a boat's rudder, what you drop into the stern gudgeons, what's screwed on the stern-post to hold an' work the rudder on.'

No doubt the old chap was correct; and Dr. P. H. Emerson, of Broadland fame, who was highly interested in Thomas, spelt it so.

'Well, Old Thomas—Pintail's father—once borrered my father's gun for a tide on Breydon. He'd got a parson to take on—Lubbet [Richard Lubbock], I think his name was, what writ about Norfik bards, as *his* gun was bein' tinkered up agin by Hicklin'. Old Thomas got one shoot on top o' the tide at a crowd o' turnstones, an' knots an' godwicks, all in the pink o' the red, an' some grey, full-eyed pluvvers, beauties! an' tew or tree pigmy ke-lews; picked up nigh a peck on 'em. That wor one "Twelfth o' May, Godwick Day", with a wengeance. Some odd years godwicks du come thick on a proper travellin' wind from the south-east. *She wuz a gun!* They don't make the likes of her nowadays.

'I 'member Father, what give me most of the odd ha'pence, and my brother Billy all the kicks, bein' out one day arter swans, five o' em, big 'uns—they was Hupers. They buffled us all day, by risin' when we was gettin' clost to 'em, and droppin' into another wake. Mind yew, they might ha' bin tame ones, but they was awful shy, like hawks. At last we chucked it; we was fed up with 'em, as yew may say, becos we'd let go by little lots of tufties and pokers, and was gettin' cramped an' cold to the bone.

'"We'll drop down home on this ebb," says Father, "and cum up on the night-flood; theer orter be a glint o' the mune. I'll slorter the lot, or I'll bust!"

'Well, arter tea we shoved off agin in the dark, tho' you

allers fare to hev a shade of glim if it's a clearish night. As we tarned the five-stake drain we got in amon' slub ice—thet's when the frost hev give a bit. But we hate the glass ice, when frosts is nippin' sharper. It took a lot o' doin', becos yew hev to keep the ice-hook handy for big lumps of dropt ice, what's fell off the sheet ice when the tide's down, and overhangin' the edge of a flat. We'd got pretty nigh into the Ham when it begins to snow; then it cum so fast it begins to lay on the uncovered flats, and *thet* buffled us, and I axes Father if we hadn't orter go back home.

'"Back be derned!" says he, low, but weighty; and gettin' a hunderd yards fudder, he lays to the gun. He must 'a' caught sight of suffin' ahead; and then I sees suffin' myself, and pinches his leg—he wos, of course, layin' lower 'an me.

'"Thet's them," I whispers.

'"*Shurrup!*" he whispers. "We're right on to 'em!"

'So he puts his finger on the trigger, easin' the click of it, gentle-like, and was jist goin' to pull when—good Laud! *some one corfed* in front of us. It wor old Punt Palmer's bark, with Jimmy Hurr aboard with him, what hed got white jumpers an' caps on, so as to look the colour of ice an' snow, an' the fowl shouldn't reckernize 'em!

'"*Good Gawd!*" gasps my old chap. "*Another tew seconds, an' I should hev blowed yer b—— hids off!*" Father didn't dew all the bad langwidgin', tho' he trimbled like a leaf; and what Gentleman Palmer didn't think of in the blastin' bizness Jimmy Hurr didn't forget. Jimmy's got the gift of pickin' the right words, like a parson—suffin' tremenjuss. Well, them tew hed gone up as sune as they'd seen us come off, and hed a go at them swans, killin' two on 'em, and woundin a third, what they lost. After we'd blowed off steam, we separated; they went rowin' down the south side, and hed a rough time pickin' theer way through the slub. Father started down the drain agin, and made for the "Bowlin' Green". And blow me tight! if we didn't fall in with that lost bird, dade as a doornail, and hauled him out.

'Now, it was jist afore Christmas,' went on Thacker, 'and Father ordered Mother not to sell it, sayin' as the *swine* (which worn't the proper name) hed, long o' the tothers, led him a nice dance, he'd hev it baked for Christmas dinner. Mother know'd how to cook wildfowl, and allers prided herself on it—she'd serve it up properly stuffed an' tender, reg'lar han'som. She sits up all night pluckin' it—and a swan take some doin'—but she made light o' the doom [down], for she put tew pokers in the fire, and ironed the swan all over with 'em, red hot, raisin' a—— What's the word?'

'Aroma, or odour,' I replied.

'Father didn't use that language—he'd gone to bed; he calls it a "H—— of a stink". I said so too, although I didn't like the word, but it was so; it reg'lar kep' the house warm all night. When you iron off the doom with a hot weapon there ain't much left, but you brown the bird before its time. Mother stuffed it with onions an' sausages, an' got Father to shove it in the small iron bath—we hedn't a dish big enough to hold a twenty-three-pound bird—and laid over it a two-inch layer of dough, like a blanket. In two hours' bakin' the crust hed tarned black, and we hulled it in the dorg-kindle, which was a cask; and then properly browned the swan another half hour. Bor! it ate delicious—reg'lar fell off the forks. Mother was a rip cookin' wildfowl; she'd make a eighty-year old pilliken out of a wild-beast show tender that way, if baked long enough.'

Thacker jumped up, and suggested we should go and look in at the bar-parlour, and as we strode across the Green I suggested to my small companion that it seemed an uncommonly promising evening for eel-babbing; several of the fellows had gone up, some even for the Beccles river, why not he?

'Idlin' pay *sometimes*,' he said with a knowing wink. 'Theer's eels around, in course, and theer's plenty others arter 'em as want 'em more'n I do—p'r'aps! I ha' got a different speckylation—other fish ter fry.'

It was mid-Maytime, and several desirable birds had been reported as seen; and it appeared that something to do with these creatures was the cause of Thacker's subtle idling.

'Bor,' he ventured on the quiet, 'you 'on't give me away, I know, but there's a couple o' spotted shanks around up'ards; I ha' bin watchin' old Ducker go down arter his grub an' water, an' he'll be safe *somewhere* till closin' time; and now's my chance. Of course I shorn't take the big gun; the noise o' the cripple-stopper'll be quite enough, though a south-easterly draught o' wind'll silence the shot—if I *hev* one. We don't see many shanks about nowadays, though there's plenty o' redlegs. Father got three or four in his time, callin' 'em "Cambridge godwicks"; some people called 'em "dusky shanks". They are werry lonely birds; old Jack Gibbs got the two best duskies in 1879, or somewhere thereabout, what's now in Cornop's [Connop's] collection. Them shanks are a bit noisy, and call "*jewty-jewty*", fairly catchin' your ear;

though theer favourite chums, them greenshanks, fairly make you jump as they start up when you're rounding the corner of a grup and haller "*plew-plew-plew*", allers three times. I'd heer'd chaps say, what hed shot 'em, and eat 'em, they'd never eat another. I once shot a warmin of a greeny what had spoilt me a shot at a black-tailed godwick ; and hevin' a couple of Arcty terns, what worn't wanted, I got my brother Billy, the baker, to make me a pie of 'em—my bein' a old bachelor. I set down to dinner to 'em, but as sune as I lifted the lid the smell of 'em was enough for me. I tried 'em, but couldn't stomach 'em, so I hulled 'em out. The on'y thing I ever tried, to come up to 'em, was a old shelduck. Give me a old harnser, or two or three kitties ; sea-swallers, greenies, and shelducks—well, bor, they ain't fit for a poleeceman's supper, they ain't.'

Slowly the gloaming blotted out the sunset and settled over the waters ; the stolid eel-men became silhouetted against the afterglow, then disappeared in the shadows and were lost to view. Had you been near to one of them you would have heard the tap of his cone-shaped lead sinker on the punt's bottom-boards, and the slap and sluss of an astonished eel as it sought to get beneath them ; or the scrunch of his heel upon a trio of long-legged shore-crabs that had come in clinging and struggling upon the threaded worms. Maybe you would have heard once in a while a gruff ejaculation of some unprintable sentence, as a pound eel let go before the bab had been slung into the well of the punt, dropping into the tide, to its great bewilderment. A fainter lead-tap on the bottom-boards of another eel-catcher, staked round the bend of the drain, might be followed by a query from the optimistic old Peg-leg Gates, an aged pensioner from the Navy, whose sole delight and occupation, when not gossiping over a pint pot, was eel-catching :

'How yer gettin' on, Fiddler, boy ?'

'There now, jist as you spoke, I now lost a whopper ; and ain't them durned little nippin' crabs a lot o' borther to-night, drat 'em ! How are you a-doin' ?'

'Middlin' like, middlin' ; getting' a few titty-totty ones, which is better'n nothin', and haulin' in a decent-sizer now an' agin,' replies Peg-leg. 'Lor ! if I'd ha' copt all the big 'uns what ha' bin pluckin' my worms ter pieces I'd 'a' hed a stone long ago. Theer !—theer's another ; I thought I should ha' landed him, but he fell off jist as I lifted him out o' the water. *His* luck was in, bust him ! Theer—I 'a' got that one ! Lor !

he's over a pound.' Then the old chap drops his babbing pole along the deck and lights up, the red glow from his pipe gleaming in the dark and winking like a star.

'Got any beer aboard?' inquires Fiddler Goodens.

'Never a drop, bor,' returns Peg-leg; 'pity we couldn't hev brought the old "Bowlin' Green" up and stuck it on the flat alongside of us. I say, Fiddler——'

'Hallo!' inquires Goodens.

'Hev yer got any 'bacca aboard on yer? Blest if I ain't got a empty pouch; what say?' asks Peg-leg, in an aggrieved tone of voice.

'*Neery a quid!*' replies Fiddler, drawing his stakes, and drifting off to another probably better spot. 'So long,' says he. 'I ain't dropped on to 'em yet.'

'I'll bid yer good——' But Peg-leg breaks off short, and the sound of his lead-tap, and the scuffle of the wooden peg-end of his leg, as he readjusts his seat, causes the retreating Fiddler to stay his oars and make an inquiry.

'What's up, Peggy? Lost another big 'un?'

'Blest if I didn't pull up a pounder and a half-pounder. Lose him? Not me. Ha ha! I could hardly make him let go.' Peg-leg only needed a big pipeful of 'bacca and a bottle of Bass to make him supremely happy, the jolly old curly-headed optimist!

CHAPTER II

TOILERS OF THE ESTUARY

FOR generations the homes of the waterway men clustered around the entrance to Breydon, which could be seen from the back doors or the bedroom windows of many of them. One quaint little cottage of two small rooms stood upon a low point of the quay at the sharp angle where the tidal water turns into the Bure. A big tide, on a strong nor'-westerly breeze that flung salt spray over the 'Bowling Green' staithe and parapet, also splashed the windows of the cottage. For some years, after the last tenants had been rescued from their beds, it stood empty and tottering, and became a mere stowage-place for the eel-pots, nets, eel-picks, and oars of a Breydoner. The Breydon folk eagerly rented the small houses near where the punts and smelt-boats were moored, making little ado when an occasional high tide flooded their lower floors: when the tide had subsided, the boat-mop soon right-sided the place. If you strode round to the back ways, the oars, the spars, and the pick-shafts that topped the walls at once bespoke the occupations of the tenants. When the back-yard door was opened, there were eel-trunks and baskets piled in the corners; and hanging on the walls the mussel-dredge and the trammel-sticks, detached from the smelt-nets. And 'an ancient and fish-like smell' pervaded the place. Wet guernseys hung up to dry, dripping from the wash-tub; jumpers just dipped in tan in the cutch copper beside them; and here and there a pair of fresh-oiled crotch boots stood in the sun to help absorb the neatsfoot lubricant. Nets were hung to dry upon the palisades, or on a fence or a wall outside. In the best room, which did duty for dining- and drawing-room, up in a corner stood the cripple-stopping gun, probably loaded; occasionally the big gun stood in another, and from it the little folks studiously kept away, for Dad was quick to correct if they went near to it. A few cheap, coloured pictures were suspended from nails, among them a favourite photograph of the gunner standing stiffly in his punt, or maybe a crude water-colour drawing of a fishing smack our Breydoner once had sailed in. A cheap timepiece ticked away industriously on the mantelpiece in front of a small looking-glass; an aneroid barometer hung near the door, but the weather-wise fellow preferred to trust to his own instincts and powers of observation. There would be an old-time bureau, that dated back at least to his grandfather's time; this, or an uncostly chest of drawers, had the powder and shot-flasks hidden somewhere inside, and on top of it stood a paraffin lamp and a few cherished trinkets of little value. A gull's wing or two 'decorated' a picture top; two or three china figures, colourful but garish, gave the little of artistic feeling that is in most men. In a cottage here and there you might discover a case of stuffed waders; a grey plover in spring plumage—facing it a turnstone that a collector would envy; a common tern, a-wing for years, but still there; a godwit in the change of plumage, for a spring bird in the nuptial attire always went to the bird dealer or to the collectors; of all the ducks that fell to his gun he preferred a shelduck for his case.

The lady of the household led a variegated sort of life: she was mother, mentor, manager. She was, as a rule, a competent beatster—a braider and mender of nets. You would find hanging on the narrow bit of wall, on a nail between the window and the door, a half-made shrimp-net, or a draw-net, at which she worked indoors at idle times if the day was wet; on fine days outside, like her neighbour next door, who, peradventure, was mending one of 'her old man's' nets. Small rents and broken meshes were occasionally mended by the men when afloat, if the tide were still young, for submerged wreckage of any sort—an old bucket in particular, if filled with mud and silt—had an unpleasant way of clutching at and tearing the delicate meshes. Smelts, chance mullet, and eels have an annoying trick of finding these holes, and so making their escape. At night, when the kiddies were in bed, mother had muddy and very ill-treated knickies and elbows to patch; little shirts had to be washed, dried before the fire, and aired ready for the morning, while their unencumbered tenants slept. 'Oh, the mud—mud—mud!' kept her busy and at high tension.

The father of the family was of necessity irregular in his goings abroad and comings home, for gunner and fisher had to work by the tides; and, moreover, things happened 'ungain' to delay him. The lady rarely worried over these particulars; although she could be furious when provoked by his dallying at some favourite pub and now and then squandering little moneys that she had need of. When after smelts he liked to be at his favourite 'draw' at the very beginning of the flood, or ready to start at the first of the ebb; the tides are nearly an hour later every day. Smelts love to be shoaling in quiet water, and the nets were then easier worked. The eel-babber preferred night-time for his labours; in the day-time he had to sell last night's catch, and dig or wriggle for worms for bait, which performance in dry weather was somewhat strenuous. At certain times, in the old days, he babbed (or bobbed) on the flats—that was when they were rarely left dry on the ebb tide for long periods, when the *Zostera marina* was like a growing cornfield, with its subaqueous foliage, and when fine silver-bellied eels threaded the labyrinths of this grass in such numbers that a score of punts might be seen moored at one time dotted about Breydon. When the tides ran low he fell back upon his short-shafted eel-spear, and stabbed the ooze promiscuously in likely places; and occasionally at the big fellows that lay under the mud of the flats. In colder months he screwed and nutted his spear-head upon a shaft long enough to plunge into the ooze in the main drains and channels. Here and there the head of the household was the owner of a small, tarry, span-roofed house-boat, wherein he turned at night or as occasion demanded.

If you called round and knocked at the front door of the nicer sort of Breydoner—for some, like other men, were grumpy and standoffish—you would hear a cheery call:

'Come in, bor. We shorn't eat yer!' No, he and the tribe of tawny-headed boys and girls had something better to masticate—it might be a brace of badly-shot wigeon, or a curlew and a mallard that, having been sorely wounded, had fluttered to the flintstone walls and died there, and had been dragged to a hole and mauled a bit by the omnivorous great rats that patrolled the walls for sustenance, and lived and slept in burrows they had tunnelled in them: such birds were detected by their wings and bodies having been too awkward to be pulled inside altogether, as our Breydoner paddled past the spot. It might be in winter that a hooded crow had disembowelled a pochard or two, or a teal that had floated to the walls after last night's discharge of some punt-gun; to them might be added a couple of black-headed gulls and some knots that had not been sold yesterday. What mattered? Here was a bake, or a stew, supplemented by the aroma of the onions, that provoked appetite and longing for a serving of it.

Now and then when better fowl than herring-gull and grey-gull were not for the Breydoner's dinner, or supper, the lady of the house had a capital way of making even these palatable as well as tempting. She would lay them, after skinning them, in salt water all night, just as she did the 'old harnsers' that some visitor gunner had 'brought down', for the mere sport of it. It mattered not to any of them if heron or gull had been the day before feasting on little flounders or water voles; or, for a matter of that, a few chunks from a dead drowned cat.

'Set yerself down,' said Pintail Thomas, one noontide as I dropped in upon him for a little chat, 'and have a gull for yer dinner.' I hesitated as Lady Thomas shot out from a steaming saucepan a quartet of black-headed gulls, with a few unfortunate dunlins, into a big tureen. Johnny stabbed a couple of gulls in quick time, as if he were eel-spearing, and pushed them off the fork with his knife on to his plate.

'Help yerself to one,' he said, and I did so. But prejudice was stronger than appetite; I put it back, and while we chatted Pintail ate all four, with the usual concomitants of a little bit of pork and of potatoes and cabbage.

'Well, bor,' he made remark, '*you* don't mind a peewit or a golden plover, what eat worrams, and leather-jackets, and beetles, and daddy-longlegs, too, jist as the kitties [black-headed gulls] do; why can't they be good enough as well? You go up to Charlie Thacker's, and it's all likely you'll see him smokin' into a big old grebe, or a hoodie crow what his brother Billy had baked in the oven for him; he dote, as you know, on any birds stuffed with sausages what give 'em a nice flavour; but in hard times an old black crow or a rook and a few hot pertaters, with a fried mushrume or two off the meshes what spice them all up fit for a king, suit old Charlie down to the ground. . . .'

Mr. Booth, of Brighton, never bought a bird for his great museum, however rare it might be, but he would pay handsomely for information that might be the means of that bird falling to his own gun. When staying at Yarmouth in the late 'seventies for a shooting trip to Breydon, a resort that greatly attracted him, a fisherman who had just arrived after a long voyage called upon him at his hotel. He, the skipper, informed Booth that he had shot a bird or two on the North Sea which he thought might please him to purchase. For a fortnight they had laid in one of the lockers of the vessel, and the bird-man could scarcely credit it that 'they were as fresh as when they were killed'. The birds were an immature gannet, a pomatorhine skua, and a bird that he could not just then determine; they stunk so horribly that Mr. Booth advised the skipper to take them away, but he could return with them in the morning, so that they could be examined by daylight, the stranger bird in particular, out of doors.

'Squire' Booth, as we all proclaimed him, however, called upon the man, but was informed that his wife had sold the lot for sixpence to an aged fiddler as 'an old and two young harnsers', and they were at that moment being cooked 'for the Sunday's blow-out', much to the scandal and disgust of the neighbours in the row, who were almost poisoned by the abominable odour.

In another little household you might have surprised a sporty shoemaker, who was a frequent visitor to the mudflats in company with the smelters, or with another gunner, and caught him in the act of turning over a fry-pan full of skinned viviparous blennies—'Lovely eel-pouts,' he described them; 'as nice a fish as any lord might want, a lot better 'an eels; and it's funny, ain't it, when cooked, you'll find their backbone as green as grass: in fact, we often call 'em "green-bones".' They certainly beat the aroma of Pintail's gulls. A second panful of fish would be some thick flounders, netted unwittingly that morning with the smelts. The next-door neighbour might be frying her good man a steak, the only sauce for which might be a bottle of pickled samphire, gathered from the flats. On high days a poached hare was gleefully welcomed; once in a while the father of a family might swop a duck or two for a rabbit or a hare at the game-stall.

The children thrived on their homely but pleasant fare, by the muddy river-margin, and in the fresh and strong salt air. The boys prowled to the mudflats, going thitherwards upon the walls with naked feet, and with dilapidated baskets, in search of flounders. They trotted in the shallowing drains as the tide lowered, knee-deep, stirring the muddy waters as they proceeded in order to disturb the flat-fish, that having spent an hour or so among the crustaceous and molluscous hordes that swam or glided among the waving acres of wigeon-grass on the flood tide, had instinctively slipped again into these 'runs', which then never ran altogether dry. The boys could feel such flounders as they stepped on, squirm under their feet, and would instantly bend down to recover them by hand before they could escape. These flat-fish were promptly thrown on to the now nearly-dry flat, to be gathered in by their chums, or were basketed by the catchers. It was rare fun, for sometimes a boy slipped leg-deep into a hole; now and again a vengeful shore-crab seized a toe or an ankle, in which case it was nabbed and in revenge for the indignity was divested of at least its pincer claws, a matter of no great concern to the cripple, who, at the next time of shell-moulting, found itself accommodated with a couple of small new ones, which, if nothing happened, would increase in size after each successive exuviation until normal. The young urchins didn't know that.

The wigeon-grass then swarmed with big, 'fat winkles', the warcry of those itinerant vendors who bought baskets or buckets of periwinkles from the boys, who kept the pence or shillings, if father or mother failed to learn of these transactions. In those days of my boyhood winkles were a much appreciated Sunday tea-table luxury; gossiping idlers used to loiter around the row-ends, in the back streets, worming out with a pin their 'pin-patches', as they facetiously named their periwinkles; the rattle of empty shells upon the cobble-stones was as common a sound as the chirp of the sparrows on the house-tops. Another interesting item, in the shooting season, of some benefit to the boys was their search for wounded or dead fowl, that had been shot at the night before in the dark and lost. Stricken fowl always make for the walls or banks, to hide in any hole that offers. A bill, a bright eye, a movement of leg or foot, or flutter of a feather caught the boys' keen eyes, and immediately ready hands captured them, and they were promptly killed by having the neck broken or the skull compressed; all such finds were popped into the sacks used as game-bags. If father or the neighbour next door had a mongrel dog, it was pressed, nothing loth, into the service. In hard times father rowed the boat round by the lee wall and gathered wooden supports, wedges, and dunnage from the shipyards and docks for firewood; in these days of iron vessels, save for a few bits of short new stuff from timber-ships that are being 'lumped' (emptied) near the timber yards, little firewood drifts up on the flood tide. If father had a roomy enough boat-shed, herring-swills that occasionally fell overboard, and came up on the tide, were retrieved and stored, until a barrow or a cart-load had been mustered, for a serviceable basket usually brought in a very welcome shilling from the owner whose private mark was painted on the end.

Before the 'seventies the boys rarely went to school. They needed discreet and persistent shepherding after the 'school-board bloke' was put upon their track. Meantime, they were serving an apprenticeship to fit them for following their fathers' occupation. In the fleet of shrimp-boats sailing out of the port the boys often found a willing employer, who could not afford to pay men or men's wages. Thus they learnt to become capable sailors, as they had already become fine swimmers—by incidental practice. Many of the boys drifted into the trawler fleets, that then made Yarmouth a busy deep-sea fishing port; some enlisted into the Navy. In after years, like others who had drifted away for a time, they reverted to their beloved old haunts, wedging in with the shrimpers, eel-catchers, wherrymen, and others.

This love of the old Estuary, its freedom, its uncertainties, and its possibilities, backed by an inherited instinct, gripped them early. These urchins frequently fetched home their fathers' wildfowl, more especially during wintry spells, when coots, scaups, tufties, and golden-eyes, in company with the 'grass-feeders', were crowding in, feeling the pinch of hunger and the furious unrest of the sea-waves. The fowl in sacks, or strung by tied feet on sticks, were shouldered home with heroic feeling; and mothers who had regular customers put on their shawls and went the rounds of the *bourgeoisie* and tradesfolk, who celebrated a wildfowl dinner at least once a week. Several of these well-to-do folk hired the men and boats occasionally and went shooting with them, to the advantage of the puntsman's purse; and collectors of the period eagerly answered the women's knocks, for goosander, merganser, long-tailed duck, even, might be found carefully wrapped in a cloth for their inspection.

The boys did not smoke as now, openly, but some did when they could forage up father's pipe and tobacco-pouch behind his back. Pintail Thomas's wife sported a tobacco licence at the little 'pork and pochard' shop; but it gradually dawned upon her that the tobacco mysteriously vanished to below profit point; and when she caught little Johnny, the head of the household, with his hand in the tobacco jar, there was an upset, and the temptation was removed thenceforth and altogether. In passing it may be said that the girls had not evolved into flappers, but were more wisely persuaded into going out as housemaids and nurse-girls. In event of being unemployed they were initiated into the useful art of trawl-net braiding; they even helped in slow wintry spells to sort the mussels shot out from father's old smack's-boat, a vessel that he had conveniently cut down several strakes, and had converted into a mussel-dredging craft, with its windlass athwart the bow end, with its belaying-pins and lengthy towing-rope. Until the end of the 'seventies tons of large mussels were scraped by dredges out of the bed of the lower Bure every winter, as well as from Breydon down-river to near the harbour's mouth. It was an interesting sight to watch the family parties wrenching stones and bits of coal and iron and stick from the mussels to which they were attached by the strong byssus threads, and which they swept into baskets awaiting them. It was a cold job in winter time, but the proceeds of the sale of these bivalves meant a warm fire for a wintry night. The men and older boys perambulated the town with barrow-loads of mussels, shouting their price at 'tuppence the quarter', which, of course, included the shells, full measure. Sewage outfalls, outcome of a municipal *happy thought*, have since so polluted the river that mussels are tabooed by medical authorities and the mussels have since become scarcer. With the extinction of this little mussel industry the poverty of winter was more keenly felt by that coterie of Breydoners. Breydon men and youths were also badly hit, when a few years since the frugal-minded Scotch fishermen, who greatly disliked the expense of counting (then known as 'telling') the herrings, introduced the 'cranning', or measuring by basket, of the fish. This system has been since wholly adopted by the Yarmouth fisher folk. Many a score of impecunious folk, including many a Breydoner, lost earnings they could ill spare.

One other occupation—that of quanting up-river in wintry days, in wherry and other craft, for loads of ice when the broads and North River were frozen—has vanished. This ice was brought to the ice-houses, which still stand near the haven bridge. They presented a busy scene when scores of men were running up and down the broad step-ladders with full or empty baskets; this ice was used by fishing-smacks to 'keep' their catches of deep-sea fish. To-day but one or two fishing-smacks using the port require a little ice, and this they get from the factory.

One other word on the Breydon boys. They were full of mischief and energy and initiative. It was no rare thing for father to go down to the boat to fish, to find that some boys had taken the boat, hoisted a rude sail of cut sacks put together by themselves, and had gone a-sailing; sometimes they hung a painter to a stake and enjoyed a swim, or else had gone a-pirating, imagining themselves buccaneers and Robinson Crusoes. One day one or two of these urchins slipped on to a boat-yard, and observing old Breydon Stork Thacker's punt-gun, gathered three or four stones and pushed them by the ramrod they had found in the punt into the barrel, adding a scrap of rolled-up paper to keep them in place. Unaware of it, this patriarch of the Thacker tribe embarked to make an attack upon a large flock of wigeon, and on getting within range of them laid-to and pulled the trigger, when a loud explosion followed, and a piece of the barrel was blown off; the fowl were scared, and took to wing, leaving a few units behind them and a blazing scrap of paper that drifted away in the wind, a sorry wad for so desperate a loading. Thacker went home boiling with wrath; but when he had simmered down a little he took the gun to Bob Flaxman's smithy, where that worthy 'gun-doctor' carefully examined it, making sure that no danger still lurked in the breech-end; and on finding the damaged barrel sound enough above the ragged hurt filed off what had been equivalent to nearly a third of the barrel; and with the remainder of it Thacker continued a-shooting to the end of his tether.

The 'accident' caused some sensation among the fraternity, who whole-heartedly and unanimously 'd——d' all boys! and decided to administer corporal punishment to all boys who should be captured messing about with their punts or boats. In those days boys were not molly-coddled—at least, Breydon-side boys were not; nor did angry parents then abuse the schoolmaster for giving unruly boys at school well-merited punishment.

Short'un Page, when a man of seventy, still stood but four feet in his stockings; as a very small boy he was packed full of mischief. He was also very daring, for when but fourteen years of age he took advantage of a very wild day in December 1853, when his father, with other Breydon men, was assisting to put out a fire at the old thatched ice-house, near the mouth of the Bure, to run off with his father's big punt and gun, to see what destruction he could do among the then abundant fowl. He had been afloat before with father and the big gun stowed in a corner of the well of the punt, and had learnt how to manipulate the boat, and knew how to use the punt-gun. He discovered plenty of game in the open wakes in the ice, and loaded and fired his gun like an old campaigner, returning home with a remarkable load of nine brent geese, five curlews, five wigeon, and over one hundred and fifty small shore-birds. By the time Short'un had returned to the 'Bowling Green', the fire had finished its work, and the Breydon men had wandered back to their favourite hotels. Great was the surprise of those who leant on the parapet discussing the conflagration, and commenting on the contrast of the ice-house flames with the arctic outlook that ended in the grey mistiness of closing-in time, to see the boy draw up to the staithe and land his first great collection of slaughtered waterfowl, an event that was much debated in bar-parlour and by the firesides of those who had not gone afloat. Short'un's father was so taken aback by the boy's audacity and prowess that punishment was forgotten.

It may be interesting to give a few of the nicknames of these Breydon men, most of whom were personally known to me. Among the Punt-gunners were: 'Old Stork' Thacker, 'Trivett' Read, 'Silky' Watson, 'Baker Stork' Thacker, 'Little Stork' Thacker, 'Huckerin' Tom' Reed, 'Pintail' Thomas, 'Miser', or 'Saltfish', Jex, 'Jiggy' Hall, 'Gabey' Thomas, 'Fiddler' Goodens, 'Strike' Sharman, 'Brusher' Broom, 'Pero' Pestell, 'Admiral' Gooch, 'Punt' Palmer, 'Horry' Press, 'Potot' Mesham, 'Short'un' Page, 'Granny' Reed, and 'Wire' Quinton.

Among the Shoulder-gunners were: 'Spunyarn' Thomas, 'Jobrey' Jessop, 'Jibro' Jessop, 'Big' Milligan, 'Trotter' Lodge, 'Dighton' Smith, 'Deaf' Hunt, 'Putty' Westgate, 'Gull' Whiley, 'Little' Wigg, and 'Cadger' Brown.

Among the Smelters, Eel-catchers and Mulleters: Ben Bessey, 'Peg-leg' Gates, 'Limpeny' King, 'Poker' Lamb, 'Old Bugles', 'Deaf Charlie' Baker, 'Dutchman', 'Sharper' Fox, 'Lucky Bob' Edmunds, 'Flea' Barber, 'Young' Barber, 'Blue' Carver, 'Chicko' Drane, 'Scrumps' Allen, 'Toby' Blake, 'Dinks' Cox, 'Fates' Bowles, and 'Stevey Bowles.

Like many other men who lived by their wits, the Breydon men in old age were sadly handicapped by poverty, as well as the aches and pains incidental to their watery domains; here and there one, whose children had taken up more profitable work ashore, nurtured and cared for the aged couple in the decline of their days, and saw them 'under the daisies' without the 'taint' attached to a pauper funeral. It was my practice when possible to see the old fellows into their last freehold. Little 'Short'un' Page lived some years, and ended his days in a one-roomed shanty in a row, to which access was gained by clambering up an outside staircase. He lived there with his kindly daughter, the cosy room being divided by a drawn curtain.

At an advanced age the old fellow passed away, and was taken to the graveyard. Some unpreventable business kept me from seeing the old chap put into the square hole of clean sea-sand. Next day one of his aged mates met me in the street :

'D'ye know, Mr. Patt'son ,' said the patriarch, 'we put poor little old Short'un under the daisies yesterday, but you worn't there.' I explained the reason of my absence.

'And I s'pose you nivver heerd the rum thing what happened ? Well, I'll tell yer. We buried him in his poor brother Stevey's grave, what wos built for two. And jist as we wos lowerin' the poor little chap inter the sile, theer come up a voice, from below, solum an' slow ; it wos his brother's woice, an' it says : "*Hallo! Boy Short'un, heer you be, then! But hev you brung any 'bacca 'long with yer?*" '

Few of the Breydon women were outstanding characters. After the fleeting glamour of a usually uneventful courtship, life for them settled down into a rather drab affair, with plenty to do, and often little to do with. They had no intellectual aspirations, and came in for long days and nights of work and contriving ; the only break was the once in a while, but somewhat regular, appearance of a new member for the family. The daughters of Breydoners usually married with open eyes and resignation.

Mrs. 'Breydon Stork', wife of 'Old Stork' Thacker, was the proud mother of two young male Storks who followed in their father's footsteps. The Brotherhood knew them as they grew to manhood as 'Baker Stork' Thacker, *alias* Billy Thacker ; and 'Little Stork' Thacker, *alias* Charlie Thacker. Mrs. Stork the elder was wont to sort over the fowl from the Estuary, looking for differentiations of colours, markings, size, limbs, and so on, deciding which should be sold to private patrons, and which should be taken to Watson the game-dealer's on Fuller's Hill, or to Durrant the dealer in the Market, who knew but little, generally speaking, about the rarer birds and their values beyond what they would sell for as table birds. Watson was bluff, sharp, and keen over a deal. He had been a shoemaker, but became a speculative game-dealer. When I was a lad his large displays of grouse, pheasants, wildfowl, even deer, upon his shop rails outside—for venison was not then rare upon local tables—always arrested my attention. Mrs. Stork gave preference to bird-stuffers and specimen-hunters on the occasions when 'likely' birds turned up ; she also had a 'duck-round', a number of private customers being waited upon with fowl and waders once a week at least—on 'game day'. They liked the old lady, and treated her with respect, and laughed over her provincialisms and eccentricities.

On her rounds, a clean cloth lined the basket; on it she laid such-and-such birds—wigeon, knots, godwits, etc.—preserved for Mr. A——; so many brace of wigeon, or so many peewits (according to order), for Mr. B——; Mr. C—— preferred wood-pigeons, perhaps golden plovers, and Mr. Stork had only fallen in with grey plovers—that mattered little enough, for with her scissors she promptly clipped off the small hind toe. Captain D—— had asked for some snipe. Good! Whiley, the shoemaker and gull-shooter, who had been on the marshes that very morning showing Captain Burch how to 'down' the erratic snipe, had brought her, only an hour since, three brace that had fallen to his gun. Sometimes she returned with a few birds unsold; but that mattered little, the game-dealers would have them; at the worst they could eat them themselves. And sometimes she had to return home for a few more birds. On Fridays she left her customers to their 'fish day'; even then, if her patrons required fish, her old man had taken flounders from the stake-nets, and maybe a few grey mullets; perhaps a brace or two of sturdy perch. Freshwater fishes drifted downstream habitually on the neap tides; and perch taken in brackish water were excellently flavoured. If they required some smelts, or a big eel or two for 'collaring', she could supply them on a short notice.

One of Lady Stork's clients was a jovial lawyer, Preston, who loved wildfowl upon the table once weekly. Mrs. Thacker would rap at the door, brush her apron down, and rearrange the ruffled feathers on the pendant head of a mallard that was dangling over the edge of the basket, and smooth its glossy breast. The elderly lawyer, all smiles, opened the door and asked her into the hall; he was somewhat of a tease, would turn the birds over, weigh them in his hand, nip their breasts, and then pretend to belittle their condition, and when the prices were mentioned would raise his eyebrows and hands, and make remark, 'Two shillings for a brace of miserable wigeon? Preposterous! Whatever will you ask next?'

'Well, sir,' she would insist, 'they was honestly worth it, without takin' into consideration my man's time and muckin' around, among floatin' ice and slimy mudflats, and *my* time thrown in a-trottin' round with 'em.'

He would bid her good-day, pretending to be going in with disgust, and throwing the birds back into the basket. Both of them were perfectly aware of an inevitable deal, both enjoying the harmless bit of fencing.

'Come, now, sir,' she argued, 'don't be unkind over the deal; tu shillin's ain't a farden tu much.'

'Pooh pooh!' growled the lawyer. 'Why, I'd take the basketful for that,' and he scratched his head.

'In course you would, sir,' she persisted, 'but give us the tu bob *and a pincht of snufft.*'

Out came the formidable snuff-box; dig into it went the lady's broad thumb and finger, bringing out a pinch of no mean quantity. Thus the bargain was struck and the lawyer stumped off to the kitchen to deliver the fowl into the hands of the cook, swinging the ducks by their necks as he went, and chuckling over the nonsense attending the deal.

When I was a small boy, Mrs. Fox 'stood the Market' on Saturdays and Wednesdays when visitors were swarming the town. On other days she made the round of visits to townsfolk who bought Breydon eels. A rival lady, known as Mrs. 'Eeley' Bowles, also 'skun' eels to order in the Market, occasionally cutting prices as well. Mrs. 'Eeley' Bowles dressed literally in sack-cloth garments, at least outwardly; Mrs. Fox was but a trifle smarter. Both ladies used most disreputable scales, constructed of inverted boiler-lids, strung with cords upon wooden beams; the weights they used were of iron, badly rusted, and never tested. Neither gave lumping weight if they could possibly manage it, weighing the eels with skin and head and entrails still attached, with a trifle of wet sand, in which they dipped their hands to make them capable of holding their slippery goods, thrown in.

Mrs. Harvey, wife of old Isaac Harvey, according to the Pagets' showing, was a valuable asset to his business as an egg-merchant, who sent 'on an average of between six hundred and seven hundred eggs to the London and other markets every week during the season'. This was when the marshes were found considerably profitable 'by the number of plovers' eggs which were collected in them'. As these Bure marshes, more especially around Acle, were then the resort of snipes, redshanks, lapwings, coots, and water-hens, and also of black-headed gulls, there is not the slightest doubt that egg-raids were made upon all of them, and were placed in the common receptacle. This busy woman also helped with the packing of the fowl, which, in one day alone (1829), had been 'brought to him on the market day, no less than four hundred wildfowl of different descriptions, five hundred snipes, and a hundred and fifty golden plovers, all of which he immediately carried up to London, and disposed of '. At that period the huxters' and higglers' carts were much in evidence all over the county. Mrs. Harvey signally aided her husband (who was also a bird-stuffer) on many occasions—once by washing a pair of badly besmeared collared pratincoles ' as she would stockings ', and hung them out on a pole to dry. They had been shot by a Breydoner named John Bessey, who sold them to Harvey for twenty shillings, and were subsequently disposed of by the astute Harvey for seven pounds. What eventually became of them is a matter of some doubt.

There was told a story of Mrs. ' Poker ' Lamb and a neighbour named Cooper, both wives of gunner-smelters, who, when the second men in the boats' crews were otherwise engaged, or loitering unduly at a river-side pub, assisted their husbands in working the nets, having dressed suitably for the occasion in their muddiest garments and water boots. When a draught was to be made these excellent ladies stepped out of the boats on to the mud, tucked up their dresses, and laid hold of the tow-ropes, following slowly on the soft ooze as their men rowed in half-circles and the tide dragged the nets, until they ran the boats in lower down, when they commenced hauling in, hand over hand, until only the bight of each net remained to be hurried in : with its mixed shoal of smelts, eels, flounders, crabs, eel-pouts, and weeds that, kicking and protesting, were drawn up the slope of the mud and emptied on the flat. It was often a lively scene—gathering in the struggling fishes, which sometimes included unexpected strangers ; the struggling crabs, which had become entangled in the meshes, gave a great deal of trouble in getting them out.

Pintail Thomas was not esteemed an excellent shot, but he was, as reported of him, ' always on the job ', and more rare birds fell to his gun in the long run than fell to the lot of better marksmen. Hence he was also known as ' Lucky ' John Thomas. When the Close Season Acts came into force he had a cute way of evading the vigilance of ' Ducker ' Chambers, who was esteemed not a bad sort, a character that ill-befits a bird-watcher. It was not an uncommon thing for Johnny to stalk and bag a rare or desirable specimen, while Ducker was ashore, ' provisioning ', or enjoying a needful doze in the house-boat. Having obtained a victim, Thomas would row round to the walls to a marsh haystack hard by, or even to a mill, and hide his victims in some secret place. He would row home innocently enough, bidding the Watcher good-day or night, as the case might be ; and whatever the Watcher's suspicions were, he never discovered ' contraband ' in Thomas's punt. Then Mrs. Thomas would be summoned to the ' Bowling Green ', where the boat was awaiting her, and in her second-best attire she would be rowed upstream by her smaller half. We who were about would give the usual hail :

' Heer ye go ! Where bound for ? '

' Jist takin' the old woman out for a blow ! ' was his invariable reply. Mrs. Thomas had certain pockets and appendages on the inside of her flowing skirts, and into these were slipped, or were suspended, the various feathered prizes that had fallen to Pintail's prowess. The pair then rowed for home, and if within hail of Chambers, exchanged the usual salutes. Neither he nor Joseph Buddery had the daring to overhaul Mrs. Thomas or to question her unduly, whatever may have been their suspicions. On one occasion Mrs. Pintail defiantly stalked past Buddery with a spoonbill stowed somewhere on her person. When Mrs. T.'s services were not available some comrade or confederate would take charge of the bird or birds, climb over the wall, and, crossing the intervening marshes, walk to the town by road.

One unquestionably true story is told of Pintail's contribution to the little business run by the lady. They kept a small shop, the front door of which divided the shop-front into two ; on one side was the lady's show of beef, pork, and suchlike, on the other the husband's game, that hung suspended outside on hooks, as in the case of geese and swans, *and gulls.* Cabbages and such-like also went that side. My friend B——n related to me the story, but B.'s henchman shall tell the tale, as he had often chewed it over.

' Of course,' began Charlie Thacker, in his odd way, ' you've often seen them rows of gulls hang in the front of Johnny's winder, an' seen him moochin' home with a string of cobs an' herrin' gulls—grey 'uns—athort his shoulder ? ' I had, and often wondered what use he could make of them—so many of them.

' So hev I ! ' jibed in Pero Pestell, who at that moment joined us. ' I ha' wondered, but Pintail allers kept it to hisself,' continued the boat-builder, with his usual dyspeptic growl ; ' must ha' got a market for 'em somewheer. No —— Englishman would eat 'em ! ' Pero lurched off with a gruff good night.

' Ain't much as *he* can't ferret out ! ' resumed Thacker ;

'and I shorn't tell him, Johnny bein' a old pal o' mine. Well, he *hed* a market for 'em, as I found out unexpect'ly. One night I was mardlin' agin' his door-steppin', when a young chap goin' into the shop run'd up agin' a string of fresh sausages, what he allers hung on a hook not far off the door. His nose jist touched 'em, when he says:

'"What the —— hev you got here?" (I heerd him my own self); "fare to be suffin' with considerable more 'an smell!"

'"Sausages!' snaps John, flarin' up at sich a remark.

'So they made haste an' served him, John lookin' at her and she lookin' at him. When she'd gone indoors, I looked at John suspicious like, and I says, "What's that chap gettin' at?"

'Johnny laughs, an' comes to the outside of the shop, and says, "Can you do with a pint?" I looks an' says, "Try me." So we sauntered down as far as Tom Reed's, at the "Lord Nelson" what he then kept.

'"I can trust you, Charlie," says he, handin' me my mug, "but for Gawd's sake keep yer mouth shut. You ha' seen me take home old gulls, and you 'a brung 'em too; I 'a' shot old gulls when no one else looked at 'em, till some on 'em fared to wonder if I lived on 'em, or sent 'em to London for hat-featherin'. Let 'em think, s'long as they don't *know*."

'"I ha' brung you dozens, I'll allow,' says I. 'I allers allowed you was sellin' feather-beds, and pillers, an' cushions—leastwise, the dried feathers for 'em.'

'"That's only half," says he. "Of course, you know my missus is a lady pork-butcher" (finishin' his first pint).

'"You can stand me another, John, if you like," says I, laughin', "and I'll promise you the next two kitties I shoot." So he shoves the two mugs for'ard.

'"You know, Charlie, the missus hev lots of meat snippin's—fat an' sich-like, sich as some makes into swurd [pork-cheese]; well, when I hev plucked a gull I skin it, and then cuts off the brists, and the meat off the thighs; well, that all go through the machine 'longer the pork snips; and they all mixes up to a temptin' mess, better-coloured than plain pork. And she puts in sage to flavour it. When I hand her the gull meat I allers say, 'Put in plenty o' sage, old gal; for Gawd's sake *don't forget the sage*!'"

'"Well," says I, "I can't see as how pigs is much cleaner feedin' criturs than gulls is; pigs'll eat the rats what fall into the pig-copper, when arter the floatin' fat; gulls'll swaller drowned mice an' young kittens washed up on the mudflats, so wheer's the differs ? "

' " Quite so," laughs Johnny.

' " Then," says I, " thet's where my old harnsers and rooks go to what you've hed off me. No, John, I won't breathe a word ; you've heerd the old sayin', ' The deceever is as bad as the thief '. But after now, I ain't pertick'ler gone on pork sausages of *thet* kidney ! " '

PINTAILS' MEAN GAME

CHAPTER III

NIGHTS ASHORE

'They were in the habit of seeing each other continually, of going to the same places, of meeting the same people. It was not exactly a friendship of natural affinity, but rather of proximity, which answers well in many cases.'

—MRS. OLIPHANT

ONE wet night in June 1888 there assembled together a mob of Breydon *habitués* in Albert Beckett's workshop on Fuller's Hill. You had to climb into the gunner-cabinet-maker's den by means of a wide step-ladder that was as ancient as this favourite meeting-place; there was no handrail to it, not even a rope hand-pull, and to mount it in safety one had to exercise some care. Any who had indulged in extra refreshment, to withstand prospective hours of pungent tobacco-smoke and heated argument, reached the door by a series of unrehearsed acrobatics, that elicited boisterous comments from those in waiting for their turn to climb, more especially when nearing the top, for the door opened outwardly.

These fellows had mustered up to celebrate what was, to them, a most noteworthy event in the history and affairs of Breydon, the cause of which the following excerpt from a local newspaper will explain:

SHOOTING SPOONBILLS

Before the Magistrates: the Mayor (Mr. T. B. Steward) and Messrs. C. Wolverton, B. H. Press, J. H. Fellows, Isaac Hill, and Daniel Tomkins.

Albert Beckett, a respectably dressed man, was summoned under the Wild Birds' Protection Act for shooting two spoonbills on Breydon water. Mr. Leach (Chamberlain & Leach) prosecuted. Defendant pleaded guilty. Mr. Leach said defendant had told him that he had waited for fifteen years to get a spoonbill, and that when he saw the birds, he shot two of them without caring for the Act. Such men would rather pay the usual fine and shoot such valuable birds as specimens, which were worth £3 a-piece, but more generally sold at thirty shillings to £2. Mr. Leach expressed regret that the birds could not be forfeited, and he hoped the bench would fine the defendant heavily. The Chairman said the magistrates thought there was no doubt it was a speculation on the part of the defendant, and he would be fined forty shillings and costs, or one month's imprisonment.

The case had caused quite a commotion among the whole brotherhood of the old Estuary—punt-gunners, shoulder-gunners, eel-men, bird-catchers, and others who had grievances, or imagined they had, against Bird Watcher, river bailiffs, 'law-jugglers', and the 'rotten Guv'mint' what made and carried out 'sich damnabill laws'. For an hour before the magistrates 'sat' small knots of Breydon folk, ignoring the call of the tides and bursting with argument, loafed around the town hall, others leaning on the bar of the 'Town Hall Tavern' opposite, and only left off debating for a moment to sip at their pewters, or to light their pipes, frequently to forget both for another spell of controversy. When the hall doors were opened they promptly filled the gallery of the court, some arrayed in their brightest blue guernseys, or their lately tanned slops. Some had never before visited the police-court, and some would oftener have been seen there had all that was known, or even suspected, of them been brought home to them and proven. Cheers were trembling on several lips as the defendant placed himself in front of the dock, at the disposal of the magistrates; and loud cheers were accorded him as he later left the court; while several who had found the court, like its 'dry-dock' in its centre, a very dry place, ambled into the nearest favourite tavern, taking their hero with them, to drink to his very good health, chiefly at his own expense.

Beckett had seen several spoonbills on Breydon on his shooting expeditions, but so far had never shot one himself; but it had happened shortly before the arrival of the spoonbills in question that a snug little legacy running into three figures had come to him; and on the strength of his access of riches he determined, at whatever cost, to obtain a couple to adorn the bar of the 'Lord Nelson', that is, if they were silly enough to come within range of his punt-gun. Neither of the birds was what might technically be termed a good specimen. They were immature; nor were they first-rate models after their preservation. One possessed a very small crest and a white breast; the other had no crest feathers at all, whilst black spots still showed upon the primaries. Both were young males. At Beckett's decease the widow sold them to a local politician, who presented them to the Conservative Club, where they now adorn the smoke-room. Beckett decorated the case himself most grotesquely with a row of short-stalked reedmace 'pokers', that curiously suggest a row of Breydon stakes. Another case containing two magnificent birds stands in close proximity: of these anon.

Albert Beckett was a vivacious, good-tempered frequenter of Breydon, blessed with a considerable share of sound common sense, but was unable either to read or write. For some years he was landlord of the 'Lord Nelson'; and tenant of the 'Gossip Shop' for a somewhat longer period. He was the designer of a superior type of gun-punt, was exceedingly handy with carpenters' tools, and was of some service as handyman in the matter of gun- and boat-repairs. He was free, too, and the Breydon men were always ready to do him services in return. It was an old eel-catcher who hastened home to Beckett and put him on the track of the 'banjo-bills' he had so much coveted. On the occasion of his going off in his punt after them he openly launched his boat, passing 'Ducker', the Watcher, near the Knowl, within a gunshot of the 'Bowling Green'. Indeed, watcher and poacher exchanged confidences quite freely as they rowed away side by side.

'Hallo!' said Ducker. 'Wheer are you bound for, Albert?'

'After spoonbills,' replied Beckett, with a good-tempered grin, 'and mean to have one, if not two.'

'But you *hedn't* better!' advised the burly Ducker, who very rarely obtained a case, and usually did not want to. In this particular instance Ducker could not help himself, as the job had been too well advertised. 'I'm comin' along, bor, to see fair play.'

'By all means, Mr. Ducker,' agreed Beckett. 'You can come along and welcome, and I'll show you how to use the big gun, only don't come too close or we might get to loggerheads, and that wouldn't be nice, would it, Mr. Ducker Chambers?'

Ducker slackened his pace but hung in the rear with perfect good-humour; and he knew the cabinet-maker's mettle. Beckett soon got within range of the unfortunate birds, which were exceedingly tame, fired at the nearer bird, but at the moment of pulling the trigger the other crossed its companion's track, and both fell dead to one shot.

The birds were carefully wrapped in a jumper and placed

FRED CLARKE SCULLING TO FOWL

BECKETT AFTER HIS SPOONBILLS

under the forepeak. As Beckett was rowing homewards, Ducker drew up, and said how very much he would like to have a look at the two birds, a little more closely. 'But you can't,' said Beckett. 'It's quite enough for you to know that I've got 'em : *two*, and don't you forget it.' They were a little later shown to several interested persons, and then hurried to Ben Dye's for preservation, strict instructions being left with them to the effect that no one, under any consideration, was to see them. Albert then walked to the police station, coolly informed the man in charge of his successfully-planned misdemeanour, and pulling out a handful of gold said he was prepared to pay the fines and costs due for such an offence. These of course were refused, but the interview was entered up against him as conclusive evidence.

Four hours after, the stolid and ponderous Ducker strolled into the police station to lay information, but was promptly told that he was a bit behindhand. In due course the summons was served, with the result already shown. In the court the defendant was fractious, and aired a few strong opinions.

One of the J.P.'s demanded to know why the birds were not produced at court.

'Well, your washups, that's impossible to let you see 'em ; besides, if I had brought 'em with me they'd have stunk the court out.' That remark applied, of course, only to the carcases that had been in the dustbin for a fortnight.

It was voted at the smoky hotel, where the whisky and ale were vanishing down droughty throats, that 'they'd all had a d—— good entertainment!' . . .

Albert Beckett was off to the workshop after an early tea, having left his buxom spouse in charge of the 'house'—as landlady of the 'Lord Nelson', for he was expecting a large and lively muster of exultant Breydoners, who would arrive chuckling their further congratulations; they would be bursting with argument, opinions, and facetiousness. Finished and unfinished furniture were stowed in the background, or they would have been monopolized by clumsy loungers, and the place was roughly tidied up. Sundry boxes and fish-trunks were planted in the 'public area' among the shavings, and an odd plank or two laid across them for seats. His queer congregation began to climb the steps and to take their favourite gossiping stations; pipes of all persuasions were loaded up for the first round.

'Go on, chaps,' said Beckett, 'but mind the shavin's: smoke all you like, but don't drop matches.'

'Righto,' said Little Stork Thacker. 'We'll pocket 'em.'

'Well, what did you think of this morning's little job at the horl ?' asked Beckett.

'Ripping'; 'Like yar pluck'; 'What about old Press ?' rattled from strong throats.

'Yes !' snapped Beckett. '*His* son Horry got *his* pair of spunebills all right, and nobody else must even look at 'em. Before he went after *his* pair o' birds Horry Press must ha' put the blinkers on old Ducker !'

SPOONBILL AND OYSTER CATCHERS

'Pint-sized 'uns !' growled the burly Pero Pestell; 'they're good for weak eyes.' The company noisily assented to this, with a little coarse laughter. Albert himself was exceedingly wrathful with the elder Press for 'bein' down on *him*.'

Beckett was, if anything, a better workman at night than he was by day. It needed a very large number of wildfowl to tempt him up Breydon after nightfall, but the least reliable rumour of good birds in the daytime quickly persuaded him to drop his plane for the trigger. He gave his mind fully to his joinery at night, but how he could concentrate on the ticklish mending of antique furniture amidst the smoke and clatter was always a puzzle to me. He seemed to revel in the babel of voices. To-night he was at work upon a new table, which had to be at the shop next morning.

Harry Collins, the cabman-punter, came puffing up the staircase into the workshop:

'Thought I must give yer a look, Albert, and condone with yer,' said Harry.

'He don't want *condonements*!' interposed Willie B. 'He wants congratulating. Beckett has got what he's long been wanting.'

'The same thing,' Collins insisted. 'You've got so nice about pernouncin' your words. Now, *I* come off a lot luckier up at the horl, as some on yer know, when I shot an' got a red-necked grebe in the river, pretty nigh agin' the bridge.'

'What's that?' demanded Beckett, who had just finished turning in a screw. 'I've heard somethin' about that little affair.'

'Why, I was goin' to tell 'em about my shootin' that grebe. All right, I'll go on, if them a-card-playin' up the corner back o' the stove'll shurrup a bit. Well, it was like this: I forget the year—I think it was in April 1873—but that don't matter. Old Gunn o' Norwich had it. I'd been to the boat-shud and was bringin' away my little double-barrel cripple-stopper. I'd got it, barrel in one pocket, stock in the other——'

'Just like you jolly poachers!' remarked Fiddler Goodens. 'When it ain't tips, it's hares.'

'Theers tips *an'* tips,' rejoined the stout little cabman, with a wink, 'in my line o' business. Well, I'd got as far as Gamblin's Mill when I see a rum bird floatin' an' deevin' in the river, on the last of the ebb tide. Not givin' a thought to wheer I was, I'd put the gun together, which happened to be loaded in one barrel, with the cap off, but I shoved on another, without ever a thought of re-primin' the nipple.'

'You're a dangerous feller!' snorted Pero; 'and I allers said so.'

'I ups gun and fired, but she hung fire for a second and then went off with a roar, killin' the bird outright, and it lay a-floatin' on the river. Theer happened to be a ship's boat moored to the quay-hid, lucky enough with the oars layin' acrost the thwarts; so I jumps in, lettin' go the painter, and in a twinklin' hed the oars out and shoved her smacksman's fashion, and we pretty nigh drifted to the bridge afore I laid hold o' my bird. People as had heared the roar of the gun was craning theer necks over the bridge-rail; and among 'em was a pal I knew by his voice, who shouted, "Cab overboard, Harry?" However, I soon sculled back and clumb the steps to the shore, with the bird in one hand, while a interferin' policeman took hold of my gun and said he'd take care of it for me, without axin' by my leave.'

'You must ha' bin a reglar pirate!' growled Pero.

'Br-r-reydon pirates was allers *curiosities*,' suggested Tom Reed, who was known as 'Huckerin' Tom', from a certain hesitancy of speech that made his animated rhetoric exceedingly grotesque. 'Th-th' breed 'on't be m-m-mopt out s'long as P-p-p-Pero's alive!' To which statement more than one agreed. Pero snorted, and lit his pipe.

'"Policemen ain't useter guns," says I,' went on Collins, "so I'll thank you for mine," I says, takin' it from his hand. He know'd that he'd no right to it. But he said he should report the case, and axed me to remember he'd had a shift up, and he worn't a *constable* now; and said he didn't know as how he orter let me keep the bird. However, he said he'd report the job, or bust.

'"Look here, Sergeant," says I, "you ain't power under the Act to take even that!" Theer was a crowd drawin' up, so I says to Jimmy Hurr, who had come at that minute, "Do with a drink, Jimmy boy?" Says he, "Nothin' I'd like better." I axes the policeman if he could do with a drop, but as he was now a sergeant he shook his head very solum; so we turned round by Shipley's, and went into the "Bridge Hotel." I axed the landlord for an old newspaper to wrap the bird in.

'Now, the weather was freshy and cold, and I worn't in a hurry to sell the bird, and, as luck would hev it, the sergeant got the summons through early, thanks to Inspector Dann, who was a good old sport and a friend of the gunners, besides bein' a rare petridge- and snipe-shooter. Besides, he was terrible anxious to see the bird, havin' heard it was a curio. So he called at mine later to see it.

'If I was you, Harry, my boy," he says, "I'd get Mr. Harvey to make it into a skin; it'll be handier to pull about and show. Alf'll do it to-night when he come from his timber-measurin'." I took his tip, and axed what about seein' a lawyer. "You 'on't want one," says he, "I'll take care an' be at the court, all bein' well, and put in a word for you; you swear it ain't a duck, and I'll give 'em a surprise when the time come, and we'll learn the J.P.'s to know when a duck *ain't* a duck."

'On the day I had to appear there was a pretty full court, and a half-dozen J.P.'s; but there worn't one as knew much about birds, though two or three on 'em used my cab now an' then. Charles Diver, the clerk, riz, and straightened hisself, givin' me a nod. Then he opens a paper, and says, "You know, of course, you are summonsed for shootin' a duck in the close season? Do you plead guilty, or not guilty?"

'"Certainly, sir, I'm not guilty!" I says, and looks at Dann.

'"Very well," says the clerk. "We'll hear what the police-sergeant has to say about it." So the sergeant riz, and starts to swear, and tells them all a yarn, pretty much as I've described to you, and I was asked if I wanted to axe any questions.

'"Sergeant," says I, "do you know a duck from a mallard?"

'"I ought to," says he. "I've bred hundreds!"

'"Very well, then," says I. "I suppose you never bred a duck with a beak like an old harnser?"

'"No!" he snaps.

'"Thanks," says I; "and where's your witnesses." He had forgot to bother about any, feelin' so cocksure.

'"You don't deny you shot the duck," says the chairman, "and in close time."

'"I deny it *in to-to*," says I. Just then up jumps my old friend Inspector Dann.

'"Gentlemen," says he—"or rather, your washups—I have here the skin of the bird in question (takin' the skin out of a cardboard box), which I think will interest you and settle at once the question of its identity. You will observe that the feet are peculiar, being lobated, and not webbed as in the duck or mallard; also that the bill is sharp and vertical, and not broad or horizontally placed, as in the duck and mallard."

'It was a reg'lar lesson in—horny—what do you call it?'

'Ornithology,' corrected Admiral Gooch.

'Well, they turned it over, and whispered; and the chairman leans over to Diver; and he riz, and says:

'"Under the circumstances, the magistrates dismiss the case." He know'd a grebe from a duck!

'I had a last shot at 'em, and I turned sharply, and axes:

'"Gentlemen, do I leave this court without a stain on my character?"

'"Think yourself lucky, Collins," says Diver, "that you leave this court without payin' a fine!" That's all my yarn.'

'Bravo, Harry!' roared the crowd.

'What become of the bird, and what did you say it was?' asked several.

'Well, it was a red-necked grebe; and I sold it for half a sovereign to Gunn, the Norwich bird stuffer.'

Gooch contended that Collins ought to have made more of the bird than ten shillings, considering how rarely these birds were observed in Norfolk: three or four at the outside were observed annually on the broads, mostly in autumn. He had never shot one—he rarely threw away shots on diving birds; and, pointing to Pero, made remark:

'It once took an old artillery militia sergeant nine shots to frighten a dabchick, and a tenth to kill it, in a low on Breydon!'—still pointing to Pero Pestell.

'Pero likes to shoot frozen-in fowl, with both feet anchored to the ice,' jibed in Willie B.

Pero grunted and said he'd like another job of the same kind, for that 'little varmin of a dabchick' beat him hollow.

'I reckon,' said he, 'half a sovereign plenty for a grebe, for poor old Overend's stuffed red-necker fetched only nine shillin's at his sale of Breydon birds.'

'And at Robert Rising's sale of Norfolk birds, at Horsey, in 1885,' put in Gooch, 'a case containing four red-necks, three Sclavonians, and three dabchicks went for thirty shillings to Norwich Museum. You were lucky, Harry, and got all the fame thrown in for nothing.'

'It ain't the first scrape you've been in, Collins,' said Albert Beckett, 'and slipped out of it like an eel.'

'No,' assented the optimistic cabman, 'it ain't by a long chalk. I once went after mushrooms on Dan Banham's mesh, and a big bull——'

'Oh, we've heard that yarn over an' over agin!' said Pero. 'Tell 'em about them swans, and shoot all marsh bulls, says I.'

'All right,' agreed Harry. 'Old Potot Marsham was up the North River walls—off to meet Powley's brick-wherry comin' downstream. On his way up—he hadn't got his gun with him as he mostly hed—he sees two swans hevin' a good time athort the river, and felt properly done not bein' able to hev a shot at 'em. Them birds hed bin givin' the Breydon chaps a lot of trouble, not bein' as tame as they might be. They *was* tame 'uns gone half wild, you know. Potot boarded the wherry, up agin' the Four Mile House, and axed the wherryman for the use of his gun—they all carried 'em a few year ago—tellin' him what he'd seen, and if they was still busy he'd hev a shot at 'em. As it happened they was, and didn't take much account of the wherry. Potot laid low on the forepeak and fired at 'em, killin' 'em both.'

'Potot sees me soon after he gets home, and later brings 'em round to my place in a sack on his back, with some mesh-grass stuffed in on top of 'em, for a blind, you know. He axed me if I could dispose of 'em for him; and as he fared a bit nervous I told him I'd work the oracle for him. I took 'em to Durrant the game-dealer's, and axed what he'd give for 'em. "Ten bob the two," he says, which I took. Somehow the country police heard of the swans bein' missin', and the owner, suspectin' foul play, instituted inquiries. Potot, gettin' the sound of it, comes hurryin' to me, and said suffin' was brewin', and he was afeard he'd bin seen on the wherry. He'd heard, too, they was gettin' a reward-bill of five pounds out for 'em.

'Off I rushed to Durrant, and tells him; and I says to him as I'd seen him put the two birds in a hamper.

'"Don't you worry, Harry," he says; "they're already on the way to Leadenhall Market; and it'll take a very clever detective to identify waterfowl when the label's tore off the packages." Durrant was a good old soldier when *he* snift anything suspicious; and he was a jolly old fence for a decent and respectable poacher, in a small sort o' way, as anybody ever wanted to see. He'd bin a gamekeeper hisself, you know.

'What fat little bags I've seen shoved round the back of his stall on a Saturday mornin', with a brace or two o' petridges underneath the peewits; and many a plump pheasant what had met with sudden death in the country, with bunches o' coots coverin' 'em over from general observation,' ventured Fiddler Goodens.

Collins was bursting to spin another yarn, when one of the card-players insisted that he should shut up for a short spell, adding, 'You'd talk a donkey's hid off!'

'There's one thing,' edged in Gooch, who so far had been fairly quiet, 'it's rarely Collins wags his jaw without being interesting.' Most assented to that. 'Now, then, Harry, you can do with a thimbleful of the real stuff?' went on Gooch, who kept a bottle in Beckett's locked cupboard for use on special occasions, like the present one. Beckett turned to the cupboard and handed Gooch his bottle. Collins raised his 'thimbleful': 'Here's to you, Admiral, and you, Albert,' and tipped his glass with the air of a connoisseur. There was just enough left in the bottle to allow Gooch and Beckett to toast him in return. Of course much chaff ensued from the company.

Beckett was well liked by the crowd; he was interested in all that appertained to Breydon, he had learnt to stuff a bird moderately well, and he was exceptionally fond of live pets. At this period he exhibited a great liking for parrots, the Amazons in particular being great favourites, and made his own parrot-cages in masterly fashion. At punt-building and gun-smithery he was an apt workman. For a number of years a wild rabbit was a tenant of the old loft, and withstood the fumes of the vilest tobacco burnt by ancient and well-seasoned water-folk without flinching; dying of old age, and much regretted by the gossip club.

Now, owing to there being a stable below and breadcrusts laid aside for the coney, mice flourished and had a good time in the workshop. With characteristic sportsman-like instincts Beckett had, for their destruction a small pea-rifle, kept in a cupboard, and with this weapon made excellent practice. There ran one or two stout wires across the workshop, tied to the beams, and these were used for hanging patterns and designs for making and adorning his furniture. The mice found this out, and it made quite a diversion when one and another acrobated across it; and very often did the cabinet-maker pot a mouse with the small cartridges he fired. It was good target practice.

Notwithstanding the riot of voices below, a mouse essayed this evening to run across the wire, and Beckett quietly snatched up the little rifle and promptly fired at it, the little victim falling upon Fiddler's shoulder and thence to the floor. So trivial an incident was sufficient to shunt the gossip on to quite a different line. Short'un Page, who had lost at the card-table—which was an up-ended fish-trunk—sagely piped in with, 'D—— all mice, say I. I've had my old house-boat swarm with 'em, but how the dowse they got aboard lick me altogether.'

'You shouldn't leave smelts and wittels about,' said Fiddler Goodens. 'You must ha' bred 'em at home and brung 'em aboard with yar old frail-basket of grub. Thet's how old Bugles started his cockroach-farm in his old house-boat. They played hoss-races over him when he was asleep, and he didn't take much notice till he woke up with one in his mouth and one in his left ear; then he got savage, took out his furniture—what you might hev put in his frail-basket—and chucked his beddin' on the rond. Then he pulled the plug out o' the boat's bottom and sunk her on the high tide. It may be true, and it may not, that reg'lar flocks of 'em like tiny black mussel-ducks come swimmin' out o' the door. Some unfortunate ones didn't jine up, but swarmed up to the roof; and when he spotted 'em he went in and slaughtered 'em with an old bit o' leather.'

'I allers say,' put in one of the crowd, 'cockroaches is like lice—they spring from nothin'. My mother allers said, when she see anything o' the sort, some one hed bewitched, or put on us the mock-moorin's.'

'Chuck all vermin!' demanded the imperious Pero. 'You're draggin' in a nice yarn now. 'Tain't respectable!'

'Well,' said little Short'un, 'Flaxman once told us that a parson by the name o' Moses sent 'em among the gipsies, and King Fairo hed 'em bad, too—so the Book say: reg'lar plagues on 'em; wuss'n rats!'

'I allers say cuss *rats*,' asserted one Liffen, a sturdy shrimper. 'Why, they play the devil with my nets. They come o' nights from holes in the quay-side, where my boat lay-to, and gnaw holes through the meshes, to get at the little soles an' big shrimps what ain't shook out clean afore hoistin' the cod-end up to the mast-hid. Careful as yer may be, some shrimps get left now an' then. If rats only got under the bottom-boards, instead of climbin' the nets, I'd thank 'em, for lots o' them warmin o' shore-crabs scuttle about there among the stone ballast, and give us plenty o' trouble takin' up the floors to clear 'em out. When we chaps sit aboard in an evenin', mendin' the nets, we know when a rat is aboard, even if we don't see him; we can hear him scrunchin' crabs to get at the meat.' Snicker and others of the fraternity sorted over another rat yarn or two, punctuating them well with maledictions.

'During the cold winter we had a few years ago,' said A. B., one of the younger generation of gentlemen gunners, 'some starving rats found their way into my house-boat on Breydon, and I couldn't get clear of them, nor trap them; I disturbed them one day as they were starting to pluck a moorhen I'd left on a settle. So before I went home in the punt I dismembered the bird and hung it up by a bit of string on a nail in the match-boarding, a good reach above a trap that I set below. Next morning I discovered that a male rat had leapt before he looked, but I only found half of him in the trap; another rat, or maybe two or more, had eaten the fore half, but what had become of the head I could not say; anyway, I failed to find it. I re-set the trap and strung up the nether half of rat number one, having rolled it among the feathers stripped from the moorhen. On the following morning I discovered the lady rat, which had been trying to get at her mate's remains, was fast in the trap by her hind legs. In her misery she struggled to free herself, but I settled her promptly by dropping her and the trap into the drain, where I had broken the ice for the purpose. I flung her carcase on the ice and went into the cabin, but was soon at the window to see what was up, and the cause of the riot. It seems that a hungry grey gull had picked up the rat, and a half-dozen equally famished grey crows were disputing possession with the gull, which promptly settled the contest by swallowing the rat on the wing.

'I had an impression,' continued A. B., 'that single legs occasionally discovered in steelfall traps were left there by the owners, who had gnawed themselves free of it. Surely he would not eat his own skin and flesh; I am now more inclined to think its surviving companions had made away with—eaten, in fact—the rest of the victim.'

'I copt one once,' put in Short'un—'a leg, the left one—and no rat to it; and two days after I ketched a rat without a left leg.

'The right one, I suppose?' puffed Pero.

'Well, the right rat with the——' Short'un was getting mixed, and subsided, having a suggestion thrown to him by Pero to 'leave it at that; lucky the rats hadn't eaten *him*.'

'I've always noticed, or heard other rat-detesting sufferers assert, that the less cunning male is the first to be captured,' interposed Beckett.

'I ha' noticed that, too,' ventured Pintail Thomas, 'that the female rat gets catched last, but not afore she ha' picked the old chap's bones.'

'*You* orter know, Johnny, if anyone do,' snapped Pero, 'judgin' by the way you've bin through the mill.' This sally was hugely appreciated, and Pero, inflated with martial, or marital pride, added, 'We ain't all hin-picked, same as some punt-gunners are!'

Albert Beckett, at this juncture, drew out from a soiled envelope a cutting from a local paper, that he had long kept in the bottle-cupboard, and told the crowd that here was '*something* as'll show you they catch the big fish as well as the little 'uns, like me.' He was referring to his spoonbill episode. Beckett handed the slip to the Admiral.

'Read that out to 'em, Admiral,' begged Albert. Gooch began :

'This cutting is from the *Yarmouth Independent*, of June 18th, 1881—seven years ago.'

''Tain't about old friend Gunn of Norwich ?" asked Ben Dye.

'The very same,' replied Gooch, and began again :

'Edward Gunn, Naturalist of Norwich, was summoned under the Wild Birds' Protection Act, 1880——'

GUNN'S LITTLE RINGED PLOVER AND TURNSTONE

'A re-spectfully dressed man, of course!' suggested Fiddler, amid laughter, and one or two strongly worded orders to shut up and listen. Gooch went on :

'For having in his possession certain wild birds, to wit, one dunlin, two plovers, and five dotterel, contrary to the above Act. The Town Clerk appeared in support of the summons. In reply to the charge, Mr. Gunn said he wished to take exception to the word " plover ", named in the summons, which he maintained ought to be turnstones, a word not within the schedule of the new Act.

'The Town Clerk said the Wild Birds' Protection Act was not a new one, being originally passed in 1872. The Chairman (to the defendant), "Do you plead guilty?" Defendant: "I plead guilty to six birds." The Chairman said they should not, at least for the present, proceed with the prosecution against him for having in his possession the plovers. Mr. Gunn, in his defence, pleaded ignorance of the new Act, and said he thought it was only intended for the protection of wildfowl in the usual sense of the word, that was, wild duck and other edible birds in this country, and not those species that are migratory——'

'Good old Tom Gunn,' broke in Ben Dye, who disliked the Birds' Act with a violent hatred.

'Gunn made a pretty good apology for a lawyer, over a clear "cop",' put in Gooch, and proceeded:

'Those species that are migratory, which stayed a short time only when passing to and fro from their breeding stations in the far north, and north-east. The minute dunlin, and the lesser dotterel were procured solely for scientific purposes, and not for their marketable value, which would be a very small sum; but for scientific investigation these birds might prove useful in assisting him to come at unknown facts in the life-history of that species, which was quite distinct from the ringed dotterel, and seemed so little known at the present time. With regard to the two plovers, he submitted that they were not plovers but turnstones, which were not included in the schedule——'

'Just a bit,' suggested Collins. 'I allers heard old gunners, an' everybody what I've seen handle 'em, call 'em turnstone-plovers. If they ain't plovers, what are they!'

'Gunn was wrong in stating they were not plovers, for they are of and belong to the *Charadridæ* family.' (In aside to Pintail: 'Fine word, ain't it, boy?' Thomas nodded absently.) But Gunn objected really to joining turnstone to plover. He was juggling!' said Gooch, who was as well versed in his ornithology as in his schooling.

'Mr. Gunn then referred to the open way in which he obtained the birds and brought them on shore, showing his ignorance of the Act, and hoped that such facts would convince the bench that he had no intention of breaking the law. He also contended that according to the new Act no person had power to search, or cause to be searched, any suspected person ; and the officer exceeded his duty to search his bag.

'The Chairman said the bench considered that the defendant could hardly be ignorant of the Act, and they, therefore, fined him five shillings for each of the six birds, with the costs.

'The bench consisted of C. C. Aldred (Mayor), and Messrs. B. Jay, F. H. Fellows, and H. Teasdel.'

'Who was the clever officer who poked his nose into Gunn's bag ? ' asked one of the crowd.

'Master Joe Buddery ! ' snapped Ben Dye, ' the weights and measures man. When old A. P. went with me in our first ratty old punt to Breydon, Joe used to lay behind the North Wall, oglin' us through his glasses. He vowed he'd nab us, but we gave him the slip every time.'

'Well, he did weigh up old friend Gunn, and he measured up Jack Gibbs, whose punt-gun they'd bin usin', when he tied the punt up to the "Bowlin' Green" staithe and went through the birds,' said Collins. 'Gunnin' is like cabbyin'—neither'll be able to earn a crust before long.' Most of the fellowship agreed with the last statement, which amounted to a prophecy that has since come true, for fowler and fisher and cabman have practically ceased to be.

Rapidly slipped away the hours, and thicker had become the haze of tobacco smoke ; tongues lagged and dry throats yearned for refreshment. One or two had already slipped down the step-ladder, and Beckett broadly hinted that the pubs before long would be closed. It had also entered their tousled heads that such was the case, and 'twas quite unthinkable that they should saunter home, and to bed, without having assuaged the drought that their pipes and patter had set up. Beckett was the last to leave, but not the first by several to stumble into the popular bar-parlour of the old 'Lord Nelson', long-since razed to the ground, with the Girdlestones' historic house next door, to make way for the brewers' wholesale storage-place.

. . . . .

'Scarboro' Jack ' had finished a final round of the red danger-lamps that hung upon triangular trestles, lighthouse-like, or stood upon hummocks of road material that had been thrown up from the trenches in the road. It was time for his 'snack' of supper; the clock had struck the hour of eleven; the last tippler had toddled off home, to be lectured by an indignant spouse upon the horrors of strong drink, an exhortation they knew by heart, and repented not.

There was more than that average 'ancient and fish-like smell' noticed by David Copperfield as Barkis, 'bein' willin', stopped his carrier's cart in front of the 'Duke's Head' just over the way. This pungent aroma was wafted up-river on the wind from the fish-wharves, where herring drip and blood trickled through the fish-swills down the quay-side to the tideway. A reflex of the oil-flares danced upon the fretted tide, as grimy fishermen, speckled and sparkling with fish-scales, hurried their catches ashore: in sweating couples racing

SCARBORO' JACK'S LURCHER

from boat to the herring-baskets with maunds of slithery fishes, from which dropped odd herrings, like flashes of silver in their stride to the fish-wharves. Raucous cries and flickering lamps disturbed the night, as if to hearten the workers and to celebrate a famous glut of herrings; and right fantastical sounded the babel of creaking blocks and sheaves, of human voices, and of wheeled traffic.

Scarboro' sat himself contentedly down upon an upturned fish trunk in front of his sentry-box, having hung his billy-can on the hook of bent wire depending from the coke stove, in order to heat his coffee; then laying a crudely fashioned grid above the clearest part of the fire, carefully placed thereon a couple of full-roed herrings to grill; these were to accompany some slices of bread taken out of the red handkerchief and laid upon his tin plate.

'One night's salt 'un's,' said he; 'prime fish like them—smooth outside as a silver spune, and full as a tick—wor a dish fitter to set before the king than that blackbird pie we kiddies used to talk about, though I reckon gentlemen and ladies as wear crowns don't see many bloaters or over-night salt 'un's, if any at all, on their golden plates. Give me a herrin' aginst all the salmon an' turbots on a nabob's table as ever was; there ain't a nourishiner jint on airth than a full-roed October herrin', unless it be the loin-chunk of a plump young leveret caught in one of yer own set snares. What the dowse is that —— riot?'

Scarboro' snatched up a lamp, while I looked after his 'two-eyed steaks', as he termed them. He shambled to the far end of the trench, muttering as he went, 'Some poor devil of a horse down, I reckon.' The sound of oaths and the slashing of a whip indicated a horse in mishap, not a rare thing in the old horse-traction times, when worn-out crocks were driven to the last inch of their strength, and when men, weary themselves and often brutal, shamefully treated their own or their employer's animals. Fish-wharf work for horses in the 'eighties, and in gluts, was merciless and barbarous. Salt grime and obnoxious aromas must be detestable to equines; yet I have watched a horse, awaiting its load, quietly munching a salt herring! To-day motor traffic is ousting the horse.

Jack came back to his herrings: their odour was pleasant to him, and without ado he sat down in his little hut before the fire, with his plate of fish upon his knees, and shortly washed down the last crumbs of his supper with his coffee.

'I had a rum visitor t'other night,' said he. 'Of all things, an old hare comes trottin' over the Suspension Bridge, and turnin' the corner, took a flyin' leap over the trunch, much to her surprise an' mine, and made off to the market-gardens t'other side of King Harry's Tower. They do stray like that, you know, now and again. I snatched up a brick-bat to hull at her, but she didn't wait; if she hed, she might hev bin a very sick old Sally. I heerd afterwards that when she got as far as the Cinder-ovens she scented the meshes, jumped into the river, and swum over. If I'd had my blissed old "Snap" she wouldn't hev got away so easy, I can assure you. You talk about hares, bor, they fare to be much scarcer on the Mautby an' Stokesby meshes, where they once run'd about by hundreds, right into the 'seventies, when they were strictly preserved, and hare-coursin' was proper sport, if you like. Me and Trotter Lodge, good old Bob Warner, and half a score old poachin' chums did our honest best in tryin' to reduce the numbers. We run'd a bit thick in times, though I preferred workin' on my own. We'd bin hevin' a drink or two one evenin' on our way to the meshes—four of us—and two of us got a bit merry, and in consequence a bit fulehardy. Anyway, Trotter's gun went off as he stumbled, and hit two of us who was walkin' in front. They smarted so that we hed to come back to the old "Victoria", where we hed the drinks. Me and Bob had to remove two o' their garments and made both on 'em bend down while we other two keerfully picked out the shots with the point of a penknife; we counted the shot, and made 'em nine all told, much to the delight of a crowded bar.

'You know, of course, in my younger time I hung out West Norfolk way a lot, where I got quite familiar with the pheasants. When I settled at Yarmouth, and got a job as flour-sack carter to old Gabriel Bell, the Ranter, I hed to be content with mesh hares, and what I didn't know about 'em I was allers riddy to learn. Old Gabriel was a preacher, of sorts, and a hot Metherdy; he often told me that follerin' hares 'ud never lead me hivvenwards. I was fond of a joke, and said as how, if there worn't any hares on that road, I'd prefer to keep to the old 'un, where there was more company, for a few years longer, anyhow. But he persisted that no poachers was allowed in, as far as he could see, and not accordin' to his programme. I used to arger, so did he, till he give it up. I never, I told him, could see as how poachin' is a crime or a sin; it's only a misdemeanour, same as brawlin' in a church, gatherin' a few mushrooms, pluckin' blackberries off hedges; or for a big swell, maybe with a M.P. to his name, or a alderman, gettin' blind drunk; with a kind-hearted policeman, puttin' either, or both on 'em, into a cab, when he find them in the doorway, tryin' keyholes with the key the wrong side up, and sendin' 'em home rejoicin'. Werrily, as old Gabriel would say, he shall reap his reward—nex' mornin'. Accordin' to the Game Laws, that slop had bin guilty of compoundin' a felony. All rot! I know'd a J.P. in the county whose kitchen-garden carrots was walked off every night by hares from the squire's land, who was a J.P. too.

The first J.P. give me a sovereign for *night-work* and three bob a day deek-fyin', and sent the hares I snared by a Norridge grocer's cart to a city game-dealer's in the know. 'Tworn't long after when the squire, who'd once fined me for nettin' petridges, give me a tip the same size as my fine and costs, and half the J.P.'s pheasants I could polish off as came into *his* place, and undertook to send 'em to Norridge in his own trap.'

'Give us their names ? ' I asked, by way of a joke.

'No, sir, unless we call 'em Mr. Take an' Squire Give. Old poachers don't give J.P.'s names away. Their little games was not thefts, but misdemeanours ; but carried out in fairness at court, without packed benches, they was both as answerable to the d—— Game Laws of their own backin' up, as they made me out to be. To pay a chap like me to poach on the cross made both on 'em poachers as well. Now, I don't hold wi' poachin' gangs—they ain't sports ; and if chicken-stealin' pay 'em better, and theer was a little excitement thrown in, they'd go arter fowls instead o' game. Real poachers ain't thieves. Them gangs maul keepers as soon as look at 'em. They usually get away by sheer numbers, with plenty o' birds, slaughtered like fat hens, without the excitement of trackin', or the joy of a hunter's heart-beats, as you might say. They hop it in a smart dorg-cart—they'd use a light steam engine if such things was on the roads. I reckon my forefathers hunted bustards, deers, wild ducks, and coneys for grub, with flintstone slings and bows and arrows, and *hed* to ; they hunted along o' the ancestors of Henry the Seventh, the greedy weasel-faced ole warmin what I've read of, what was so mingy that he used hawks instead of weapons, instead of properly follerin' up his game, like a poacher, on foot. Them flint-slingers owned the land, till stronger folks snook it, and put up notice-boards about spring-guns and man-traps ! And if them old kings—say, like King Harry the Eighth—worn't downright thieves, who snook churches, and who robbed the Catholics and gave the land to some of his pals, then a round-shouldered, wore-out old poacher like me orter bin a archy-bishop.'

Had Scarboro' lived in the present free-speaking era the reddest Socialist could scarcely have been a match for him, without the bitterness, or with the same good-humoured twinkle of his eye. I gleaned from Jack, somehow, that he had been a keen reader of books lent him by a clerical ' client ,' and also of the newspapers.

'Look here, young Patt'son, you can't kill in a jail the instinck bred in a true poacher, nor yet his love of wild nature ginerally. If one don't come of a royal strain, like King Charlie's span'els, likely as not we come in a roundabout way from Ishmael, or in a line from Father Adam; though *his* mate wasn't perfect, for she went in the garden and pinched an apple, so some parsons tell us. Come to that, we all fare pinchers—of sorts.'

'You're a queer chap, Scarboro', with your historics and your philosophies.'

'Well, if you mean my rigmaroles, I must ha' caught 'em off old Gabriel Bell. Ain't it about time you made for home? Not tired you yet? Well, let me load the old briar agin. You'll find some jolly hard nuts among game-preservers; why, a little farmer dussen't shoot at a pheasant, a hare, or possible a miserable little rabbit in some places, though they be a-robbin' him night and day, because the landowner, or somebody over his head, hev let the shootin' to some red-whiskered, freckle-faced, soap-bilin' nabob, or a clever, money-makin' pickle-mixer. I knowed a poor devil of a farmer who dussen't even drain the water off his lower mesh-levels because a unedjicated money-stuffed bookmaker had hired the *rights* of shootin' the snipes what come to 'em.

'Of course, you know, when I went poachin', I preferred to breed my own dogs, like old "Snap", what you knew. We was real pals; 'twasn't often as I poached in company—some fule is a'most sure to make mischief. I never stopped to arger with a keeper, because "Snap" could prognosticate him a hundred yards away; I never carried a nobbler; and I left my nets behind if I couldn't clear 'em. I wasn't ever too proud to run—*skute,* if you like it better. If I was copt, I paid up, and took the *interest* when I came out of court, as sune as possible.

'You'll think it very funny—lots of folks do—how it is that when petridge or pheasant shootin' come in, on the very day mornin' you'll see game hangin' up in the game-shops, quicker 'an traps or trains could carry 'em. Look 'ere, there's sich a thing as nettin' 'em a day or so before; of smugglin' them alive to a game-dealer who's got a long chicken-run at the back, or a cellar behind; also a little muzzle-loader pistol or shot-gun—what's to stop him murderin' them hisself and hangin' them up in the shop with blood on 'em? Most people what buy game prefer to see the feathers a bit blood-spotty.

'You know some o' the little tricks o' the trade; how

eggs is nicked from one game-preserve and sold to another; of leverets trap-netted to stock a "shoot" what's short of 'em. Boy, parsons and lawyers know a trick or two, if they be sporty men. Jest one yarn, to wind up, like:

'A report come from A's farm to the police at the village of B—— (name in full don't matter), to say that six turkeys hed bin stole. Police-Sergeant Beans (yes, Beans'll do) says to Constable Sniffs, "We must get on somebody's track, but first let's go to the farm and see what's what!" They see the farmer, who showed 'em the shud wheer the birds was snaked from. The constable shoved the straw about with his foot, unearthin' one dead turkey with a broken neck; and off they goes, takin' the turkey, for a pattern, in a sack with them.

'"Now, who," says the sergeant, scratchin' his hid, "whose work do it look like? Don't look like Billy Horner's, nor Jimmy Rayson's, nor Teddy Barlow's: *they* prefer long-tails, and two or three each fare quite enough. Chicken-stealin' ain't in their line. What about Tibby Jessup?"

'"Let's try Tibby *first*," says the constable; "he's all likely to be abed"; and off they marches, afore most people was up, to Tibby's cottage down the pightle. Without a word they carefully tried the latch, finding the door undone, and heerd Tibby snorin' upstairs like a 'potamus. Constable Sniffs tiptoed through to the wash-hus, and plumps the dead turkey in the copper, puttin' the lid on; and tiptoes back agin, and shuts the door, both standin' outside. The sergeant knocks at the door with a stick.

'"Hullo!" says a rough voice upstairs. "Who the divvil's that a-knockin' my door in, enough to wake the dade?"

'"It's only us, Tibby," says the sergeant. "Come down sune as ye can; we jist want a word or two with ye."

'"What's that you, Sergeant?" says Tibby. "I'll be down in a minute; but you've come to the wrong house this time. I come to bed early arter a hard day's work in the garden; besides, if I'd bin a-poachin', d'ye think I'd come to bed and leave the door undone? You try it."

'Both on 'em tried it, and told Tibby as he was comin' downstairs they could see he'd left it undone.

'"If you suspect anything," says Tibby, "you're at perfeck libbity to overhaul the place. Whatever's missin' now?"

'"Turkeys," says the sergeant. "Chris'mas turkeys."

'"Turkeys!" says Tibby. "Only turkeys? Oh, I thought you was after long-tails, but you 'on't find even *them*; turkeys, bor, ain't in my line at all."

'So the two started searching the pantry; upstairs under the bed—apologizin' to the old lady, in a white nightcap, and sittin' up indignant in bed, like a queen; then they inspected the dickey-shud, the hins' roost, and up the chimbley; and then starts right tragic-like to scratch theer hids.

'"Theer you are, gents," says Jessup, grinnin' athort his features like a laughin' hyeeney. "Didn't I tell yer so?"

'"Jist wait a bit, Tibby," says the constable. "We'd better try the wash-hus." So into the wash-hus they marched, Tibby behind 'em, with his gills turnin' a bit whitish.

'"Try the copper," orders Sergeant Beans, in a starn voice. "*Try the copper.*" The constable goes to the copper, and liftin' the lid, catches sight of a turkey, and holds it up by a hind leg.

'"What's this?" roars the sergeant, turnin' to Tibby.

'"Gawd's truth!" said the crestfallen old chap, "what a d——d fule I must ha' bin; blessed if I didn't think I'd buried all the lot *under the coals* in the coal-shed!"

'Axed why he'd left the one dead in the farm-shud, he meekly replies as how six turkeys was more 'an a man's load, so he'd left the tother under the straw, to be called for when required. He hoped they wouldn't charge him with stealin' *that* one.'

CHAPTER IV

CERTAIN GUNNING MATTERS

' Since the introduction of breach-loading and hammerless weapons, accidents never should, and never would, happen, were ordinary precautions taken, and a few simple precepts attended to.'

—' 20-BORE '

A NUMBER of deplorably faulty guns were formerly in use upon Breydon, and the marshes surrounding, in the palmy days of the earlier, and even the latter, half of the last century—guns with rust-pitted barrels, defective locks, often made worse by amateur tinkering, and glued and patched-up stocks; these were made the more dangerous by often careless and grossly incompetent handling. There were guns in my early days which had passed into the third generation of ownership. There were rickety weapons that necessitated a layer of paper or cloth placed between the barrel and the stock; more than one gun was known to be minus a cock, and more than one lacked a trigger-guard. Some of these guns were undoubtedly marvellous killers; others were distinguished as remarkable ' kickers ; even then, most of them were superior to the bulk of the jerry-built foreign fowling-pieces that to-day flood the gun-shops and the iron-mongers.

' Pintail ' Thomas for a long period used a fowling-piece whose lock was so weak and unreliable that he carried a small iron door-bolt in order to use it as a hammer when the cock obstinately refused to crack the ' patch '. Peacefully-minded curlews and knots, bent upon lunch or dinner, not only raised their heads in wonder at the clicking sounds of it, but promptly took heed and flew to a safer mudflat. For a number of years a little tailor friend, who straightens his legs gladly in what he terms ' wood-cock time ', holds the longest local list of successive shots at his favourite ' long-bill '. If he is using the same weapon to-day, it has one barrel in excellent order, but the other owns to a rusted hole, half-way down it, that in no way endangers him; for this one he never uses, and rarely indeed has he missed with the former. In my younger and sporting days it was thought a sign of superiority to carry a double-barrel.

Carelessness has been provocative of much mischief. Two

young fellows hired an open boat on the morning of the last day of the close season; they laid the gun forward, 'out of harm's way', but managed in changing seats to fire the gun, the whole of the charge going through the bows of the boat below the water-line. One of the youths was a baker, and had taken a flour-sack with him for a cushion, and presumably for a game-bag, but very gladly made use of it as a plug by ramming it into the breach to keep out the water, which had already let in a considerable quantity of Breydon. They had to sit aft to tilt the boat up as they paddled back to the boat-letter.

Local pawnbrokers took in and also dealt in all sorts and conditions of weapons; and to them many a young and penurious would-be sportsman was glad to go for something likely or cheap. An eccentric gunner visited one Mouse, a pawnbroker, and selected from an armoury of good, bad, and indifferent guns one of them for a trial, with an understanding that it should exchange ownership for three half-crowns, providing he was allowed to test it in the open. With the airs of a musketeer he marched with it to the north-east corner of Breydon, near some timber-rafts, and, having loaded it, stood in wait for a passing gull. In what proportions of powder and shot this novice used he could not have told himself. A gull unconsciously coming within range, he clapped the gun to his shoulder, pulled the trigger, and the gun misfired, the nipple being foul. Remembering a little trick of Fielding Harmer's invention, he sharpened the end of a match, and, to use his own words, 'progued the blinkin' nipple', a process he had to repeat two or three times. For a fourth attempt he gave the gun-nipple a fresh stirring up. Another gull was looming up, and the gun was raised again to his shoulder; this time the charge exploded, killing the gull, which floated away on the tide, but the ancient stock burst into fragments on the rebound, filling his eyes with dust. The worms had practically eaten and hollowed out the butt. The barrel had fallen in the ooze, from which the much-surprised gunner retrieved it, as he did a few splinters of wood, to take back to the pawnshop as evidence of the untrustworthiness of the weapon.

Two punters went to the mudflats—one a novice, the other a professional. The fowler sculled the punt to within distance of a couple of fowl, and the amateur laid to the gun, forgetting the instructions he had been given; but in his excitement he placed his shoulder much too close to the butt, and on pulling the trigger he received a kick that nearly dislocated his shoulder. It stunned him. He never after tackled a big gun again. Another gunner who by lapse of memory had failed to 'lock' the swivel in its socket effectually, received a great scare, when on pulling the trigger the gun jumped out and flung itself backwards in the narrow space between himself and the punt's side.

One more example of thoughtlessness. A young gunner of my acquaintance had pawned his ancient muzzle-loader, with a hope that before the next shooting-season he would be able to arm himself with a more respectable weapon. The end of August saw him without the ready money for the purchase of a breech-loader, so he repaired to the pawnshop to have a look at the old gun, in order to decide whether to redeem it or go without one for the coming season.

'Do you mind me having a look at my gun?' he asked, showing his ticket of ownership. It was handed in and the gunman was allowed to examine the condition of his gun. He lighted a match and dropped it inside the barrel, knowing it was not loaded, yet forgetting that the dross of burnt powder has a way of candying and drying when not in use. Before the match had gone out he had hastily applied his eye to the muzzle, when, on the instant, there was a mild explosion, which burnt off his right eyebrow and gave him a blackened eye into the bargain, and that required tactful explanations when his friends met him in the street.

Breydon fowlers frequently went at night—more particularly during the spring passage of the wigeon—to get a shot or two. Once in a while the excitement of the expedition was heightened by a mishap, when the linguistics of the sufferer were strained by the selection of his choicest epithets. On one night two gunners slipped out for a pot at the noisy wigeon that could be heard 'smeeo'-ing and babbling in the shallows where grew the luxuriant wigeon-grass. Moving around in silence, neither knew of the proximity of the other, and it chanced that they sculled to the flock from opposite directions. Fiddler Goodens laid his gun and took aim at where he considered swam the bulk of the fowl by the sound of their prattling; the tumult of the terrified fowl as the survivors rose was for the moment tremendous, but was closely followed by a shout from Sergeant Crowther, in the other punt, whose head had come into contact with a single pellet of shot that ploughed a line along his scalp, and there remained for the rest of his life. Explanations followed, with a few choice remarks interspersed on either side.

6

On another like occasion Little Stork Thacker and Jack Gibbs were, unnoticed by each other, laying in one of the drains at a number of whimbrel, irregularities in the mudflats screening each of them. Gibbs fired, bowling over two of the birds, but unfortunately dosing Thacker's skin with several shots—in face, ear, and forehead. Gibbs expressed his great regret at the accident, and waited for Thacker to give over his rather drastic opinions of his—Gibbs's—crass stupidity, when he did his best as an amateur surgeon with the point of a penknife to extract the pellets with which he had unwittingly punctured Thacker's interesting physiognomy.

It is astonishing how far individual pellets will sometimes travel. I once lay on the wall, hidden by the tall grasses. A gentleman gunner was insidiously drawing up to some grey plovers that I was also watching. I happened to be in a line with the shot, the punt being much more than a hundred yards away from me; but three or four pellets whisked through the herbage on either side of me.

Some years since the redoubtable little John Thomas was lying moored near the old ship *Agnes*, waiting for something to loom up to shoot at. Charlie Carr and Snicker Larn were higher up the Ship Drain, smelting. A dense fog descended upon Breydon; so the two smelters dropped downstream a short way, and lay-to a long gunshot off Thomas, unseen by him. Carr, thinking to have a bit of fun with Pintail, began softly to quack like a duck, as he and Snicker squatted down below the level of the row-locks. Thomas, like many of his compeers, often ventured a shot at fowl guided to some extent by experience. He fired, a few of the shots striking the smelt-boat, but with insufficient force to penetrate the strakes; and it was fortunate for the two smelters that they had lowered themselves below the gunwale. A yell, as of pain, came from one of the jokers, to the great horror of Pintail.

'Good Gawd!' said he, 'whatever hev I done?'

'Oh, Johnny, you've gone and shot me!' piteously wailed Carr, 'and you'll hev to row me off to the hospital.'

Pintail sat spellbound for a few minutes in his punt, mopping perspiration from his temples, but presently began pushing his way through the fog towards Carr's boat, where he found the two ready with certain uncomplimentary remarks. Pintail was shown several pellets that had gone at least through the paint into the wood; he saw no damage had been done to either of the smelters, but after the reaction following his fright he loosened his own tongue. Carr assured me that of all the language he'd ever heard on Breydon, Pintail's topped the lot.

Genial George Blake, sea-fisherman and poacher by turns, was a magnificent old man when I first knew him, with the limbs of a giant and the beard of a patriarch ; he was a mixture of gentleness and forcefulness. He was liked as well as feared by the gamekeepers up-river. They took pains not to cross his path, or if they did, not to get to cross-purposes with him. With his sealskin cap and his long white jumper, he was an outstanding figure. He used the marshes on either side Breydon ; and it was a delight to me to fall into chat with him, for the insight one got from him into the ways of hares, wildfowl, and whatnot. He was an excellent shot ; he took his gun to sea with him in fishing-time, and his fine old retriever. In winter he lived, like the bear, on his summer-time savings, eked out somewhat with the earnings of his duck-gun.

An ancient four-bore gun was going the rounds for a purchaser ; one after another tried it, but its peculiar bent for bruising their shoulders warned them from making too close a companion of it. It passed into Blake's hands for trial ; it fitted his shoulder and his liking to a nicety. A cynical friend met him out one day when he was after snipe upon the marshes.

'A nice old crock you've got, Blake,' said the friend. 'You won't get any snipe with that.'

Now Blake was a noted snipe-shot.

'Hold you on, Toby,' demanded Blake, and putting his hand into a side pocket he drew out, one after the other, four full snipe. 'How's that ?' he asked.

'Well,' replied the prevaricator, not liking to have his judgment thwarted, 'a charge of three ounces of shot don't ought to miss a poor little devil of a snipe, do it ?'

Blake put them back in his pocket, said nothing more, and went after another snipe or two.

In *Nature in Eastern Norfolk* I have quoted Girdlestone's account of a serious gunning accident to Joe Thomas, in 1827. His son, who also became a noted fowler, had a narrow escape ; and Thomas the third, little Pintail, had more than a fair share of accidents. On one occasion he lent another Breydoner his punt and gun, the latter being returned to him loaded. Not giving this a thought he, with characteristic carelessness, placed another charge over the first, with the result that the next discharge not only blew the fowl in front of it to pieces, but knocked Johnny senseless into the after part of the boat, breaking his collar-bone.

Once again, when firing his 'cripple-stopper', the wretched weapon burst, blowing two of his fingers to pieces. Not only did the accident resemble his grandfather's, but his spirit too. A chum rowed him home, not without some protest on his part, because he wanted to retrieve the duck he had killed. His face remained in after-life speckled with powder burns. His mutilated hand, except the thumb and remaining fingers, was always encased in a woollen glove. Often it gave him terrible rheumatic pains. He was a merry, optimistic little fellow by nature, with a saucy twinkle in his eye, when not overtaken by his favourite liquors. In his cups he was extremely argumentative and pugnaciously inclined.

A lively crowd had gathered in the bar-parlour of the 'Staff of Life', on the North Quay. You stepped down into it from the pathway, and a tall man's hair all but touched the low, smoked ceiling. Pero Pestell leaned lazily against the counter, cynically contemplating his favourite measure, now empty, and eyeing sharply each new-comer to the bar. He was anxiously awaiting the mug's second filling, and inwardly execrating the landlord's gossipy dawdling. Fiddler Goodens was more attentive at the moment to his black clay pipe than to his pewter. Snicker and Mouldy Pillar were discussing rat experiences, for these scurvy pests had been recently troubling the house-boats, into which they had gnawed their way at the door corners, or beneath the cockpit floor-boards, where the aroma of the smelts caught yesterday still clung to the nets, although dry, and had damaged many meshes by their nibbling. Billy Thacker, who thought more than he said, edged in an anathema on a pair that had found their way into his tarry old ark.

'D—— all rats!' said he. 'Why, I left a couple of wigeon on the settle last Saturday, while I sailed off home for fresh water, meanin' to spend the Sunday theer——'

'The old woman,' interposed Pero, 'tend to the bakin's on a Sunday, don't she?'

Thacker made no reply, and the interruption fell flat; and the publican, filling Pero's mug to overflowing, curbed the cynical boat-builder's flow of speech.

'Well,' went on Thacker, 'when I got back, and opened the door, two blinkin' great rats bolted out; and I found they had gnawed the innerds out o' both them wigeon. Thinks I, if I leave you one each of them hids, you warmin, I shan't lose much: I shall hev the bodies left for my Sunday dinner.

B—— told me how he caught *his* couple o' rats by fallin' in love with a water-hen ; thinks I, I'll set my traps in the same way.

'So I laid a sack on the settle, set two steel-falls close together on it, and covered 'em with a thin layer or two of torn smelt-net. Then I druv a couple o' nails into the side o' the cabin, a foot or two above 'em, three or four inches apart, and hung the two wigeon hids jist dangling low enough so's to make 'em reach up. Closin' the door, I shoved the eel-pick in the punt and rowed down to the sunken wherry drain, and did a bit o' pickin', gettin' a few pound o' nice eels, one on 'em jist over a pound, that I meant to keep for breakfast.

'I was back in a little over an hour, and afore I opens the door I could hear rats a-squakin', as they will do when they gets pannicky. On openin' the door I found both traps on the ground, with one rat held by his two hind legs, the tother by one ; and they were fightin' and tearin' each other like the dowst, with fur torn out and blood on 'em, and on the floor, all nicely mixed up with torn bits o' net.'

'Rats is the werry devil!' commented the rubicund, pleasant-spoken Roman-nosed old Snicker, 'though they fare as knowin' as human bein's. Last fishin', durin' a spell of frost, I was butt-dartin' for a mess of fish on the south side of Breydon opposite the yacht-sheds when I see a couple of French mavishes fly off Punt Palmer's willer-tree, and 'light on the edge of the water, against what I took for a lump of Scotsman's suet puddin', or it might be duff off a foreign ship——'

'Them —— foreigners!' growled Pero, 'don't often chuck even fusty grub away till a dorg wouldn't sniffle at it. I can't a-bear foreigners.'

'When you've done,' said Snicker, 'I'll tell the tale.'

'Do shut up, Pero,' demanded Pillar, 'and let the man go on.'

'While them birds,' resumed Snicker, 'wor pickin' that duff, a big rat drawed out from Little Wigg's shed, and made a run at 'em. They flew away jist in time, and the warmin nabs hold o' the duff, and was a-pullin' it, when a starling, shinin' like a strake o' metal flew towards Master Rat, and made as if to pick at it, and started flutterin' round it, when another starlin' jined it, and they went for him tooth and nail. Them two bustled the rat and he slunk off under the boat-shed. After he'd gone a dozen or more old starlin's dropped off the tree and jined in with 'em, and soon made that duff go to rack an' ruin.'

'Werry plucky on 'em, too,' assented Pillar 'for I've know'd them brutes tackle a wounded mallard on the ronds as soon as look at it.'

'Now, chaps,' said the landlord, 'I've got a little rat ditty to tell you, as you'd scarce believe possible. But you'll admit seein's believin'?'

'Certainly,' agreed all but Pero, who happened to be at the moment lighting his pipe. The landlord brought in a small wooden box from the back room containing what he declared to be 'the biggest curio rat-trap ever known.' He lifted the contents carefully on to the counter in a clear space free of mugs and slops.

'There,' said he, all the fellows drawing round to look at it. 'Bob Townrow dropped in here last night and left me a ped of "smack's" oysters as he'd brought from the smack *Albatross*, knowin' a fresh fat oyster allers appeals to me.'

'Look who you are,' sniffed Pero Pestell; 'you must be one of them philantropist fellers.'

'No such thing,' said the publican; 'though I ha' done Bob more 'an one good turn, I'll own, when he's been on the rocks. And he's a chap as isn't above showin' a bit of gratitude like.'

'One for *you*, Pero!' nodded Snicker, 'Bob's got gumption.'

'Well,' continued the landlord, 'I laid them oysters on the bricks in the wash-hus to keep cool till I wanted 'em. We went to bed and left 'em—locks, bolts and bars, oysters and all—all serene, as we thought——'

'No one ever supposed you'd take 'em to bed with yer,' said Pestell, as he drained the last spoonful of his favourite liquor.

'It might be two in the morning when I was woke up with the rummest noise you ever heard. The missus swore it was burglars, and insisted on me goin' downstairs to see, suggestin' it might even be a overlooked sleepin' drunk. The noise continued, so I hed to light a lamp and go down, takin' a pair o' tongs in one hand. When I got down the noise stopped. While I was lookin' round, a passing policeman, seein' my light through the window, rattled at the snack, and wanted to know what was up. So I undid the door, and in he walked. Afore the door could be shet a big rat shot from under a settle and made for it, but the policeman, who'd got a truncheon in his hand, made a mow at it and killed it.'

'"Lor' lumme!" says the policeman, "an' if that old rat

ain't got a big oyster clingin' to his tail. He's reg'lar hand-cuffed, as you may say. Thet's genuine enough. You ain't hevin' any oysters off Breydon, are yer ? "

' " No," says I, and I told him how I got 'em. " I reckon the oyster had felt a bit faint, and had opened hisself and peeped out of his shell, to see where he'd got to ; just as mushels will do in a shop winder when the sun break out. That rat must hev been prospectin' ; then stopped and hed a look at it, and while movin' around it to see if it was all right, had drawed his tail between the open shells athort the oyster's eyes ; when, objectin' to bein' tittled, it shet itself up instantly, same as you might shet a purse ! '

That the landlord's oyster caught the rat in the manner stated was talked and joked about for years after by the Breydon-siders.

' As for them tarnation rats,' put in Short'un Page, in his mild, feminine-like voice, ' I could tell yer suffin'.'

' Then don't,' demanded Snicker ; ' it'll keep, and it's about time we got the smelt-nets into the boat and earnt suffin' ; it's gettin' pretty well on for high water.' And the twain passed out, Snicker drawing hard at his pipe, Short'un's bright golden ear-rings swinging as he trotted by the taller man's side.

They had scarce turned the corner of Goffin's Buildings, when Harry Collins, short, stout, and vivacious, dropped in at the ' Staff of Life ' ; there seemed to be a constant ebb and flow of humanity at these water-side pubs. Harry, who in turn had been a donkey owner, was now a veteran cabman, full of native wit, and was a lucid teller of spicy sporting stories.

The landlord, who was leaning on the bar counter, sprang to attention, placing a hand on the lever of his beer-pump, and merely asked, ' *Stout ?* ' Harry nodded. A round-shouldered seaman, with folded arms, lolled against the counter, an inverted pipe held between his lips. Pero, having no copper nails to clinch at the moment, leaned with his back to it, now and then eyeing the lowering of the tide in his favourite pewter mug, and, with his usual audacity, hinting his inability to refill it. Two shrimpers, who had been early out with their dredgers and had disposed of their catches, sat in a corner forefronted by an empty, up-ended barrel for a table, upon which they were planking down their cards with heavy thumbs.

Harry greeted Pero, and asked him how things were going, receiving a pessimistic reply ; and turning to the landlord, told him to ' load him up again '.

'The game ain't worth the candle nowadays,' snorted Pero, lifting his mouth from the beloved pewter, 'they're still usin' copper nails in the boat-shuds. There's one thing, Harry, *you* look fit and fat; and I reckon you wouldn't care to change bank-books with me.'

'No,' said Harry, 'but *that's* mine!' (proudly pulling out of his pocket a fawn-covered little book). 'I have worked hard, and I hope as honest as any man; and have done what *you* might have done. There's enough there now to buy the little cottage in Row 85, what I live in; and when, if please God take me fust, the old gal 'on't need to go to the Union.'

Pero grunted, but with the remainder of his cherished liquor he held up his pewter forehead-high with:

'Here's to your health, Harry boy, and the missus's'; and lowering the rim of the vessel to the level of his lips, he added, 'may this not be the last pint o' good stuff I shall be able to drink yer good health in.'

'Thank yer,' responded Collins, 'she was glad enough to see me back home from the Wash.'

'And werry likely you needed it, didn't yer?' suggested Pero, with a grin.

'I'll tell you what, boys,' said Harry, 'I've brung home from Boston the dinkiest little punt-gun you ever see!'

'Well, where's this duck of a gun to be seen?' inquired Pero. 'I'd like to set eyes on her; and borrer her now and agin.'

'She's over the water, in the boat-shud,' replied Collins, 'and if you like to run round and have a look at her, besides airin' your opinions on her, I'll be there afore tea-time, say, four o'clock. And what's more I'll bring and broach a bottle of the right sort, and you shall all drink to her good health, and mine. . . .'

Collins was exceptionally good company: he had many a bright story of sport 'up his sleeve'; we often chatted in the street, and in his latter years by his fireside. He lamented the passing of his 'hosses', the decay of Breydon, and the dropping-out of old sporting chums, but never with the acrid sentiments that soured the worn-out gunners and fisherfolk, who, having found their occupation gone, had drifted mostly into the Infirmary. Harry had not depended upon eel-pick, net, or fowling-piece. He carried on until he and his old lady came in for their old-age pensions, which also removed the sting of poverty from the last of the decayed Breydoners.

I called at his cottage in the row on the eve of Christmas,

1925, and found him cheery, but ageing rapidly; I sat in a proffered chair by his fireside, and edged him into reminiscence.

'Well, Patt'son, I'm in my seventy-ninth year,' said he, after a spell of coughing, 'and if my old asthma worn't so wearisome, I'd hev little to grumble about; but when them spells come on, my poor old hid fare fit to bust. But Breydon, and cold nights and days, and wet, done that for me; and cabbyin' was a bit tryin' too. I ain't the only one as Breydon left its mark on, though it's funny so many on 'em lived so long. But some on 'em crocked up and out awful roughly—Billy Sampson months a-dyin'; poor little Billy Thacker, drowned out of a punt in a fit; poor old Fiddler Goodens, smoker's cancer; Noah Nicholls the same; Pintail screwed to dade with rheumatics; while Scrumps Allen pegged out of sheer old age, like several more on 'em; and little Charlie Thacker, gone his eighty, fare never so much as to hev hed a headache, and still a bachelor.'

I had called ostensibly to hand the old lady a Christmas cake, which she immediately enthroned upon a suitable plate to admire; but my desire was for Collins to re-spin the oft-told tale of the loaded gun, whose strange behaviour had marked an era in his life.

'It's not an over cheerful Christmas Eve,' said I, 'and I want you to chip me up with a spicy tale or two, say, of the *dinky little punt-gun* of yours, once more. Give me the whole rigmarole, Harry boy.' And he started to tell me the yarn, and, as it happened, it was the last time he spun it, garnishing it with many side-issues as he proceeded.

'You know, young Patt'son,' he began, 'when the summer season slowed off, I laid the old cab up in lavender, and migrated off to Lincolnsheer, for a time. I sat the market with kippers, bloaters and reds, and wet fish of sorts—had 'em sent up to Boston to me. That's how I come to get into tow among the gunners and the fowl-netters of Boston—got, as you may say, reg'lar among my own partickler sorter kidney. I hobnobbed with 'em at Boston and Spalding, and roundabouts. I jined in with 'em o' nights settin' the shore-nets for plovers, stints, knots and other birds: I went out with a gun now and agin, and met 'em bad days at a favourite pub. Law! the yarns they told. Then the game-dealers' stalls, and little shops where they used to hang up fowl; I used to nose round all on 'em, and sent poor old Hoppy mor'an one or two good birds; and bein' p'raps a Wash-shot specimen, might pass for a Norfolk one. That's not my bizness. The stalls sometimes sagged and squaked with the weight of fowl on 'em ; and the hooks a'most bent under the strings of geese, ducks and shorebirds.

'I know'd one feller—Jeffrey H——, who was the artfullest and cleverest of all them many fellers.

'Theer come on a bit of a blow,' Harry continued, 'and a briga'tine named the *Ethel*, with a green-painted hull, what traded out of Yarmouth [I well remembered this rakish, daintily-built little vessel] was run ashore. She was loaden with grain. You know the tides run very strong there, and very far out. Well, the wheat got scoured out of her damaged hull, and fritted away on the tide, ground-baitin' the place, properly. The old Scotch geese, them black geese or brants, as the gunners used ter call 'em, when they worn't so scarce in Yarmouth Roads in winter, as nowadays—they found it out, and crowded the place, and had a right proper good time of it. I sees Jeffrey slippin' off in his old punt one night down the Drain.

'"There ye go!" says I.

'"Yes, Harry," says he, "I'm off arter 'em."

'And if you can believe me, Mr. Patt'son, he come back with that old tub fairly loaden with black geese; sich a load of 'em, that he didn't know what to do with 'em. You see, afore that slice of luck, the geese had been feedin' foul, as they say, on shellfish and marine stuff, bein' hard-up enough; people couldn't eat 'em, they was so rank-flavoured. He had to chuck a lot back into the Wash.'

'But the gun,' I hinted.

'Oh, I'm comin' to it d'reckly,' said he.

'Punt Palmer,' I made remark, 'used emphatically to tell me that no fowl on earth would compare with Scotch geese when put on the table. He used to sail down to Scotland for the goose-shooting.'

But Harry insisted that such brents as he had tried were rank. He continued:

'What most of the fowlers used on the stakes were wore-out 'long-shore herring-nets; these poles were seven feet high above the sand, planted along-shore, and were inspected early next mornin', for the various wild birds that hed become entangled in the meshes when flightin' durin' the night. Sometimes they got a rare mixture: dunlins, knots, plovers, godwits, stints, dotterel, whimbrel and sich-like; now and agin a kitty or a turnstone; even larks struck 'em. Some was nicely crumpled up and dade by strugglin'; others not so badly meshed, and still alive and strong, were sent to Zoos, and to the Leadenhall bird-dealers. I don't tell you *all* the nets was herrin'-lint, for some was braided specially for the job. I got B—— a new net for Breydon, but that's another yarn ; perhaps you know it—all right, I'll tell it.

'Pero,' continued Harry, 'went and got a job at boat-wrightin' and repairin' at Boston ; and *he* naturally got among the fowlers, bein' an old Breydon man. By some means, fair or foul, he got hold of a properly made nine-inch meshed net, and sold it to B—— (Ulysses), who dabbled in everything you

BRENT GEESE

could think of—eel-catchin', song-bird nettin', and all the rest—the biggest experimenter you ever come across, and also the biggest chump at 'em all, but gettin' more pleasure out of his failures than all the crowd got out of their successes.

'You see, he didn't get his livin' by 'em ; makin' all the differs, didn't it ? He and a chum took them nets one night up the Acle New Road, on to the meshes, and staked 'em along a bank-side for plover-flight. First night's work—nothin'. They set 'em agin, the meshes bein' damp and misty at sunset, but it froze afore mornin' like old nails, makin' the net like wire-nettin'. Next morning they found any amount of peewit and golden-plovers' feathers, but no birds ;

they'd struck, but not got entangled, and had flown away, no doubt very much surprised.

'Pero returned to Yarmouth, and borrowed B——'s net, and stuck it up on the edge of the Lumps off the five-stake drain ; he'd "get some stints and knots or know the reason why ! " B—— was up an hour before Pero had started work in Reed's workshop, close ter Breydon, next mornin', and on the quiet rowed up through a thick fog to the net, findin' one poor ragged old hooded crow in a dowse of a tangle. B—— rowed back, leavin' it there, and sent word round to Pero by a smelter "in the know", that he'd better hurry up to the Lumps and save his net afore the strugglin' wildfowl had busted it all to pieces. Pero came to the quay-side with an old field-glass, but couldn't see many yards ahid ; so he jumped into Snicker's smelt-boat which laid handy, and rowed up against a strong ebb-tide, and on reachin' the spot, discovered the wretched bird, whose neck he twisted, and then chucked it overboard. He chowed up a good many hard words, no doubt, as he took down the net and laid it in the boat. Away he come, puffin' and blackguardin'.

'"A nice thing to do—gettin' a feller off his job, for a d——d old crow ; and make me lose my work on two blissed corfins." Pero never forgot to stretch his mouth.

'The net had one more chance. B—— comes along, sayin' what he'd do with it ; he took it up and set it on the edge of another flat the same night, for there were a number of migrant waders about the mudflats ; to find it in the mornin' a mass of tangled sticks, broken meshes, seaweed, and smashed up herrin'-swills and maunds, with one poor little devil of a stint hangin' up in the meshes. B—— was disgusted, and left the whole bilin' of rubbish there : "tworn't worth takin' up."'

'Why don't you get on with the gun, Harry ?' asked the old lady, 'you *do* go wanderin' around the candlestick.'

'You know, Mr. Patt'son, I always loved a gun ; why, when I was a kid truantin' from school, I used to slip up Breydon along o' the Thomases, and Salt-fish Jex, or any of 'em as 'ud let me go. Well, it was the last time I went to Boston, that I made up my mind to go in and axe the price of a dinky little punt-gun, what for months and months had stood up in a pawnshop window. Every time I passed I'd stop, and wish that there gun was mine. My fingers fared to itch to pull the trigger, but I allers fancied and feared the pawnbroker would open his mouth a little too wide, if I went in about it.

However, the day afore I was due to come back to Yarmouth, I plucked up courage, and went in.

'"Guvnor," I says, "you ha' got a dinky little duck gun in the winder; would you be so good as to say the lowest price you'd dare to axe for it." The pawnbroker takes the gun out o' the winder, and rubs the dust off with a bit of rag, then puts his forefinger in the muzzle, jist as a hoss-dealer might in his hoss's; that's a silly way some people hev, and p'raps he was feelin' what dust was inside: and then like a bloomin' amateur he lifts the cock and pulls the trigger, which went with a click. If that gun had been loaded, and spiteful, it *might* hev drilled a hole in the ceilin'. Still, that sorter made me feel it was all right.

'"You shall hev her for five pound," says he.

'"Then she's mine," says I. "Now, I'm off to Yarmouth to-morrer, and'll take her with me. Wrop her up in plenty o' paper, and if you can spare an old sack, put that round, too."

'So he wrops her up; and I lays down five golden sovereigns on the counter, and axes for a receipted bill. "I've bin savin' 'em up for her," and I puts her on my shoulder.

'"I hope you'll hev some sport with her, Collins," says he, for he know'd me, hevin' sold him soles and kippers. Off I hops to the station, and hands her in to the bookin'-office, tellin' 'em what it was, and axin' 'em to see that she was all right. Next day, as I was comin' away, I sees the guard of the train, and axes him to lay her up a safe corner in the brake van; promisin' him if she arrove safe, I wouldn't forget him. I gave him a knowin' wink, and he returned me his.

'When I gets home, I collars her, shoulders her, for she worn't so over heavy as them as shot a pound o' lead at a time, and over; but I sweated by the time I'd got to the "Bowlin' Green" pub, and axed for a drink.

'"Got a curio?" axes the publican.

'"Yes," I says, and ups and tells him all about her and the deal; and several of the clique gets round, and wants to know even more. But I puts 'em off with a promise that they might all see her when she was mounted, and ready for business. Jimmy Hurr hed come in for a drink, leavin' his punt at the staithe; and him and me walked athort the Green discussin' guns, for Jimmy was a crack shot, and a good judge of shootin' irons. He stepped aboard his boat, and I handed him the gun, and we rowed athort to the boat-shud, undressed her, oiled her down, and put her on the gun rests on the wall. . . .

Four or five of the gunners, who considered themselves

experts, dropped in at the boat-shed at four ; they were Fred Baldry, Lucky Bob Edmunds, Fiddler Goodens, Strike Sharman and Jimmy Hurr. Baldry drew in more by way of a joke, and called the crowd a ' crowner's inquest ' ; and wanted to know who Harry had knocked down to obtain the gun. Bob Edmunds hinted that to drink the health of the gun, before ' crittercisin' ' her, would give a business-like air to the proceedings. They all agreed. On this, Collins unlocked the ammunition cupboard, and produced a bottle and a couple of wine-glasses, that were hailed with evident pleasure. Bob Edmunds extracted a well-chewed quid ; the others pocketed their pipes ; and spat in honour of the event.

' " A good drop o' port ! " exclaimed Goodens, " and here's luck to little dinky ".' As he handed back the wine-glass, in popped Pero, with a gruff command, which the Army had made him master of, to " fill up that there glass, Collins, it smelt temptin' ! "

' While they were bent on emptying that bottle,' said Collins, ' they also discussed the gun.

' " Do you think she's loaden ? " axed Lucky Bob.

' " Well, bor," says I, " I never thought o' that, not after she'd bin standin' up in the winder all them months. Surely the pawnbroker worn't sich a fule as not to know."

' She looked clean enough outside, without a rust-speck ; and down the barrel, as far as I could see inside, she looked middlin' bright. If she *was* loaden, the pawnbroker handled her very careless.

' " I'd hev the breech off, if she was mine," says Hurr ; " you can't be too careful."

' " I ha' blowed down her," I says ; " put your lug agin the nipple," I says to Pero.

' " You 'on't see *me* put my ear agin the muzzle ! " says he, " now, Collins, *blow* "—and I blowed, on which he says, " Well, there fare a bit o' went, but I'd hev her breech off, anyway."

' " I would, too," put in Sharman, " and give the barrel a jolly good cleanin' ; I'd stand no nonsense jist for the sake of a little trouble."

' " All right," says I, " I'll run no risks ; she's very likely got some caked powder-dross inside, and might kick or hang-fire, and play the dowse."

' So Jimmy lays her in my punt, and we shoves off to Bob Flaxman's. We found Bob busy makin' a new eel-pick for Billy Sampson, and he looks up—

'"Hullo!" says he, "so that's the dinky I've heerd of. What's wrong with her?"

'"Nothin'," I says, "only she fare foul a bit; and I want you to warm her at the breech end, and unscrew her."

'"You're *sure* she ain't loaden?" he axes, lookin' werry serious, "I'm gettin' cautious of guns nowadays."

'"If she *is* loaden, it's a miracle!" I says.

'"Let's try her, then; put your lug agin the touch-hole, and I'll blow down her," he says.

'"I fare to feel a draught," says I, and rewersin' the barrel, "you try *this* end, and *I'll* blow down—how's that?"

'"Well, I fare to feel a vent," says he, "let's shove her in the fire!"

'You see, Mr. Patt'son, a gun's breech is made of sich fine tempered metal, and a breech-screw is so ready to fly, if you tamper in the least with it; she must be made warm, so much, and no more.

'Bob began to blow the fire: his old monkey, Jack, was a-sittin', watchin', on the cinders t'other side the forge, scratchin' hisself soothin'ly, and sayin' "*Oo-ah*", as the flames flickered up, when all on a sudden, like a earthquake, *bang*! she goes, the barrel jumpin' out like light'nin', and turnin' two summersets reached the door, what was shut, and struck it like a baggernet, and went half through it, stickin' there. The sweat run'd down Bob's smoke-grimed face: my hair fared to stand upright, and my knees trembled like as if I'd see'd a ghost; and Jack the monkey had wanished. *The old bounder of a gun had bin loaden all the time.*

'Somehow, Bob's flow of language didn't work to fit the job: he fared stemmed, an' all he could muster up was:

'"Well, Harry, thet's a rummon: let's go athort to Pamminter's pub, and hev a drink; I can do with one."

'"So can I," I says, and we went.

'When we come back to square up, and looked at the breech, she fared to hev taken no harm; and we had to warm her up agin to the proper temperature. Bob said, "No more loaden guns arter this, not if I know it!"

'"So you've said afore, Bob," I says, "only you be a bit more careful!"

'We missed the monkey, and wondered where he'd got to; but while Bob was workin' the bellows, down from the chimbley come the warmin', like a sweep; he yelled, and danced on the warm cinders, jerkin' them between his hind-legs with his hands, as he jumped, smotherin' us; and then, takin' a flyin' leap out o' the smithy winder, dashed down to Houghton's row-boats, and pulled out all the rowlocks, hullin' them one by one as he went, into the tideway, to be fished up hours later on the bottom of the ebb.

' " That —— monkey ! " says Bob, as he managed to overtake him, and catchin' him by the tail, " blest if he ain't gone dotty. . . . ! " '

Collins, seemingly well wound up, continued yarning.

' We had a rum accident once, in Jimmy Hurr's boatshud, next door to mine. He'd jist come off Breydon one wet day, and axed me if I'd give him a hand in with the big gun, as he wanted to swab down the boat before he cranked her in. She weighed several stone, and she was loaden, I knew, and the oily cover was tied over the breech-end, to keep out the wet. Hurr had got hold of the breech-end, I had hold of the muzzle, which lay on my shoulder, the muzzle-end bein' about a foot in front of me. Now, I allers took care to hold so as a gun in any mishap shouldn't slip. Afore we'd got the length of the boat-shud, Jimmy's foot slipped on one of the muddy rollers on the slope, and the breech-end fell off his shoulder, bumpin' on the floor ; and I'm blessed if she didn't explode the charge, the shot strikin' the angle of the gable, blew the woodwork to smithereens, and the gun, jumpin' back, broke a board in the shud door. That silly fule Jimmy hadn't taken the cap off, and had left the gun on full-cock.'

Mrs. Collins followed her old hubby's yarns with evident interest ; and edged him into telling all about his record shot.

' I was up the South Breydon Wall,' went on Harry, ' and see a tremdjuss lot of stints, the largest flock I ever did see. They was on the edge of a rond ; law ! we used to see thousands in them old days, afore the flats so grow'd up and went dry most of the tide, killin' the little red worms in the mud. On a open day in the late autumn, you'd see 'em, a thousand in a flock, like a regiment of soldiers flyin' this way, then flyin' that ; showin' white and grey in the different lights, twirlin' and twisterin', without you hearin' a word of command ; and right pretty it was to see 'em : and I ha' lost more 'an one chance watchin' 'em, and forgettin' I'd got a gun in my hand. Well, I worn't out for bird-watchin' *this* time, no further than I might get a poke in at 'em. Cabbyin' ain't a over flush job arter the season. The stints was only anxious to 'light upon the best spots for grub, which was them little red worms. Them on the outskirts of the flock fared to be watchin' me, and kept runnin' in among the crowd ; but as the water was risin' and likely to be over the flats d'reckly, they was makin' the best of their chance of a feed—and so was I.

'I called my spaniel close to heel, or rather signalled her; and Minnie wanted no twice tellin'. Then we crawls over the wall slowly, like two slugs, so as to get along the lower side of the wall, with my back to the meshes. I marked the spot, and found when I got opposite to 'em, it would be likely to be a poor shot, as they'd gone runnin' at right-angles to me. So I crept back, Minnie follerin' me like as if she was my own shadow; and I waded along, bent a'most double, along the drain, the dog havin' to swim behind me. I got in a shot, killin' scores; the winged birds flutterin' away, the dog catchin' them and bringin' me two at a time: the dead ones she'd gather up by fours and fives, and bring 'em. I put in another cartridge, and had another shot at the survivors as they wheeled past to see what ailed the others. Now, I'd left my bag in the boat-shud; and had very few pockets on me; you don't hev many in a blue woollen guernsey; so I took *that* off, and tied the bottom so as to make a bag of it, poppin' them in at the neck, and so brought 'em home with the arms athort my shoulder.'

'Law!' edged in the old lady, 'and I plucked every one of 'em. I like pluckin' fowls, you know, particularly coots. We hed pies, dumplin's, stews of 'em day after day, till they was done. They was alright too, and I should like to 'a' hed some now!' . . .

'Chicko', or as he was as often called, 'Chickey' Drane, combined a number of water-side professions. He was so expert a swimmer that for rescuing a number of persons from drowning, the breast of his guernsey is smothered with medals and clasps. To-day, he is a white-haired shrimper. Of the hundred odd persons he has plunged into the water to rescue, he never brought one out dead; even so, and he has never hesitated to fetch out for decent burial the sorriest of corpses. He sails out of the harbour in a cranky old boat after sand-shrimps and the abounding Æsop's prawns; and when things with him get to dead low ebb, gladly turns night-watch lamp-tender, when the roads are up.

Drane dropped into the cabin of my houseboat *Moorhen II*, when she lay berthed at the Bure-side quay a few years since. One of the yarns he told me, which comes under the heading of this chapter, is worthy of narration. It referred to a dilapidated muzzle-loading gun:

'Me and Lucky Bob Edmunds,' he went on, 'and two more

on us, bein' stumped up for a shore job and for a salt-water job too, come to that, went well up the North River in an old ice-wherry, quantin' our way up through floatin' slabs of ice, which the tide happened to be carryin' in the same direction, and when it came on to the gloamin' we was as high up as the Stokesby meshes, so we laid-to, and got the grub on the way. Bob lit a nineses tallow candle, same as they used to use in the malt-housen, and stuck it over the little mantelpiece in the cabin, and then laid on the settle his hunk o' bread and biled pig's hand [forefoot]. Nicholls shot out a bone with a bit o'

HERON

meat on and some cold potaters. Four in a little cabin didn't leave much elbow-room to set a supper table ; and we didn't worrit much for the want of a table-cloth. I lit the fire, for we'd plenty of driftwood in the settle locker. Short'un Page had a warp of over-night salt herrin', and laid 'em athort a grid ; and some other little jints as I took no stock of in partickler. Bob Edmunds had also got some onions—Spanishers—and our missises hadn't forgot pepper and salt.

' There ain't much furniture in an old wherry what ha' hed her day. I'd lost my knife.

' " Look in the cupboard," demands Lucky Bob, " you'll find a rat if you don't find nothin' else."

' I looked and foraged out a rusty fork, with one tine, two

iron spunes, three cracked plates, and a couple o' teacups. There was a hand-bowl, for washin', you know, but no kettle nor teapot. So I handed the bowl to Nicholls to rinse out in the river, and fill it ; and Bob Edmunds follered him outside.

' " Look out ! " yaps Bob, " hand me the old gun off the bulkhead pegs ; blessed if I didn't see an old hare over on the mesh ; mind, she's loaden, but very light on the trigger ; handle her *carefully*. Righto ! let's hope we'll hev an old Sally for to-morrer's dinner."

' She was one of them old converted rifles ; I believe they called her " Old Queen Anne " ; I know that, to stiffen the friendship between barrel and stock, there was a coil of tarry twine. Noah Nicholls popped his head out, and axed Bob to be very careful how he let her off, and be sure that she went off before he lowered her agin from his shoulder ; and to hold tight to her.

' " You talk to your grandmother ! " insolently came back a comment from behind the ditch. But Bob sune came back, for the hare hadn't stopped to investigate our doin's. We'd set down to tea, or supper, whatever it was, and Bob steps aboard the plankway. The cabin didn't smell half bad, what with raw onions and the grillin' of over-night " salts ", and that.

' " Here, take the old gun," Bob sings out, as he comes to the cabin-door, and was handin' in the gun ; but afore I could lay hold on her, cuss the old beast, the leastest jar of the stock agin' the door lintel, and off she went, blowin' the candle out, and fillin' the cabin with smoke thick as London fog, Short'un upsettin' the bowl of water on the fire what we was bilin' for the tea, and the place goin' in darkness. We couldn't see each other ; no one said a word ; each on us thought the other was killed, all round, as you might say. Then after a bit Bob spoke, and the others answered up, and begun to use language suitable to the occasion. But it worn't on the lines of a thanksgivin' service.

' " Strike a light," says Bob, " and let's count heads ; blessed if I didn't think I'd killed the lot of yer." I strook a light, and you never see sich a lot of powder-blacked faces, in your life. The candle was about done for, and Noah's old turnip watch, what he'd hung up for the time, was properly busted up ; and when we found another tallow dip, and nailed her to the cabin end, we see that a new bit of plank was wanted in the bulkhead.

' Bob took it wuss'n we did, and kept on repeatin' : " That was a d—— nigh 'un ! " However, we got the fire on the way agin, collected the grub off the floor an' settles, biled some more tea in the old hand-bowl, and drank a cup or two in turn.

'Then we sat and yarned on all the old guns we'd known as cripples and man-slaughterers—in principle, as you might say; and Pintail's, Jex's, and Thomas's, all the whole regiment of crocks we'd met with.

'At ten we was all snorin' as if nothin' had happened; and as daylight broke we was hevin' breakfast on the way. We slipped into Ranworth Broad, loaded up with ice, and made a fair day's work of it, and wanted it.'

CHAPTER V

HOUSE-BOAT MARDLINGS

With field glasses rather than gun I have sought and followed the birds of the marshes, the sedge-warblers of the river-sides, the reed-warblers of the broads. . . . Night has come upon me as I sat in the small cabin of some fisherman's house-boat, watching . . . and listening to the harsh crowing of cock pheasants . . . the calling of the curlews. Dawn has found me among the ooze-flats of the tidal waters, where the waders come to feed at the fall of the tide.

—W. A. DUTT

WHEN I first went to Breydon, the mudflats were very much lower than they are to-day; the tidal water remained much longer on them, whilst the *Zostera* flourishing in an easy alternation of the tides, was so abundant and so dense that fish and crustacean life was luxuriant in its variety and plentitude, even so late as the early 'nineties. When I towed up my house-boat *Moorhen I*, at that period, and laid her in a gap in Duffell's rond, she floated almost continually: when I sold her to an amateur fowler as a sleeping and shooting box for his week-ends, she was perched high and dry, and shored up to keep her in position. There she remained until 1912, when an abnormal tide filled the estuary basin almost to its brim, and a violent gale so beat her with the swell of the waves, that the hull burst, and the cabin collapsed into it, and she was dashed to pieces. I had many happy days and nights and week-ends aboard her, when eel and flounder of my own catching, with mushrooms from the marshes to my own bacon, played an appetising tune in the gallant old tub's fry-pan.

It was under these happy conditions when in August, 1899, Mr. W. A. Dutt visited me, and spent the night with me in the old *Moorhen I*, which is recorded in his *Norfolk*.

One night early in August 1921, I embarked for a fortnight's holiday on Breydon with Jary (the recently retired bird-watcher), whose house-boat lay moored snugly enough, on normal tides, in a cross-drain running at right angles to the Ship drain, immediately opposite the few weed-clothed timbers of the good ship *Agnes*, a small old-time brig of some two hundred tons burthen, as round a-bow as any Dutch galliot; she traded in and out of the Mediterranean as a fruiter in the days of Nelson. The morning had dawned with an angry red sky, which in late summer portends a spell of wind. The gulls flew restlessly, clamouring noisily. A mud-brown current raced upstream from the sea, an almost sure precourser of a gale from the north-west.

Jary, who for as many years as myself had 'followed' Breydon—myself for the joy of it, he for the hard-earned, fluctuating livelihood that he had wrested from its tides—had gone home as soon as I had stepped aboard. He had ostensibly gone home for provisions and water, but undoubtedly to escape the coming 'blow', which he knew as well as I did was then on the way. He found a rough sea in the channel, but crept along by the flats as near to wind'ard as was possible, and spent a quiet night ashore. I had stowed away my provisions in the lockers, hung my spare clothing on the hooks, or tucked them under the rough canvas mattress on the settle, and had arranged my books and trinkets in a cupboard that had been emptied for their reception. The latter, among other things, covered bottles of formalin for interesting specimens, besides household utensils—knife and fork, tins of tea, of salt, a pepper-box, etc.

The hull of the house-boat, had been a smack's ferry-boat, a species of vessel that gets many a hard knock when ferrying fish upon the North Sea; and owing to the constant wear and tear of such craft, had been put together with iron nails, in lieu of copper fastenings; an economic bit of workmanship that would have rejoiced the heart of Pero Pestell, because rust set in earlier, and helped to shorten the life of a boat.

Our Noah's Ark was ancient and dilapidated, and I found its condition even worse than I had suspected. As I sat to a frugal supper, I was entertained by the music of the billage water splashing to and fro under the floor-boards as she rolled; and on lifting two loose boards, I found some buckets of almost clear sea-water, that had percolated through in divers places. It seemed to me that all hands should be put to the pumps, but as there were no such appliances, and I was all the crew aboard, it was for me to use the hand-bowl, until the old sailor-cry was on my lips, 'here she sucks'. It might be remarked that nightly, after this, we had to bale out ten or a dozen buckets of salt water, renewing the task each morning. Even before the tide had risen above the level of the flats, she wallowed and shook herself in the drain, or creek, like an enraged sea-dolphin. The tide rose surprisingly fast, and sent rollers across the flat a couple of hours before high water, making the tethered smelt-boat dance in the wind's eye, more than merrily, giving unpleasant thumps at the house-boat strakes.

Jary was back in the early morning, having made a lively run of it, to find the smelt-boat quarrelling with the parent ship, and flinging aside the cokernut fenders, as a disputatious couple resent the interference of a third party. My old punt was as restless, and the addition of Jary's made matters even more uncomfortable; with the increasing wind, the unrest of the boats became intolerable.

At length it was decided to shift the smaller fry around us, to leeward; the smelt-boat was lashed to the house-boat's stern, Jary's small boat being tethered behind that with a long leash, and then my punt with an equally lengthy halter farthest astern. The wind was so forceful from the nor'west, that although the tide was boiling up from the south'ard, our little fleet streamed out in a line *into* it, and undulated like the tail of a kite. Had the house-boat drawn her stakes, there would have been the novel sight of four boats tied together floating against the tide! Such unexpected disturbances on Breydon may occur even in the height of the summer days. The danger of being rammed, however, was over. We rather anxiously watched for the top of a marked stake—now under water—for its reappearance would have at once proclaimed that the time of high water had passed. At length it showed, and from that moment the disturbance gradually lessened, and a sharp ebb raced towards the channel and down to the sea in sullen mood, silt-brown in colour from its disturbance of the ooze. Never before had I felt myself, even when crossing the Irish Sea in a gale, so nearly realizing the unpleasantness of *mal-de-mer*. Towards low water a bright, peaceful evening set in.

Breakfast preparations had been a farce; teacups and plates refused to give over sliding and falling; and frying the breakfast bacon was a lively task, although a salt-water appetite made light of untoward incidents. Jary, like all the Breydon fraternity under such circumstances, sought consolation in his pipe, and having thrown himself on his mattress upon the settle, started to spin yarns of other days of special stress. In June he had been so storm-beaten that the house-boat pulled up three mooring-stakes, and was left tethered by a single rope; fortunately, before the fourth stake was drawn out of the mud, there came a welcome lull, when he was glad to collect the stumps, and, scrambling on to the slippery flats, with a sledge-hammer drive them in again. Whilst he was yet moored so precariously, Jary had scrambled into the smelt-boat, prepared to make an effort to save himself should the old boat founder, or smash herself up, as a runaway, on the flint walls. On another occasion he had such a 'jostling-up', that the house-boat swamped the smelt-boat, and rode over it. He awoke next morning wondering where the latter had gone, until the smelt-net, streaming out on the ebb tide, caught his attention, having been saved by a strand of the rope still attached to the seat of the boat, below-water. Bottom-boards, oars, and other gear had been drifted more than half a mile, to the South Wall, where he gathered them together as he came to them. Fortunately he used tholes rather than rowlocks, in that boat; these were swollen with wet and stuck in tenaciously. The punt had come off very lightly.

Extremely fortunate was Jary to right-side boat and gear so quickly, for after that particular 'blow', and tide, there came up-river from the sea to Breydon an extraordinary number of smelts on their way to spawn in fresh waters. He netted in an hour no less than three-quarters of a bushel of these delicate fish; in one draught of the net alone he secured fifty score—a thousand big, full smelts!

These summer storms are apt to break out unexpectedly; the shorter-lived, but often mischievous outbursts, are known as 'Rogers'. One fine day I was myself overtaken by one of these in my little punt; I lowered my sail in an instant, and merely held to the tiller; my slender mast, collecting as much of the wind as was needful, carried me down homeward to the boat-shed. Yachts and sailing boats are sometimes blown to a lee shore, when a topsail goes for it, or a topmast smashes like a stick. On the rivers the soft bank or a rond does no harm, and the crew may lay-to till the little summer storm eases—on Breydon it may mean a stay all night on the edge of a mudflat, necessitating a tow-off, even a dig-out, next morning. Amateur yachtsmen experience some discomfort from them, and most of them dread crossing Breydon in order to sail the Waveney and the Yare; hence not a few prefer to confine their voyage to a cruise on the Bure and its tributaries. This apprehension is now and then encouraged by a certain type of skipper, who finds the river-side hotels so few and so far apart.

Our little gale had put two or three yachts on the mudflats, on the wrong side of the stakes that line each side of the channel, and their navigators anxiously hailed any craft that

FRED, THE WILD-FOWLER, AND JARY, THE BIRD-WATCHER

TYPICAL NORFOLK GUN-PUNT

came-to near them, or passed them unheeding.

On the last of the ebb it was my turn to sail down to town for provisions, to return on the beginning of the flood-tide to the house-boat. There came back with me a very old and intimate chum, 'Brusher' Broom, since gone to the Happy Hunting Grounds. He was a genial, hearty fellow: his favourite hobby was a bit of wildfowl shooting in the winter, and flighting in idle hours in autumn. 'Brusher' plied the oars thoughtfully, as the little trip conjured up old memories, and he chuckled good-humouredly as the punt dipped her nose in the rounding swell. As we drew up to the house-boat, little Charlie Thacker peered out, pipe in mouth, and took hold of the painter, Jary helping in with the stores after he had moored the punt in safety. Tobacco smoke, which is one of my pet aversions, but must be tolerated in such company without demur, made the cabin interior as hazy as a mist.

Jary had just recently observed a great grey gull, resting on top of a stake, surfeited with dead eels: for the tail of the last one swallowed was still hanging from its mandibles, a great temptation to passing comrades, who snatched at it as they swooped and sailed around him. It developed into a scrimmage, when the gull in question vomited that eel: eight other saddlebacks on swift pinions darted to retrieve it as it fell into the water, to float to the surface again to tempt another skirmish. Dead and decomposing eels have a curious way of floating in the water in the shape of a horse-shoe. This recalled to Jary's mind that he once knew a dog which was partial to dead eels, and was sorely tempted at the sight of a live one: he would also 'scorf' one flounder after another, while they were yet alive; and a dog kept by the keeper of a lock on a Suffolk river once robbed his eel-bucket, temporarily left on the bank, of sufficient eels to distend his body. He averred that 'the dorg's body stood out like a blamed balloon'. He made complaint of this robbery to the dog's owner, who was well aware of this animal's weakness for fresh fish—eels in particular.

'Never mind, old Jary,' said the lock-keeper, 'I'll get yer some more in the place of 'em;' and he at once repaired to the eel-net at the sluice gate, and with a scoop of the landing-net brought up half a stone of eels, to replace the others, which were then irrecoverable. Piscivorous dogs are not rarities in Broadland, and animals with perverted tastes were now and then noted: a cat that boldly plunged in a ditch and caught water-voles, otters that cracked and enjoyed nuts, and squirrels that enjoyed fried fish.

'Brusher' had noticed the curious propensity shown by marshland partridges, and sometimes pheasants, for the vicinity of reed-beds near a river, and as for Broadland ducks, he said, 'they was very innocent and confidin'', and would follow slow-going and sailing yachts for the scraps thrown overboard.

'I was once workin' on a yacht,' said Broom, 'and one of the swells had laid his rod on the cabin-top, while he took a sprawl and a nap, what he called a "sun-bath". The baited hook fell over the plankway into the water, and a parcel of ducks raced for it, one of 'em catchin' and swallowin' it. What the devil was I to do? It run'd nearly the whole line off the screechin' reel, and I had to save the rod by snatchin' at it. Well, bor, I hed to play that blinkin' duck like as if it was a bloomin' carp, to save the poor thing bein' choked. It made a pretty bit of flutterin', and I wondered it didn't break the line. At length I cranked the duck close to the yacht, and catched it in the landing-net. I couldn't clear the hook, so I broke the duck's neck to get it out. Now, I didn't know the owner, and if I *hed* found him, he'd hev kicked up a hullabaloo. Mind ye, that worn't the only fule of a duck I've know'd with a weakness for a worm or a bit of bread-crust. The owner of the rod woke up over the rumpus, and mightily enjoyed it, like he did the duck afterwards.

'The owner of a yacht I once sailed with,' added 'Brusher', 'shot some kitties [black-headed gulls], and three or four wood-pigeons. He asked me to pluck a couple of pigeons for his dinner; and while I was about it, I plucked two of the kitties. I handed the two gulls to the cook for to make the pigeon pie, she not noticin' the differs between the birds, and got her to stew the two pigeons for *my* dinner. So the gulls were served up to the gentleman, and the others to me. Things went on all right. After dinner I says to the owner:

'"How did you like the pigeon pie, sir?"

'"Oh!" says he, "the pigeon pie was excellent"; bein' unawares of the swop. So that was all serene.'

Broom recalled to mind a gentleman who saw a seven-pound pike, hopelessly floundering in a marsh ditch, and got it ashore with the 'crome' of his walking-stick. It looked fat and tempting, and was as fresh as a daisy, so he carried it home and handed it to the missus, with a request to serve it up for dinner next day. He came home expecting a fish on the table nicely flavoured with anchovy sauce, 'and the dowse know what ', to find the pike in the rubbish-bin, with three fat water-voles recovered from its stomach lying on the ashes with it.

'That worn't nothin',' said Jary; 'I remember bein' at Hoveton Broad one time, when an old eel-babber, I believe it was old Bugles, caught several jolly great eels, which, on bein' opened, wos found to be packed with nestlin' young gulls—kitties, that hed bin drowned by heavy rainstorms, and washed out o' the nests. If you was to catch pike at that time, you'd find a lot in them too.'

It was now Charlie Thacker's turn to jibe in, for he had been very busy with his pipe, and somewhat impatiently listening to his chum 'Brusher'. Said he:

'I hev shot over here for nigh fifty year, and ha' *seen* suffin'; I ha' muddled about amon' ice-slabs, with icicles hangin' to my whiskers; been blow'd a'most outside-in, for Breydon, being four mile long, and a mile athort, catch a gale suffin' proper from any quarter, but a nor'ard by west'ard blow is the wust. I was only a kid when I come up 'longer Father, as they useter call Old Stork, though you mustn't ha' said it in *his* hearin', or he'd ha' come for you! Ginerally speakin', Breydoners rather like their nicknames, and get used to 'em. I remember once bein' with Father when goin' up Breydon with the big gun, when we met Lawyer Preston comin' down. He bid Father good mornin' and Father grunted it back to him, when Mr. Preston says: "I passed a white stork up there, near 'Berney Arms'," which wos *true*, but Father, thinkin' the lawyer meant suffin' else, flew in a tiff, an' rowed off, bitin' his tongue to keep his temper down. That was Father's funny little way.

'I fust fired the big gun when I was twelve. I think I once told you, Mr. Patt'son, how we made our own flints for the gun; never mind, I'll tell you agin, and how we snook great flints out o' the walls, to work up. I tried my hand at it, but couldn't somehow catch the run o' the grain of 'em: unless you hit the right spot, you might as well try to knock chunks off old Bob Flaxman's anvil with a rollin'-pin.

'You don't get the birds now as we useter. I once shot seven spunebills: you'd sceercely believe that, though you was once up Breydon when seventeen was feedin' all at once. Old Fieldin' Harmer put 'em in his book as only three. He'd have made it seventy if he'd 'a' shot my seven. I made a pound of one, the best one. Them spunies allers fare a-sleepin' or a-feedin': they feed wonderful *small*: I hung 'em up by the legs in the wash-hus, outer the way o' the cats, and some shrimps and two or tree gobble-bellies [gobies], and a white-bait or two drained out of the mouths on to the brick floor. You can't, you know, ram your little finger down the throat —so they must feed small.

'Old Harvey, the stuffer, took two o' the others for a quid, and told me arterwards as how his cat ate the head off one on 'em. All us chaps what took him good birds was scary of his old tabby cat, because he was so careless, or that there beast wor sich a cannibal. Du you think cats last as long as tharty-four year ? '

I assured the little man that I had seen a cat which was still going strong at twenty-three.

'That's more likely ; but I allers vowed he must hev a kinnel o' cats, all as bad as the old 'un. Durrant took a lot o' my birds, and worn't half a bad 'un ; Watson on the Hill took some ; and poor old Hoppy Smith follered all on us, like a faithful span'el, to get the rare 'uns. I used to like shootin' fowl under the mune, but we used to lose a lot o' cripples what fluttered off out o' sight an' sound, to scamper to the flint walls, and inter the holes and gaps, wheer they hid. We used to make allowance for our persitions and the time o' the tide on the next mornin', and find some on 'em with their bills peepin' out, and watchin' *you.* Golden-eyes was the wildest of all on 'em, barrin' a wounded pintail ; and if you moved arter 'em, they deeved and turned under-water, so you never fared to know which way they was comin' up to breathe agin. Father an' me hev reg'lar sweated arter 'em, specially when they got amon' the ice. I ha' took gentlemen with guns, and others with spy-glasses, but them without a gun made a derned sight more fuss over one turnstone throwin' the wigeon-grass over an' snappin' up them sea-lice, than others did over a hamper o' fowl tucked inside it—dade. Funny tastes some folks have ; can't reckon some on 'em up.

'Allers muckin' around in them good old days, we picked up other things you didn't expect ; I ha' seen big skate, t'ree or four large brills, and a whoppin' codfish in my time stranded on the flats ; and run'd my pick-shares into more 'an one big pike in a drain. What was my largest eel ? Why, the two largest together, what I copt in one night, weighed exactly nine pound, and a conger eel of twelve pound, I run'd a share through him. Once I follered a floatin' hover [broken-off clump of reed-bed] on Breydon, with the reeds and rushes still a-standin' green as it left the broads, and took a pail full of them mottled lampreys workin' underneath it, and ha' took them little green river lampreys too. Them smaller hovers with eels a-workin' under 'em 'mind me of them big jellyfish with the strings movin' under 'em.

'We had reg'lar customers for all we laid our hands on. Mother took a basket round with godwicks, pluvvers, pokers, mallards, and smee; she often come back for a second lot. Once in a heavy snow, when snipes was starved to shadders, a mighty big wisp settled on a rond huddled up with cold, lookin' terrible dumpy, as if they'd got wery little life an' no more hope left; so I shot a shoulder-gun into 'em, pickin' up two score. The brist-bones was like a knife, a'most sharp enough, you may say, to shave with. Breydon, I might say, was full of ice, and everything on it fared hungry. Watson took a few of the snipe at thrippence each, after feelin' on 'em, and grumblin'; the worst 'uns he only sprung three-ha'pence each for.'

Broom and Jary thought it a miserable shot, and a very unprofitable deal. They loaded and lighted their pipes after a jug of coffee, brewed by myself for them, had been emptied; and the twain returned to town with the Watcher, who landed them at Cobholm, shortly after coming back alone to the house-boat.

. . . . .

For many years, a few yards to the south'ard of Vauxhall Bridge, rode an aged and dingy oft-tarred, home-made house-boat, the head-quarters of Billy Sampson, erstwhile ship-caulker, punt-gunner, marsh-ranger, eel-catcher, and eel-merchant. The hull of the unnamed craft had been built by honest workmen, or she had not endured for decades the swirling of the tides, the 'bumps' of passing craft, or the scrape of the ice-floes lumbering down-river. Before her conversion she had been tender to a fishing smack working 'nor'ard of the Dogger'. Billy built the pitch-roofed cabin of raw, unplaned wood, covering it wholly with a condemned schooner's sail, that had been heavily tarred at the start, and annually ever after. The roofing boards were not tongued, or the edges would have licked up the vagrant tar that hung like black ear-rings overhead inside for a long period after she had been finished. There was trouble even in her old age when the heat contracted the edges of the boards, due to surprisingly hot weather or an overheated stove. There were no windows, for quay-side urchins to use as targets; the open door admitted light, except when during a heavy rainfall which drove in, and the door was shut. But a closed cabin rarely disagreed with such men as lay sprawled behind a big gun in blizzards, motionlessly watching tufted ducks and mallards; and crowded themselves in the cabin whose temperature was above the normally tropical.

The fittings of the cabin were bald and grimy; a mop, or a part of one, doing duty for the housemaid's touches. A largish skeleton stove was built in a setting of bricks, the former innocent of black-lead, the latter of whitewash. A stalwart bit of iron pipe ran up from an arch of bricks, and covered by a sort of wainscoting, poked up through the angle of the roof, and around the outlet was plastered some cement, then an old hard crownless hat was run down it, fitting tightly, and cement was placed around that: a frequently-heated pipe had thus been made innoxious to the woodwork. Several old house-boats as ugly, as useful, though as badly finished, dotted Breydon and the river-side in the long ago.

A trapezoidal bit of glass was tacked on the wainscot, and on the little mantelpiece a clock, very much dilapidated, ticked away the hours; a comb and a strong jack-knife were the only other ornaments. A large spring-balance hung near the door, and its inverted eel-bucket stood just outside it. The rest of the furniture comprised a rough mattress, stuffed with feathers from many a victim of Billy's gun. This was rolled up by day, and spread along the settle at night. In a recess below a corner cupboard, that held the crocks and provender (in tins and pickle-bottles), lay a heap of dried firewood, which served as a bolster beneath a cushion. Coals were shot in a bottom locker under the settle, where ropes, sacks, and other lumber were also packed away.

Billy Sampson in mid-life had acquired a lame leg, and a slouching foot, the result, no doubt, of many a winter night's duck-shooting on the damp marshes near the old Black Boards. When he took up the business of an eel-merchant, he practically lived in the aged tub: his fellow eel-men, who brought their catches to him, also ran his errands for water and provender, and dispatched the eels to London in the eel-boxes for him. In idle times he read his newspaper, and gossiped in a high-pitched voice of the gunning adventures of his earlier life. Old comrades of the powder-flask often drifted into the cabin, and compared notes with him; it was fine, even in the heat and the smoke and smell of heated coarse clothing, to listen to these gossips, several of whom figure in my other volumes. Poor old Billy made a bad venture when he took into a sort of partnership a slimy-tongued, greasy-fat German, named Housmann, with his patched old steam-launch that was known as the *Fly*. The German was a great grumbler, and often cursed the speed of his boat, and her cost for repairs. Said he, 'She haf ze name of *Fly*, but by mein crikey, she is von vasp, and haf stung me!' She also stung Billy—badly. Our spectacled Prussian trawled against all rules and regulations, up and down river, with an eel-net at night, making great hauls now and again. How he and his engine-man Jary eluded the river bailiffs remains a mystery, when a keener river-poacher, the noted Flea Barber, was waylaid and prosecuted, as often as not to escape conviction. Housmann monopolized poor old Sampson's scales, eel-boxes, time, and most of the returns. He had a contemporary, an equally 'slim' Prussian, who was a great Broadland angler; and both aliens knew not the meaning of the commonplace word 'probity'. As an instance of the angler's trickery: at a fishing match he and another angler each caught a three-pound bream. At weighing-in time Herr Slim's fish scaled an ounce more in weight than the other angler's, although the two fish were exactly the same in dimensions, to the thousandth part of an inch.

'Let me weigh his fish, Mr. Umpire,' said the Englishman.

'Nein, nein!' said Slim, 'I vill not let zis man touch mine preem! It ish not ze sing for von man to handle von oder man's fische!'

But the umpire allowed the testing; and 'ze Herr' Englishman hung it to a spring balance, tail upwards, when from its mouth fell an ounce weight German bullet! 'It vos dam bad luck!' said the much chagrined German.

To Housmann: he complained to Billy one day about the returns from Billingsgate—'Mein Gott!' said he, 'Vy vos ze money so leetle? How vos it ze Beelingsgate puyers dip zeer fingers sho deep in ze returns? Dem feesh-peeples vos ze very defil, and skveege ze very pludd out of von gate—vat you call ze post?'

Poor old Billy, who had worked himself up to sticking-point, retorted: 'You d—— German! Go to hell!' said he.

'Damme!' returned the German, 'dat is veer I haf been all ze time in dis vicked country!'

'Then it's d——d well time,' snorted Billy, 'you went back to your own wonderful country,' throwing ashore the German's own spring balance with which that gentleman had somewhat tampered in its machinery, and flinging after it the German's eel-bucket, assuring him, if he did not hop it, he would get his chums to chuck him in the river.

'Oh, mein Gott!' wailed Fritz Housmann, tumbling ashore over a slimy eel-box dropped in his way by an eel-chap, to the great amusement of a small crowd looking on, one of whom suggested that the waterworks people were after his uncharted eel-tank taps.

Sampson, like many others of his kind, enjoyed the Sundays and high holidays in his own fashion, which meant an overdraft on the ale-bench. One Christmas eve saw the men at their favourite taverns; and Billy, with two of his favourite cronies, Peg-leg Gates and Limpeny Joe King, sitting in the old house-boat. A big stone bottle of beer had been shipped, and an extra supply of tobacco: they intended making a night of it. At the 'Railway' tavern across the quay a lively crowd was at the selfsame game. As night drew on they closed the cabin door, and started to sing the coarse songs of the sailor-men, chorusing them lustily. 'Poke her up!' shouted Limpeny, as Sampson stirred the fire: 'Pile on the coals,' demanded Peg-leg. The cabin had become hazy with tobacco smoke; and the old rascals exceedingly merry, as they sang their songs of marshland folk-lore and of the sea, and of 'beer, glorious beer'.

The riot of their voices in the still night air was heard at the tavern, where kindred spirits were holding festival; one of these, known as Jack Calver, suggested mischief, and the others, nothing loth, turned out with him to perpetrate it. Jack found up a deceased cat, stale carrion, and as black as ebony. This was carried by the tail across the quay to the river-side, and having quietly secured the carollers in the cabin, by thrusting a stick through the hasp of the door, by another adroit manœuvre dropped the cat down the chimney, and pushed a handful of grass sod, pulled from the bank, into the hole by way of a bung.

'Poke her up agin!' demanded Limpeny, and the weapon was thrust into the—cat—to the puzzlement of the stoker, whose eyesight had become somewhat impaired by the smoke. A horrible stench was emitted, and gradually the situation dawned on them, more especially when the jokers outside started to violently rock the house-boat. Some more than sublime language, the smashing of mugs that fell on the floor, and the stumbling about of the tenants, could be heard across the river, as well as the loud hammering on the door inside, and hoarse demands to open it.

It was only for fear of suffocating their victims that the door was unfastened; and the perpetrators of this coarse, un-Christmaslike joke made themselves scarce. Limpeny and Peg-leg shambled ashore with some arrears of profanity, leaving poor old Sampson to get ashore as best he could, and by good luck he managed to do so, angry enough at the moment, but his usual good temper returned in the morning, when his tormentors took him into the tavern to laugh over the joke.

CHAPTER VI

THE LEISURE HOUR

' Oh, it is great to shake off the trammels of the world and of public opinion—to lose our importunate, tormenting, everlasting personal identity in the elements of Nature, and become the creature of the moment . . . one may take one's chance of all characters in this romantic state of uncertainty.'

—Wm. Hazlitt

ALBERT BECKETT, one-time landlord of the 'Lord Nelson', and overlord of the Breydoner's Athenæum, needs no introduction. Night after night, for several years, a medley of gossips found their way up the step-ladder —fewer in summer days than on wild winter nights, when funds were low, and the elements forbidding. The shavings of the workshop were a change from the sawdust in the bar-parlour. More gunners than fisherfolk gossiped in the workshop, and fewer gunners, perhaps, joined in with the droughty eel-men in the pub; but proportionate numbers were always a matter of accident, or excitation.

One day Sartor (our tailor-gunner) brought into the shop a certain noted old punt-gun, of unduly short length, and hung it upon the brackets on Beckett's wall, giving out the fact that he was very desirous of securing a big old marsh duck-gun from whose barrel a section could be cut, in order to be brazed upon, and to lengthen, the gun aforesaid.

Every one of the fraternity who heard about this project made a point of visiting the workshop and discussing the matter. Jimmy Hurr thought the aged weapon was not worth the trouble and expense; the Admiral thought differently, and much argument and discussion ensued, ere the novelty wore off the suggested experiment, although each new-comer or absentee who chanced to drop in invited a slight renewal of the problem.

Curiously enough, Sartor's near relation, Ulysses, heard of a big 'marsh-rail' gun in a certain country village, and inquiries were instituted. A visit was made to the owner, and the gun was discovered standing in a low-roofed outhouse, with its muzzle-end sticking out of a hole made by the removal of a tile; it had been roughly protected by a bit of floor-cloth round the barrel, and ended in a sort of waterproof cap. It was examined and found desirable as a speculation. Ulysses was much taken by the weapon, but pointed out every little fault, real or imagined, to the owner, who climbed down in price in proportion to the disparagement of the would-be purchaser. Ulysses was, like the late Police-Sergeant Barnes, ludicrously fond of messing about and buying and selling fowling-pieces. A case in point will show this. When looking at a heap of scrap-iron in a marine-store shop, I noticed a double-barrelled gun with a rather short pair of barrels. The iron-merchant told me I might have the old crock for a shilling. I purchased and cleaned it, and had a new hammer put on it, one being absent. A bird-catcher took a fancy to it, and offered me a half-sovereign for it; he sold it to Ulysses, who shortly after offered it to me, as a 'clinking little snipe-gun', for two pounds. I offered him a shilling for it, which seemed to stagger him, and when I proved to him how it had come into my possession he was exceedingly wrathful.

Ulysses, however, bought the marsh-gun, and brought it to Albert's workshop, with a view to obtaining a profitable customer for it, or a lucrative exchange. It was hung near to the punt-gun; and it was only natural that these two guns, suspended before the eyes of the crowd, should be of recurrent interest and entertainment.

Harry Collins came up, and the guns immediately attracted his attention; one and another explained to him the meaning of the guns being put up on exhibition. Said he: 'Why, that old marsh-rail is jist the dinky thing to dock [cut down], and solder on to Sartor's old piece. I never see a better chance!'

Those within hearing all agreed to the proposition; and thenceforth the interest grew apace, and insistence was made, providing the 'relation', as they called him, was agreeable on carrying out the job; and if he was not, to do it in spite of him. Even Sartor had come to a tactful consent to this.

'Right you are,' said Beckett; 'we'll saw the old joker in halves, and there's enough of you to take turns if you don't feel over-workish. It's a rum thing, but you chaps fare half afraid to go eel-pickin' and shootin' jist after a gale.'

'The g-g-gale ain't b-b-bin over twenty-four hours,' said Huckering Tom, 'and t-t-tain't summer-t-t-time now!'

'Then let's get on with the job—a little work won't do you any harm now you've got a leisure hour.'

One of the fellows, who was a carpenter, and thought himself somewhat of a blacksmith, suggested some one should go over to Yeoman's smithy and borrow a hack-saw; and if

Yeoman could not oblige, he'd buck off to Bob Flaxman's, and he was sure to lend him one. In a short time he was back at the shop with Flaxman's newest saw, and the two weapons were taken from their pegs and laid upon the carpenter's bench. The punt-gun was lashed to the bench, immovably, and Tom Reed and Albert carefully made measurements upon the barrel of the other, so as to cut where the circumference exactly tallied with that of the muzzle of the punt-gun, and great care was given to marking the place of severance ; the part of the barrel that was to be taken off the muzzle-end would be marked and cut later. Fiddler suggested that it looked like a very dry and thirsty job ; the owner of the big gun, who was present, thought there would be no harm in getting in a can of Beckett's best ale ; and so it was decided. Two or three hands were readily held out for the cash, but Beckett said he'd square that job. A droughty eel-man was sent to fetch it.

'You 'on't see him back afore tea-time !' growled Pero.

'You wouldn't have turned up afore to-morrer mornin'!' remarked another ; 'we've seen you afore. I hear you ain't gone on copper nails.'

'No, bor, no, nor half-pint pots !' assented the old ex-sergeant-major of militia.

Tom Reed soon got warmed up, and offered the hack-saw to Pero, who refused, until the can came in. Beckett now had a hand at the sawing. Just then a well-known footfall was heard upon the step-ladder.

'Fare to sound like yer relation,' suggested Pero, turning to Sartor. 'You'd better take my tip an' get out o' the way.' The owner of the punt-gun thought so too ; and while one jumped to the door and barred it, Beckett lifted the little trap-door, situated behind the work-bench, which opened into the stable below, just then in possession of an owner of beach donkeys. The said occupier seemed to have been unaware that this outlet was still usable ; and Beckett's weighty tool-chest, as a rule, stood upon it. The worm-eaten old steps below it had not been removed. Amid a shower of sawdust and shavings, Sartor descended, and the trap-door was shut.

It was the excitable owner of the marsh-rail that the workshop door was opened to let in ; he facetiously wanted to know what conspiracy was on, as Harry Collins closed the door.

'Keepin' draughts out,' blandly replied Collins. The amateur gun-dealer turned to Beckett, who was oil-stoning a plane-iron at the moment ; when, to his horror, he espied the gun—*his* gun—fastened to the bench, like a victim strapped on the guillotine. Not happening to be present at the time myself, my friend Sartor, whose ear, notwithstanding the grains of sawdust that were in it, and the cobwebs, was at the crevice of the trap-door listening, shall tell what ensued.

'Bor,' said he, 'Ulysses foamed and raved ; he flung his arms about like a windmill in a fit. "My d——d gun bein' murdered !" he yelled. "Who the —— started that game ? I'll be hung for him—that I will." He stared round like a wild hawk at one and another of the crew ; you never heard such a row in all yer life ! "I'll see a lawyer. You've spoilt my best gun. Who'll buy half a gun ? Somebody'll have to pay pretty smart for it ; you've ruined the gun !"—and out he went, all of a muckwash with perspiration and shaking his fist at all of them, so they told me. All the time I was holding myself on the rotten steps with one hand and my crutch, and pretty nigh exploding with laughter.

'"You can come out now, Sartor boy ; your pretty six-foot chum is gorn. If he'd 'a' seen you he'd 'a' killed ye—I'm sure he would." It was old Charlie Thacker that lifted the trap-door and helped me out, while he chuckled like a laughing jackass just beginning its song. "Went clean off his nut, he did," added Thacker.'

Beckett suggested that they should finish the job now they'd started ; this they did ; and the next morning the punt-gun and the chosen portion of the marsh-rail were carted over to a certain engineering works at Cobholm, to be bevelled at their junctures, for the purpose of brazing them together. Meantime, the owner of the despoiled gun, who had survived a night of unusual unrest, had gone off in his punt to Breydon, taking his other fowling-piece with him, having received an intimation that thousands of lapwings had descended upon the swamped marshes from which the flood water was being drawn off by the pump and steam-mills.

To revert to the misadventure that happened to this composite gun : the engineering folks had welded the two sections together, and a rather heavy bill came in for the job. Neither Sartor nor Beckett was well pleased with the juncture, so the devoted weapon was taken to Crowther, senior, the amateur gunsmith, who, having divided the sections, laid them on his bench and proceeded to prepare the parts for the forge fire, an exceedingly delicate operation ; and also made a sort of bed to take them after being lifted out of the fire. Having finished the job, to the evident satisfaction of himself and the owner, it was carted to the punt-shed and fixed in the chock for work.

Highly elated, my friend Sartor pushed off from the rollers adjoining the 'Bowling Green' staithe to give it a trial on Breydon, where a few fowl were busy upon the wigeon-grass. Fielding Harmer, who had been watching the gunner launching, presently called to him; and on drawing to the landing-place the keen gentleman gunner complimented him upon the advent of his gun, that now looked more workmanlike than when it was of a shorter length.

'But,' said he, 'I don't think, young man, I should care to fire that weapon. I presume you have loaded it?'

'Yes, Mr. Harmer, I have; but what's wrong with her?'

'There's a decided drop at the muzzle-end of her,' replied Fielding Harmer.

'Dear me, I hadn't noticed it,' admitted Sartor.

'If you will allow me to step aboard,' said the sedate Mr. Harmer, 'I will, I think, very soon convince you that there is. I will bring a straight rod and show you.' Mr. Harmer stepped on board, and laying the rod along the barrel pronounced it to have three-quarters of an inch drop out of the straight. So it was decided to take the gun to 'Jiggy' Hall, who was a clever mechanic, to whom it ought to have gone at first. He made a real good job of her. The barrel was painted to keep the metal waterproof, and its owner had some good shooting with it. Later it was advertised and sold to a Ross-shire sportsman. Many years after I obtained the real reason of Sartor's parting with the gun. He was on the eve of getting married, and the temptation of a handful of golden coins at such a period was greater than that of a fresh supply of powder and shot. Beckett managed to patch up an uncertain peace between the 'relations', and the owner of the desecrated gun recovering the original value of the old marsh-rail, was glad to hear the last of it.

To return to the workshop. Tom Reed and three of the others were still engaged in a game of cards in a corner of the shop where the tool-chest usually stood. Tom had shifted it to make room for the card-playing quartet, forgetting that he had uncovered the trap-door. The game had become exciting, Tom Reed exceptionally so, until a climax was reached by all the coppers staked coming to him. In exultant mood Tom rose to declare his good fortune: 'Boys,' said he, 'the b-b-blinkin' g-g-game's mine!' and he made a jump to celebrate the event, coming down with an extra forcefulness upon the weak trap-door, which was smashed to pieces beneath him; and through the hole he went with the fragments, falling upon the back of one of the donkeys, to the amazement of the other asses, who set up a roar that was even eclipsed by the riotous laughter of the Breydonians, who were equally astonished. The owner of the donkeys was not a little astounded, when he came into the stable below, to find broken pieces of the old door lying about, and saw to it that the tenant above permanently filled in the floor with stronger boarding, remarking he 'farmed quite enow beach dickies, without others comin' in without bein' inwited.'

. . . . .

A wet night and a blowy had set in, with the promise of an increase of rough weather as the tide made up; a south-easterly wind had brought upon its wings, and their own, a number of waders to the Estuary. Pintail Thomas had brought home a bunch of nine grey plovers and a couple of black-tailed godwits as the result of one discharge of the big gun, making for him at least a fair day's work. The plovers, at sixpence each, 'covered four and sixpence', and a little bartering might probably bring a crown apiece for the godwits to the lady chancellor of the exchequer of the Fuller's Hill gull-shop, minus a shilling for the droughty little fowler, who needed 'a bit o' 'bacca' to solace his mind, for few of these men had had opportunity for 'larnin' tu read print'; and there were few mental relaxations for men of his sort, save what the public-houses afforded, and such institutions as the cabinet-maker's workshop. Other gunners had done better than Pintail, some not so well: Charlie Thacker had fallen in with some curlews, and missed a 'black curlew' (glossy ibis) that was consorting with them, for which fluke he was not a little wrathful, for it meant a loss to him of 'harf a quid, what wos half a week's work hulled away, all through a tarnation stroke o' bad luck'.

. . . . .

Soon after the tea-hour Beckett unlocked the workshop door, and three or four of the Breydon men, who had each been lingering over a slow-emptying pot of ale at the 'Albion' tavern, a few yards from the cabinet-maker's place, and watching for the advent of Beckett, were ready for an evening's warm shelter and a miscellany of gossip.

Collins turned up early, and within half an hour nearly a half-score were busy with their tongues, or their playing-cards; most were filling the atmosphere with grey, acrid smoke.

'How's eels ?' asked Collins of George Sampson, a hard-visaged, canvas-clad eel-picker.

'Wal, Harry, they fare wery spotty nowadays, since them silver-bellies hev done runnin'.'

'Breydon fare rotten nowadays,' sympathetically spake the jolly little cabman ; 'and I don't wonder at you a-grizzlin'. What a spree I had when I was down at Hartleypool, some yeer ago, when I was cabbyin' for a bit for a relation I had livin' there! I was on the water one Sunday when two Dutch schuyts drawed into the harbour and dropped anchors. I got a boat, and made some excuse to board one of them, to see what I could learn from the Dutchies. They had cargoes of some sort, but I forget what it was. However, I spotted a couple o' big eel-pots layin' on deck, which I pinted to and axes, partly with my hands, if they'd sell 'em.

'"No, no, t'anks," says the skipper. "I feesh wid ze pots ven I come in ze port for zum eels meself."

'Howsomever, by a little cajolery I managed to coach him into lettin' me have 'em. I rowed off and laid 'em, baitin' with some red herrin's I had left from a deal ashore, and next mornin' I found no less than three stone of eels in 'em. But since I left Hartleypool the eel-fishin' fare all messed up—what with chemikils and sewerage and other muck pourin' into the harbour.'

Thacker thought, and said, 'Them eel-sets laid about our rivers wos playin' the dowse with eel-babbers, for them poor eels hedn't harf a chanct to come down-river to winter in the sea, and us poor devils get wery little at all nowadays.'

'You fare to have chucked the Beccles river,' suggested Collins. 'Several of ye used to draw up there o' nights and do pretty good business. What ail the blissed eels ?'

'Old Housmann fare to me to hev cleaned 'em all out with his trawl-net ; anyway, there don't fare the eels there wos; there ain't a single eel-set on thet, or on the Norridge river; although theer's plenty in the North River, what'll show how things is. It's only by sheer luck we get amon' a few of 'em nowadays.'

'Nowadays of a night,' corrected Collins.

'If I could get a pound a week reg'lar, pig-killin', and my sausages throw'd in, I'd chuck up Breydon to-morrer,' insisted Thacker.

'What's that ?' demanded Bellin. Charlie repeated his remark, Pero overhearing it.

'You'd look nice a-doin' it !' growled Pero. 'You'd want to take the old punt-gun into the slaughter-house, you would. You can't shave yourself, let alone cutting a hog's weasand !'

RINGED PLOVERS

'You'd hev to be like old "Scientific" Fuller, up there at Rockland Broad,' edged in Collins. 'When they wanted to make a butcher of him——'

'What's that ?' snapped Charlie Thacker.

'Why, they shoved a knife in his hand and bundled him and the pig into a barn and shet the door.'

'And then what happened ?' interrupted Pero.

'W-w-why don't yer shurrup !' demanded Huckering Tom, 'and l-l-let Harry g-g-get on with his y-y-yarn ?"

'Well, I was a-sayin',' went on Collins, 'they shoved both the warmin into the barn, and told "Scientific" they'd never let him out agin till the pig wos dade, and a mighty good time he an' the pig seem to hev hed of it, for when they opened the barn doors, " Scientific " come out smothered with blood, an' the pig nicely mauled about.'

Baker Stork, Charlie's quiet brother, who was not much of a talker, made some remark on the crab nuisance, which in those days was a great annoyance to eel-babbers.

Now, I happened to have been somewhat interested in these little crustaceans, the green shore-crabs that sometimes boasted a ruddy tinted carapace, and proffered my observations, which cover the next paragraph.

These vicious creatures swarmed the muds of Breydon, and abounded in the channels, as they were aware ; eels largely preyed upon them, and their stomachs were often packed with them. This was not to the disadvantage of eel-sellers, who sold them by weight before skinning them. Little comes amiss to *Carcinus mœnas*, from shrimp to drowned dog ; it seems to devour carrion and freshly dead shrimp with equal avidity. When the water flowed they shuffled about everywhere seeking prey ; when the tide fell they hid below the *Zostera* or any flintstone or wreckage that was handy ; failing these they would wriggle into the ooze, leaving but the tips of their stalky eyes unburied [like periscopes] showing above water. At low water, in times of scarcity, great grey and black-headed gulls patrolled the flats, sometimes in extended line, turning the wigeon-grass over and snapping up each small stowaway with alacrity. Near shore they burrowed in like manner, often to fall a prey to rambling, mouching rats. Older crabs when hungry made no scruple in devouring those of a younger generation.

Pero had been intently listening, and made remark that he didn't know why folks who set eel-pots shouldn't smash up crabs and use them as bait for eels, just as the Wells and Blakeney folks used them for the whelk-traps. He'd seen tubs of ' them little witches ' caught by kiddies for their father's fishing.

' F-F-French people eat 'em,' ventured Tom Reed, ' though there ain't much meat on 'em.'

' People as eat frogs,' put in Harry Collins, ' will eat 'most anything—even dorgs.'

' Dorgs ? ' exclaimed little Charlie.

' Yes, dorgs—dorgfish,' explained Harry ; ' and spotted dorgs ain't bad tack, nicely cooked. Down Kent way they call 'em " Husses ", and most fishermen eat 'em.'

' They're welcome to 'em,' said Charlie, shaking his wise head. ' I'd be bloomin' hard up to try 'em.'

'You wait till the North Sea fish scarcen,' assured Collins, 'and get too dear for the poorer English people: they'll eat 'em fast enough—specially if sold to 'em ready skinned—and get to like 'em.'

Reverting again to my crabs, I called to mind a beautiful sunny June day when staying in the *Moorhen*. I was idling on a rond beside a shallow drain nearly emptied by the ebb tide, the water in which would not have floated a match-box, when a movement caught my eye, and I stooped down in order to watch a pert little crab that was too busy to pay much heed to me. This crab, the size of a half orange, was scuttling about, his mud-bedaubed carapace now and again slightly above the muddy water; he ran, he shuffled, halted, and sprung by turns, like some little water ogre. He was out for a dinner of small things that were quite as alert as himself. Now he would stop a moment, and the dull eyes of him came above the surface, like two unstruck lucifer match-ends. Then a brown shrimp on whose track he seemed to be, made a movement, which was instantly observed by him, and he lowered himself on his bow legs, and—but the shrimp had sprung backwards a distance several times its own length, and off he ran to seize it, but it again eluded him. A freckled goby next caught his eye; a short run, and a shorter spring—but that goby had sunk well into the ooze, baffling him with the silt stirred up by its powerful ventral fins, that covered it as in a cloud. This move the crab did not seem to understand. Had he stabbed the ooze with his wicked, two-pointed claws in the spot where the fish had vanished he might now have secured it, but it did not occur to him to do so.

Next came the turn of an immature, halfpenny-sized flounder, which, like the goby and the shrimp and even the crab, was working hard to capture a little dinner. The flounder eluded the crab's rush, but this movement sent it up the tiny slope of mud, though the fish, with another smart undulation of its chief fins, was immediately in again and had covered itself in the ooze.

There were no other crabs about in this shallow drain to dispute our client's right of way; had there been, undoubtedly there would have been a quarrel and a fight, and a great show of retreating and advancing. In a slightly deeper pool through which the drain meandered some ditch prawns had taken up their position, also on the hunt for a meal. On perceiving them, the crab, who had continued his explorations in that direction, made a dead set at them, but they threw themselves helter-skelter out of his way, and all but one made their escape. Our crab captured him, and took good care that he did not escape by breaking him in two with those two strong pincer claws of his ; he then crammed each piece alternately into his hungry maw. And there I left him.

A mixed ' atmosphere ' of contrarities usually pervaded the old workshop when tenanted ; mild argument, heated disputation, coarse laughter, and rude merriment intermingled ; hot heads and spicy comments rarely gave opportunity for a dull moment. Two of the eel-babbers present seemed much interested in the little dissertation upon shore-crabs, but Charlie Thacker in particular made remark : ' I allers say damn all crabs ; but they do bite the babs to pieces, and even keep off eels from havin' fair play ; and when you try to shake 'em off in the boat, they cling like the dowse, and you hev to bump the lead on the floor-boards, losin' time, till you set yer foot on 'em, and smash 'em one arter another, and so get yer own back.'

The subject now turned to snipe and snipe-shooting. Whiley, a noted snipe-shot in his younger days, had dropped Breydon marshes for the—to him—nearer south beach, his favourite beat lying between the Wellington Pier and Gorleston harbour mouth, where rare gulls, skuas, divers, and other marine birds fell to his gun, to the occasional benefit of his pocket. His sedentary occupation as a cordwainer so tended to enlarge his waistcoat that as an antidote he stumped the sands merrily with his double-barrelled muzzle-loader ; he had the accuracy of aim of a sharp-shooter. Woodcocks in their season made appeal to him.

' I was on the south beach t'other morning,' said he, ' when I see three woodcocks, close together, come over the waves fairly low, as if they were tired—which they were. They fared on mountin' above a little sand-hill, as if they intended to light among the marrams. Consekwently (a favourite word of his) I looked to my caps, and crept to the top of the low sand-hill, to find all three in the middle of a little bit o' marram, apparently asleep : I tried to get all three together or in line, by a careful bit o' shiftin', but could only cover two. So I shot, killin' them two. Consekwently the other woke up and made off like lightnin' to the west'ard, my second shot missing him ; consekwence wos, I lost him.'

' *Consekwently* you fared disappointed ! ' put in Pero, who had just thrown his last card on the box. Whiley glared at him.

'You used to trot over the south Breydon meshes with old Captain Burch?' suggested Harry Collins.

'I did,' said Whiley. 'Conse—I mean, he wanted a bit of learnin', too, he was so nervy when a snipe rose and wobbled. I went with him one day to the South Wall and on to the reed-mesh. There was plenty o' snipe about, and he said he badly wanted some for a dinner he was givin'.

'"Very good, sir," I says; "you go just ahead of me." A snipe was flushed, and the Captain took aim, but not until the bird had towered well in the air and was zigzagging. He fired, and (turning his eye on Pero) consekwently missed it!' Whiley was great on his 'consekwences'.

'*Consekwence wos*, he didn't get it!' growled Pero, shuffling a fresh pack of cards.

'"Now you try, Whiley," says the Captain to me, stepping behind me. In a few minutes I stopped and fired, killing the next snipe that riz before it reached the top o' the reeds.

'"That's a rummon," said the Captain, on looking at the dead bird lying on its breast, its wings spread out. "You must have shot it on the ground."

'"Nothing of the sort, sir," I says. "You ought allers to shoot at a snipe after it hev squeaked *but once*, afore it's above the reeds—like this" (and I pulled at, and killed another). Captain Burch put the bird in his pocket, and he downed the next he saw; he had learnt his lesson.'

'*Consekwently*,' ventured the facetious Charlie, 'he left skule!'

'Howsomever,' went on Whiley, 'of the next three or four birds he killed two, and later one or two more, till we'd made up nine.

'"Well, Whiley," says he, "I've killed hundreds of snipe in my time, but I've missed thousands"; and after that he took me to his boat-shud, and treated me handsome.'

'*Consekwently*——' edged in Pero.

'No, I didn't. I'm not a boat-builder, nor an ex-militia-man; I know my limits when a bottle is broached.'

'I was once out shooting,' said Admiral Gooch, who had come in while Whiley was yarning, 'when I all but stepped upon a snipe, but its beady eye caught mine, and up it jumped from under my foot, momentarily startling me, but I let go without aiming, and it fell dead near my feet, without a single shot-wound; it must have been the concussion that did it.'

'Have you noticed snipe helpin' themselves up a bit on

the wing,' asked Whiley, 'by leverin' themselves a bit by the bill?'

'I don't know that I have,' answered Gooch; 'but some birds, like gulls, will run on pattering feet as if to get themselves under way; others bend their legs, probably for a sort of leverage.'

'I've seen a woodcock,' said Whiley, 'light on a fairly level sea, in a thick morning, with wings stretched out as if it was resting, and suddenly lift itself from the top of a roller and fly off inshore. I've seen them flying low and apparently bewildered in bad weather, but I've an opinion they fly very high in fairly decent weather, lowering when near the shore if it's a bit thickish. Odd birds what I've seen flittin' in up till midday and have now and agin shot, I've found were heavy ones.'

'One of the queerest things I've seen in snipes,' said Bellin, 'was on one occasion when up the North River Wall, nearly opposite the Black House. A snipe towards eventide rose from a reedy dyke, and I let go at it before I realized what I was doing. The wind was from the east. I had not brought my dog with me, she having hurt the pad of one of her feet, and it was useless for me to hope to secure the snipe, which had fallen in the river with a broken wing. It swam across the river, and, getting on to the muddy margin, scrambled up and vanished in a clump of thick herbage. Now, snipes have a curious propensity even after several times being disturbed for returning to a favourite feeding-ground; so next morning I was on the same beat with my dog, and when I had reached the reed-patch I sent her in, when, after a little splashing about, out she came with a snipe in her mouth with a broken wing.'

'That bird had swum the river,' suggested Gooch, 'and I have observed myself the queer way they have of returning to a spot from which they have been disturbed. It was a nice little dog you had.'

'She was,' admitted Bellin. 'She was with me one late evening on the North Breydon Wall when I shot into a bunch of teal, securing two, and missing one or two more that I thought had been brought down. I returned to the wall in the morning, on my way up to the house-boat, the dog following me. I was proceeding, thinking, when I felt the dog's nose nudge the calf of my leg, and found she had a dead teal in her mouth. Soon after the same thing occurred with another one. Little "Rosie" knew her work.'

Admiral Gooch seemed to have been much interested in

Whiley's snipe-shooting experiences, and declared that he himself enjoyed a bit of snipe-shooting, although he possessed a modicum of pity for a species against which every man's hand was raised, from the duke who slew his hundreds in a season to the lout with a converted rifle, who rested his gun on a marsh-rail to knock over a starving *Scolopax* that he found pottering about in front of him in a field of beet or cabbages, whose leaves were white at the beginning of a spell of frost that, in a couple of days, would clear off the survivors to more saline places. As to roasted snipe—he knew no titbit upon the dinner-table more dainty.

'As to cooking a snipe with its trail,' said he, 'I greatly dislike it. Let me have a bird *stuffed* with grated beef and suet, breadcrumbs, and a pinch of salt and pepper, with a little chopped parsley and yolk of an egg.'

'How d'you roast 'em?' asked Pero—'on a jack or a toast-fork?'

'Jack be blowed!' said Gooch. 'Give me two or three yards of worsted, one end tacked to the mantelpiece, the other attached to the snipe's skewer, and a twist of the thumb and finger now and again for about twelve minutes, and they're done. I never even let the missus interfere with them.'

'I don't hold with cookin' anything with the guts in,' protested Pintail, 'neither plover, cute, cur-lew, a young herrin'-gull, or even a rabbit. There's suffin' to pick at, without scorfin' bird-trails, as they call 'em, what fare more like putrefyin' macaroni.'

'I can't abide gentlefolk, as they call 'em,' remarked Billy Thacker, with that feminine voice of his, which he was slow to use, 'scorfin' baked pheasants with maggots cooked in 'em; nor green-bellied four-legged Sallies. If that's bein' genteel, I'd suner sit down to a baked poker [pochard] or a couple o' stewed hoodie crows. Gentry fare to want flavour and giblets, instead of clean, honest pickin'; and with all them got-up sauces, they might as well eat their game with eyes shut. What do you say, Johnny?' The gentleman addressed winked wickedly.

Tom Reed and Collins, with one or two others who had wearied and thrown down their cards, bade the rest good night, presumably making sure of a little light refreshment before the pubs closed. Pero shortly followed them.

'Now off, Pero?' asked Whiley, with a veiled sneer.

'I've got suffin' else to do,' grinned Pero, 'or I'll hev to take the *consekwences*.'

Hoppy Smith and Harvey, who had heard of Thacker's brace of godwits, had met at Charlie's door simultaneously, to be told that Charlie was out, and where they'd most likely find him. They naturally bent their steps to the gossip-shop, and each seemed to be inclined to mount the steps first ; but they entered as if nothing had happened to provoke business rivalry, and having passed a few incidental remarks on weather and fowl, and things in general, gave Charlie a hint to come out and show them the birds.

'Another stroke of luck, Thacker,' remarked Beckett, as Charlie bade him good night, and then in a half-whisper added, 'and don't you jump too quick to an offer, old man.'

'No avocets about, I suppose ?' asked Gooch of Fred Clarke, who had been enjoying the chatter, but as usual having very little to say.

'A few wigeon,' said Fred ; 'but it don't look much like avocet weather. I got one just afore the close season ended—a youngster of not much account, quite a baby.'

'I hadn't heard of it,' said Gooch. 'Who did you sell it to—Lowne or Harvey ?'

'Neither,' replied Fred. 'I let Hoppy Smith have it. I didn't expect to see a bird of this sort so late in the season ; but Pintail and me were rowin' down in our punts on the ebb tide when I spotted the bird among some kitties, lookin' very much like a kitty on stilts—different coloured legs of course. I made sure I was right by usin' my field-glasses. I reckon as how that bird had shifted from Holland on a stiff easterly breeze ; anyway, there it was, leg-deep in a pulk, jist off the "Lumps" ; and neither on us had a gun aboard, as we'd bin doin' a bit of eel-pickin'. I wasn't goin' to lose that bird for want of a try, so I rowed up the North Wall drain as near to it as I durst, for fear of puttin' it up, though it fared to me mighty tame and innocent ; so I moored the punt agin' the rafts, crept over the wall, and bolted down the line to the station, what you know is only a few yards from my house, and snatchin' up a loaded shoulder-gun, goin' back round by the wall, through Moy's coal-yard, to have a shot. A bloke on the line, one of them navvies, says to me, "I bet I know what you're after !" I says to him, "Then I don't need to tell ye." I slipped into the boat, and sculled up within shot, but on the first pull the cap didn't explode. The bird only lifted his head and looked round, but didn't take to flight, bein' innocent of Breydon ways. I put on a fresh cap, and pulled, and winged the bird. Law ! didn't the poor little devil shriek—almost like a kicked puppy. I ran him down and settled him. But I was more 'an half afraid to take him home, Buddery bein' somewhere about, and ye never knowed where he might drop on to yer, so I rowed up to the Dickey Works, and slipped home at dusk. Hoppy got sound of it, and come to see me next mornin'.

' " I hear," he says, " you've got a avocet."

' " I hev," says I, " but I ain't showed it to nobody yet; however, you can see it, if you like." So I showed him.

' Says he, " Thet's only *half* a bird—a mere baby."

' " Well," I says, " it was a *whole* one when I shot it ; and there's my price, hev it or leave it." I forget exactly what I axed him for it, but never mind ; he wanted it, and so he paid for it.'

Beckett, having finished the job in hand, took off his apron and hitched himself on to his bench for a little mental recreation and a bit of tobacco-burning with the others. Dye and Lowne, who had got hot-foot upon the trail of the black-tailed godwits, had come in a few minutes before ; and having hinted at their quest, were told that they were a bit behind time, and Charlie looked like making a bargain. The two, like the others, sat down to seek a little comfort in a soothing smoke to get over their disappointment.

' Not the first bird bargains we've lost, and hope it won't be the last,' enigmatically responded Lowne.

' Why ? ' asked Clarke.

' Why, because it would mean that rare birds have not yet altogether left us,' said Lowne.

The subject now turned on rare and desirable birds, always a strong feature in the debates.

Ben Dye, who was always ready to analyse, even to take exception to the introduction of a new species of bird to the British list, wholly negatived it, if it were only seen and recognized by even a competent authority, unless a decided inquest had been held upon the little dead body. Times and often had he argued and protested against the admission of Allen's rail (*Porphyrio alleni*) into the Norfolk list, because, at a not remote period, this very slim and elusive member of the rail family had been advertised in a London bird-dealer's list at thirty shillings and sixpence. I was not altogether in favour of admitting the bird as a reliable British species, for at the time I received one of the lists, and saw the figures mentioned. I therefore put brackets to this bird in my *Nature in Eastern Norfolk* (1905).

'I reckon,' said Ben, 'you may get twenty spotted

redshanks, even in spring, and you won't find a pair to come up to my birds, which were shot in the 'sixties, on Breydon, in the pink of condition.'

'We know all about 'em,' said Lowne, 'who shot 'em and got 'em, in 1866, and where *you* got 'em, and *how* you got 'em! I'll admit what you say about 'em, but I contend that the right place for them is in the Tolhouse Museum.'

'And so do I,' remarked Admiral Gooch, 'but they're very nice birds. The Pagets describe the species as the "dusky sandpiper"; the old punt-gunners in my younger day called them redshanks and Cambridge godwits, and sometimes "shriekers", for they disturbed all the other birds with their yelping; but they were never very common, especially in the fully adult spring plumage. The pair shot in 1862 Mr. Harmer wrote to the *Field* about; one was shot from a punt as it was feeding on the mudflat, and the other was shot on the marshes. It seemed a pity to kill such beautiful creatures. Harmer never watched 'em, only with the eye of a bird of prey.'

'If we don't shoot the rare birds that come here,' interposed Dye, 'somebody else will.'

'Two wrongs won't make a right,' said Gooch.

'You'd have shot 'em yourself,' said Lowne, 'if you'd had the chance; but opportunity's a fine thing!'

'A bird collector,' went on Gooch, 'is always chary of publishing his own good fortune, in either shooting or securing a rare or unique example, save in some exclusive journal, or circle, for the sake of marking its authenticity. A report of such a happening sets all the gunners and collectors on the alert for repeating a record, generally much to the annoyance of the latter, for repetition has a tendency to lower the prices of birds already killed and embalmed.

'I consider the prices,' continued Gooch, 'that have been paid or asked for rare local birds an abomination, although dealers and gunners may think otherwise. It seems to me preposterous to give twenty-five guineas for a buffel-headed duck and twenty-one guineas for a red-crested whistling duck, let alone asking three figures for a Mediterranean black-headed gull.'

'What about the night heron shot in Youell's garden in 1824?' queried Ben. 'It fell into old Harvey's hands, and was sold by him to a collector named Thurtel, of Fakenham, who refused the elder Gurney's offer of thirty pounds for it. It's all right with people with big pockets. What say you,

Pintail ? ' Pintail didn't answer, for he was having a comfortable nap.

' There's one handsome little duck,' remarked Bellin, ' the Steller's duck, now in Norwich Museum, presented to the city by the Rev. Steward in July 1831. The bird had been shot in February the year before, and the *Norfolk Chronicle* made a lot of fuss about it, stating that " One of the greatest treats for those interested in Natural History is to be seen at . . . Mr. Harvey's . . . shot near that place " (Yarmouth). Stevenson gives a racy chapter to it in the *Birds of Norfolk*, stating therein that our Harvey—the second—saw one George Barrow carrying the bird, and followed him home with it ; then ran home to the old man to go back with him to see it. The general opinion has been that the bird was shot on the shore at Caister—Stevenson merely says " at Caister ". My father, who knew Barrow, got it from the man's own lips that he was on the Caister marshes, not a great way from the Bure, and the Black Boards, where he saw it sitting in a pool of water, and to use Barrow's own words, " I crept on my hands and knees, as close as I could get, but it was still too far off for a shot. My hands had become numbed with cold, and well nigh frozen ; so I says to myself, ' If I don't get a shot now directly, I shall be too cold to get a shot at all.' However, the bird came within range, and I let go. One shot struck the duck just above the eye. I took out my handkerchief, and rolled it up, put it round the bird's neck, and strangled it "— an absurd way for any man to settle a miserable little fowl, you must admit. The Barrows of that period were noted for their eccentricities. I understand that Stevenson instituted a lot of inquiries about it, but omits my father's description.'

' Barrow must have been a mug,' observed Fred Clarke, ' and I suppose we ought to make allowances for queer people in our own time.' This comment apparently passed unheeded by the others.

' The old days,' said Lowne, ' must have been rare and exciting, with all the attractions for fowl in full blast, as you might say, when common birds dropped in wholesale at times with many a rare one mixed in the crowd. The Pagets must have revelled in the unexpected arrivals of good birds. Harvey's old chap had fifty stormy petrels in at one time ; and the Pagets record that in November 1824 nearly 300 were shot after heavy gales. To see a couple in a sharp winter to-day dodging the billows as they go would make a prowling gunner sit up ! '

'There must have been a frequent and an interesting sorting over of birds sent to the folks who then studied ornithology,' interposed Bellin, 'who had comparatively few text-books to refer to. And what a book old Harvey and others who dealt in birds could have written had they the brains to do it! We are lucky to have had the fine little book of the Pagets, in which you may look long and carefully to find an error of naming or of judgment.'

'Some of us could put together a menagerie of species if we had kept alive all the birds we have stuffed,' asserted Lowne. 'In my little tinpot way I've had brought in eight grey shrikes in one year, twenty Pallas's sand-grouse in another, and a pretty good mixture time on end; but I'm no scribbler—we leave that to old "A. P.".'

'Did I ever tell you,' asked Whiley, 'about me and Brusher Broom goin' a-shootin' up the South Wall of Breydon? It was blessed cold weather, and we see flyin' in from the east within easy shot a couple of mergansers. Brusher shot and missed; I shot and killed one, hitting it under the wing in the soft part of the body. It so happened that a certain gent, whose name I don't need to give you, was in a punt with another gentleman gunner a-rowin' up-channel, when Mr. Knowall fired *over* the floatin' bird, which was drifting on the tide with wings stretched out. I see his shot strike the water yards ahead of it. They picked up my bird and placed it on the floor of their boat, paying no heed to my shouting, or my offer to pay 'em for their trouble if they brought the bird ashore to me. Instead of that they turned about and raced off home to old Aldred's, where they'd hired the boat; and they got off with my bird. So me and Brusher hurried homeward over the bridge, and went to the boat-yard; but we found the birds were flown. Consekwence is, knowin' where Mr. Knowall lived, we trotted off to St. George's Road, and cum upon him outside his house, showin' our sawbill to another gent, tellin' him all about its rarity and value, and no doubt pitchin' up a yarn as to how he shot it.

'We draw'd up to the two,' continued Whiley, 'and I said to Mr. Knowall, "I'll thank you, that's my bird, and I'll take it."

'"The devil you will," says he, "be off, you silly, ignorant fellow. Who do you think you are addressing?"

'"You, sir," says I. "You've got my bird; consekwently I mean to hev it!" Brusher began to draw up the sleeves of his guernsey, and the gentleman gunner, seeing that the owner and witness were determined to have the bird, if only by force, seemed disposed to listen to reason, and to allow me to tell the other gentleman my version of the story.

' " Very well," I says to the stranger. " We'll leave you to judge when you've heard both sides."

I told him the size of my shot, and the way Mr. Knowall shot at a bird that didn't belong to him which was already dead. I axed Knowall what sized shots *he* used, and he replied " Sixes ".

" Well," says I, " mine were fives." I then made them witness my extraction of a shot, which, surely enough, was a number five. The gent sided with us, and suggested to Knowall that he thought we were in the right. Mr. Knowall with a snap, said, " Here, take the mucky bird ; it's worth nothing to me," and almost flung it at me.

" Thank you," says I. " Here's a tip for ye," offerin' him the price of a pint of ale. He turns as nasty as poison and went into his house. I made seven and sixpence on the bird next day.'

' This is all very nice and interesting,' said Beckett, as he shook Pintail into wakefulness.

' What is ? ' demanded the discomposed little gunner, and yawned.

' Bird talks,' replied the cabinet-maker ; ' but time's up, and I've got another little job on, what you can guess at ' ; as he drew from a corner a canvas-covered package that looked uncommonly like a wee baby's coffin.

' Some poor little mite seft a world of trouble,' said Thomas, in a more than usually subdued tone.

' Yes,' said Albert, as he took down the key ; ' but little birds don't need little boxes, do they ? '

' No,' said Pintail. ' We can pack them up and away to Leadenhall in hampers much better.'

CHAPTER VII

NOTABLE SNOW-TIME HAZARDS

'It is most imprudent to adventure these frail craft among the drifting floes, where they run a serious risk of being stove, to say nothing of . . . working a big gun under such conditions.'

—ABEL CHAPMAN

THE late R. Fielding Harmer, an ardent fowler in the latter half of last century, his record as a punter extending from 1854 to 1901, was undoubtedly an authority upon wildfowl and fowling; but lost, for want of a certain ambition, a unique opportunity as historian and naturalist of Breydon, which in his time had been matchless as a resort for wildfowl and shore-birds. He rowed and shot over the Estuary with the airs and imperiousness of a Tudor lord; and in personal appearance, when 'rigged' for an expedition and wearing a pointed beard, he very much reminded one of such. He slavishly dressed as recommended by Colonel Hawker. The rank and file of the illiterate, unrefined horde of fishermen and fowlers were, I think, more amused than awed by his assumption and self-assertion.

Harmer had no great gift of expression, and beyond sending an occasional note to the *Field* he wrote very little, and that of small ornithological interest, but rather from a sportsman's point of view, being more ready with his gun than with his pen. It is a matter for regret that with the opportunities he had for enriching local bird-literature, and preserving the records of a strange and uncommon race of most observant men—the Breydon fowlers—he failed to rise to them. In Dr. Emerson's *Wild Life on a Tidal Water* Mr. Harmer wrote a barren essay dealing with the birds of Breydon, which savoured more of a butcher's record than a bird-lover's diary. Beyond the name of a species, we get a constant repetition of 'seen', 'shot', 'not shot', with dates recording these three facts, but no descriptive observations. In Nicholas Everitt's *Broadland Sport* an interview with Harmer forms a chapter worth reading, but how much of it was Harmer's, or how little, must be left to the reader's imagination.

Mr. Harmer, however, gives us a jagged account of certain spells of severe wintry weather, as affecting Breydon. When referring to that which occurred in the winter of 1887–8, he states that 'Breydon had the appearance of a miniature Arctic Region.' He went on to say that he left his boat-shed at the corner of the 'Bowling Green' Quay and cautiously worked his way upward on the flood tide, through drift-ice of unusual thickness and of formidable dimensions, through jostling floes that scraped and pounded the strakes of his punt, which he had had the forethought to case in protecting copper sheeting where desirable. His punt, of whose lines and qualities he was so proud, was somewhat undersized, and far behind in beauty and utility to the type evolved by Albert Beckett, cabinet-maker and amateur fowler, and 'Little Billy' Harrod, carpenter and handyman and water-side humorist. Poor 'Little Billy' died in October 1927 at a very advanced age, the last of the Breydon boat-builders. This type is fast vanishing, for punt-gunning is a thing of the past on local waters.

Had Harmer's punt been unprotected at the lower strake and bends, it had been madness to attempt what he actually accomplished, for a 'nip' would have crushed the boat like an egg-shell. He managed to reach the edge of the Main Channel by an expert use of the ice-hook, a weapon very like a shortened boat-hook, by means of which he fended off floes, diverted jagged lumps, or pushed his way between them; and on coming to the 'fast' ice-floe, of considerable extent, that the tide had not yet swept from the flat, he shoved his boat to leeward, held on a bit, 'and had luncheon'. Harmer was not the man to overlook his luncheon 'nose-bag', nor his well-filled bottle of liquid refreshment that defied the frost, in a handy locker. Nor was he careless of his winter attire, that consisted on such occasions of a series of woollen under-clothing, oilskins, waterproof helmet, and stockinged crotch-boots; in these matters he also very precisely followed the Colonel's 'Instructions'.

To return to his adventure. He pushed and pulled through 'floes and pancake and drift-ice', now and then reaching an open wake where starving pochard and hungry wigeon and golden-eye fell to his gun; and so, by as careful a descent on the first of the ebb, ended his rather hazardous trip, tersely remarking, 'which I did after four miles of such'. Luckily he arrived at his boat-shed in time to escape a very dense snow-storm that covered all Breydon and the marshes with a heavy pall of snow, and the rush of the ebb tide with its mass of grinding, pounding ice-floes.

On this occasion Mr. Harmer saw three stout wherries, each

of twenty-five tons register, that were laden with ice from the rivers for the smacking fleet, caught in the whirling masses, and spun round like shuttlecocks, then left stranded on a lee shore, two of them being considerably injured. No other fowler had dared to venture out, preferring to drift to a less inhospitable spot to seek comfort and warmth, and be quite content in the snug parlour of the 'Bowling Green' pub or the equally popular 'Lord Nelson'. . . .

Fred Clarke, on another wild day seventeen years before, met with an equally exciting experience. At that time he was living at the Lock-gate Farm, two miles up Breydon North Wall. He kept his antiquated punt in a little grup cut in the rond, hard by the wall, where it lay smoothly in peaceful times, but ramping on the rollicking waters when a gale broke over the place. Breydon was just then perplexed with roving ice-floes, which a violent wind from the northward had taken charge of, and was driving towards the southward wall, leaving a widening wake of dark waters in the rear of the moving mass.

While Clarke was breakfasting a thick squall of snow began to fall, blotting out the retreating ice-pack; he promptly ended his meal and strode out to the wall to take a look at the prospect, when to his great surprise he saw that the wind had also released his punt, blotting it out from view, as it had also shrouded the ice with thickly falling snow-flakes. As the storm passed over he espied his craft rocking broadside to the ice edge, and quickly made up his mind what to do: he bolted into the farm kitchen, seized a hog-trough, in which the slaughtered pigs were scalded, launched it, and essayed to propel it by means of a 'shoving-pole', when to his great discomfort the improvised boat wobbled hopelessly, and presently turned turtle, throwing him into the water nearly up to his middle.

Just as he had waded ashore, Jack Gibbs, punt-gunner, came into view round Stone Corner, taking advantage of the clear water, in which fowl began to crowd. Clarke begged him to fetch back his punt, but the selfish fellow pointed to the waterfowl, promising him that after he had had a shot at them he would row to the ice and fetch back the boat. This Fred was quite sure would be farthest from Gibbs' intention, so, having been already well soaked, and the water not too deep for safety, providing he could avoid slipping into a deeper 'drain', he waded out to the runaway, and shortly brought it

LITTLE PINTAIL THOMAS
WILD-FOWLER

R. FIELDING HARMER
GENTLEMAN-WILD-FOWLER

back to its moorings, vowing with an oath never to tether it again 'with anything under two half-hitches, stem and starn alike!' While in the act of securing the boat a large flock of some hundreds of lapwings, flying low and undoubtedly just come in fatigued from oversea, passed over him, making him for the moment imagine their shadow but the passing of a cloud-squall. 'Beggar me!' he assured me, 'if I'd only had my cripple-stopper with me I must hev filled a skep with a double shot.' Such are the uncertainties and precariousnesses that variegate the fowler's experience.

Gibbs was off homeward, elated with a profitable shot or two on his way down; the results filled a herring-maund with pochards and other fowl, besides a score knots; and, on arrival home at the Green, was not slow to give idling 'pals' in the bar-parlour a highly coloured picture of Fred Clarke's adventure, well knowing that, had the punt been ready to his (Clarke's) hand, he would have had precedence, according to a time-honoured Breydon usage, with the fowl Gibbs himself had made such a profitable shot at. A breach of such precedence, it is as well to state, was never passed over without reprisals, sooner or later.

Later in the day Fred walked to town with a *rara avis* carefully tucked in a basket, and made his way to the 'Bowling Green' for refreshment before taking it to an eager collector of local birds. Much curiosity was aroused among the several gunners idling at the counter, but the victim's identity was not divulged. This reticence was resented, and a few cynical remarks respecting the story retailed by Gibbs thrown out; but Clarke was content with laughing last. When Clarke had left, 'Pero' Pestell brought his favourite pint measure to the counter for refilling.

'It's a rummon,' said he to Pintail Thomas, who sat half-dozing in a corner of the parlour, 'how Fred stand this sorter weather in his old house-boat. He gets his meals mostly at the Lock-gate Farm, but spend his nights in that ratty old tub stuck in the corner of Duffel's rond. He must hev a con-stertution like a polar bear!'

'It's use,' volunteered Pintail, 'and plenty o' coal.'

'And red herrin's,' put in Little Stork; 'though *I* couldn't live on "two-eyed steaks" three parts of the year, and fresh an' salt herrin's from the Fish Wharft the other part on it. Bor, he was born in a snow-storm, and raised on a rond; he's as hard as nails, though I reckon some fine mornin' they'll find him pegged out on the settle, if nothin' wuss happen tu him.'

'If we only got spells of weather oftener like this 'ere,' said the landlord, 'and every winter, you chaps 'ud 'a' earned more outer fowl than ye do nowadays; and we might get ten times more on 'em if we was to close them decoys at Fritton.'

Assent and dissent followed Bessey's expressed opinions. Boniface is an adept at starting an argument, but leaves it for his clients to continue it.

'I can't see that!' snorted Pintail Thomas. 'I think them decoys is a great draw. The decoy ducks, what they train to work around and inside them pipes, fare a reg'lar temptation to wild flocks comin' in from the Borltick, when they're froze out there. Them hundreds what drop in there in the early mornin', and come back to Breydon a-nights to feed, give us our chances, as well as the decoy folks.'

'Yes,' jibed in Pero, 'and hundreds never leave the decoys except packed in peds and hampers for the London markets. I don't see why the rich orter hev all the sport.' And he took a long draught at the mug; then turning, challenged Thomas with a defiant glare. Thomas held his peace.

'I can't see," ventured Admiral Gooch, 'how decoys can be a help to Breydoners, when you come to know what a slaughter takes place in them. Take this for a sample' (pulling out his note-book): 'in 1872–3 they took 215 ducks, 138 wigeon, 66 teal——'

'That worn't much of a cop,' sneered Pintail. 'I ha' took pretty nigh that in a winter with my old punt-gun.'

'Well, in 1874–5 they netted 1,053 ducks and mallard, 23 wigeon, and 28 teal.'

'That fare to show duck and mallard is bigger fules than wigeon,' commented Snicker Larn. 'We fare to get thousands o' them smee [wigeon] on Breydon to a very few on the decoys.'

'You never shot any in yer life,' snarled Pero Pestell. 'You know more about smelts and grey mullets.'

'I *du*,' assented the placid Snicker. 'We ain't all so bloodthirsty as you and Pintail.' Pintail was nodding, or he would have resented this comment with some emphasis.

'When I was down in Boston,' said the old boat-builder Pero, alias the militiaman, 'I met a chap who lived near a big decoy; he told me that in thirty-five seasons they netted over 95,000 ducks; out of that lot forty odd thousand was wild duck and mallard, forty odd thousand teal, 2,000 wigeons, over 200 shovellers—nigher three hundred than two—pretty nigh 300 pintail, besides a few score gadwall and garganey teal. How's whatcher call *Nature* to stand agin a racket like that?'

'How big was that decoy ?' asked Snicker.

'About two acres,' said Pero.

'Gosh !' ejaculated Snicker, 'and on Breydon, now, a feller is lucky to get two to an acre, and now and agin theer ain't that number to be seen on the whole blissed two thousand acres. How many decoys d'ye reckon theer is in Lincolnsheer ?'

'I've heerd,' replied Pero, 'theer wor thirty-eight one time ; but only about one nowadays what's workin'.'

DUCK AND MALLARD

'Look like shuttin' the stable door when the hoss ha' bin stolen,' commented Larn, clucking, with a gesture of indignation ; 'an' when wuz them decoys inwented ?'—turning to Pero.

'Now you've *axed* me suffin',' said Pero. 'Try *him*'—referring him to Admiral Gooch, who was an acknowledged authority—a well-read man—on fowling matters.

'No doubt the Dutchmen claim the honour,' said Gooch—'if it be an honour ; and Yorkshire prides itself as the first importer of these duck-shambles, by establishing one near Doncaster, in 1657, though I think Norfolk may claim it with some show of——'

'Deep regret !' growled Pero, amid laughter.

'Du shut up, Pestell, an' let the man talk,' admonished the urbane Snicker.

'Anyway,' went on Gooch, 'the decoy was introduced into Norfolk by a William Wodehouse.'

'William Woodhouse!' interrupted Pintail Thomas, who was now quite awake. 'What, the twine-spinner?'

This stupid remark just tickled the crowd, who knew such a gentleman then living in the town.

'I ought to have said *Sir* William Wodehouse—probably another spelling of the name—in the reign of James I. James died in 1625, so Norfolk must have got in ahead of Yorkshire.'

'Why don't we get the fowl now?' asked Fiddler Goodens. 'I suppose Breydon flats growin' up, like they hev bin for years, account some way towards the sceercity?'

'No doubt,' admitted Gooch, 'it has done something towards it; but you forget how the fens in Lincolnshire and Norfolk, round there by the Wash, have been drained—acres by the thousand. Then, locally, the broads have grown up, and where water stood—packed with pike and bream—scores of acres, less than a hundred years ago, barley and beet crops now grow. Look at the marshes—miles and miles of them—all a few centuries ago under water; to-day they're below the rivers' levels, with thousands of clean-cut, straight, shovel-deep, spade-width little gutters, into which drain the surplus rainfall. These feeders lead to larger cuttings—call them dykes or ditches—that empty into the *main* ditches that draw the water down to the "mill-deeks", to feed the wheels of the tower-mills, and the suction pumps of the steam-mills that lift it into the river through the sluice-gates in the river-walls, which save the marshes from inundation by the highest tides.'

'A reg'lar house that Jack built,' edged in Pero.

'The feed of the fowl,' went on Gooch, 'is vastly depleted, for fowl want swampy levels, not bowling greens.'

Gooch paused to take a sip at his glass. More than one had intelligently followed his deductions: others were bogged by his eloquence, and merely grunted assent.

'That's right what you say, Admiral,' remarked Thacker. 'I ha' followed yer argiment, though we ain't got the edjucation to put it so pat and plain. We see it workin' every day, and take no note on it. Breydon's growin' up fast—we can't get away from it; we've seed it comin' on for years. Wheer I once see a dorg—old Parmenter's big retriever—sink in the slub, on Rotten Eye Corner, you can now shove a barrow without the tyres sinkin' in. It's grow'd as hard as bakers' rusks——'

'You orter know!' snapped the blustering Pero.

'Know what?' demanded the little Thacker.

'Rusks!' roared Pero Pestell. 'You was brung up on 'em, or you'd bin as tall as a man by now!'

Thacker sniffed, and continued: 'An' it 'on't be long afore the wigeon-grass'll perish, same as the reeds hev done all along by the walls; so constant dry, 'cept when the salts come up, and perish 'em. Breydon *is* done for!'

Conversation drifted to the decoys again.

'The decoymen,' resumed Gooch, 'were a class of chaps by themselves, just as Breydon gunners are; and from what I've seen, and read, some were rare hands at decoying and netting fowl. Old Pettingill at Herringfleet, I knew well, and old Page I just remember. But I've heard that old Skelton, who was a Lincolnshire man, was a don hand at the business, and took more fowl on the small decoys of his own design out there at Winterton than many of the bigger ones destroyed. He came to Norfolk in 1840, when I was a kiddie. You'll find his grave a few yards to the north-east of Winterton Church steeple, for his stone still stands there.'

'And theer let it stop!' commented Pero. '*He* never done Breydoners any good: I'd bury all decoymen alongside of him!'

'I never heerd o' King James afore,' said Stork. 'I hev of good old King Harry, but not *him*. I reckon he worn't much cop—not for Breydoners anyway.'

'I never read much to James's credit,' assented Gooch, 'and Guy Fawkes was of a similar opinion. The only remark I ever read that had a spice of wisdom in it was, when on seeing a soldier in steel armour, he said, "It was an excellent invention, for it not only saved the life of the wearer but hindered him doing hurt to anybody else".'

'I don't set no store on kings,' said Thacker, ''cept old Harry the Eighth; he'd catch sight of his missus in a temper, and say, "Saw her head off", and it was off afore you know'd where you wor. He was a don hand with a saw, but I reckon Pintail's old woman wud ha' bin a match for him!'

'If Pintail *wos* a king I reckon he'd hev *his* missus's off to-morrer!' growled Pero. To which all of the coterie assented, and Johnny wisely held his peace.

In the finer months of the year, before the Wild Birds' Protection Acts came in, the Breydon fowlers had a free time of it as they sailed or paddled about the shallows of Breydon. The flats were oozy, for before the silting-up had become so noticeable the commoner fowl and waders visited the place in astonishing numbers. Rare birds, too, put in more frequent appearances ; and as collectors of Norfolk birds were an eager crowd close following on the heels of the gunners, the men made a tolerable living at the game. It was a pleasant life—drifting about on sunny waters, reclining upon the grassy walks like picnickers when meal-times enticed them ashore, where they opened the red handkerchiefs which their women-kind had filled with bread, a half-picked bone, with a few cold potatoes, and a hunch of shortcake. The stone bottle under the forepeak usually remained there until the skipper was once again afloat. Rarely a gunner owned field-glasses, but here and there one used a brass-bare, shaky old pair that had probably been for years at sea on board a fishing-boat ; most of the men had excellent eyesight. I knew but one man who had need of spectacles, and they were for reading his newspaper ; the majority of the men could not read at all. From the top of the walls they viewed a vast expanse of the flat, and perchance now and again an avocet or a spoonbill arrested their vision in the sunnier months. Most of the men resorted to eel-catching when the birds were away at their breeding-stations. Eel-spearing, babbing, potting, and lining for eels, as well as the netting of fishes, varied their activities, according to the seasons, or whatever method was most profitable at the time. Those halcyon days are past, and for ever. There are frequent periods to-day when the tides do not cover the mud-flats at all ; whereas in the earlier half of the last century they were as frequently covered with water as to be sufficient in depth to sail a yacht or a wherry thereon.

For years after the Protection Acts came in, when July came along the big guns were ready for flapper-shooting, i.e. the young flighting fowl of the year.

With the advent of the wintry days and nights fowl of all sorts came hither in considerable numbers. Then did these hardy fellows brave the snow and storm and stinging frost in their pursuit of them, often to their own advantage. When continued frosts obtained they did not do so well while they lasted, but even then some with bared throats dared the elements, for they were as hardy as Arctic walruses and polar bears, with a dash of their characteristics.

Fred Clarke, the last of the professional punt-gunners surviving, assured me that fifty-six years ago, in the terrible winter of 1871, as a young fellow of twenty, he made his first essay with a big gun in a punt belonging to the doughty 'Old Stork' Thacker, whose two sons, 'Baker Stork' and 'Little Stork', were following in the aged man's wake as promising punt-gunners. Fred at the time was an excellent shot with the shoulder-gun, when the '*whizz-whizz*' of the duck and mallard's wing was as familiar a sound as the call of the godwit and the squawking of the gulls. Clarke was by occupation a millwright, one of several men who found almost constant employment in repairing the big mill-sails, the pumps, and the mostly wooden machinery that reminded one of the gigantic works of a monster clock. For several decades steam has been slowly ousting the windmill. The marsh millwrights also made and mended the gates, repaired the sluices, 'fyed' the ditches, patched the embankment walls, and assisted in an emergency in cutting and stacking the marsh hay.

But to Fred's adventure: Breydon was smothered with jostling ice-floes. On this particular morning day broke sullenly, with a faint touch of redness in the western sky, on a typical wintry outlook. There were only two or three boats afloat, for there was little open water to tempt them save in the lower part of the main channel; and there was a promise of wind that might drive the loose floes together. Woe to any belated fowler whose frail craft became surrounded. Cobbold's youthful fowler, lost and unconscious in his punt on the Aldė, in *Margaret Catchpole*, presents a lucid picture of such a calamity.

'I was allers trottin' around in spare time, or bad weather—and bad is the best for fowl, you know—with a gun in my hand,' Fred assured me, when recently chatting with him in his one small room, which had a slight resemblance to a Breydoner's house-boat's cabin, 'in them days, when you could almost make sure of gettin' two or three fowl. But *that* morinng! Lor', it come on to blow and snow a rummon! Breydon was smothered with ice, thick as planks. I drawed out of the Lock-gate Farm, where I was livin' then, jist to hev a look round, and over the wall, and who should I see but Old Stork; and he was in a devil of a frap, pushin' and muddlin' among a lot of loose stuff—ice as big as table-tops, with others scrunchin' agin' 'em smaller, down in size to half-bricks. Thacker was tryin' to poke his way up to the rond forefrontin' the house, the wake bein' corkscrewy, showin' black water here and there among the twisterin' pack-ice. I certainly thought he'd never get up to the rond—and he wouldn't ha' done if I hadn't run for a rope and hulled him one end of it. I then lent him a hand, and between us—pullin' and shovin'—him and me sune had him and his old punt out of danger. And though it was dowsedly cold, we was both in a molt of sweat with the exertion.

'" Got any fowl ? " I axes him. " I ain't heard you shoot."

'" No," says he. " I've had enough to look arter myself."

'" I thought as much," says I.

'" May I shove the old punt-gun up in a safe corner in the house while I go athort the meshes home, to get a bit of help for gettin' thet theer old punt back to the boat-shud ? " says he.

'" You'll find the meshes mor'an a foot under snow," says I, " and you on't know which is deek and which isn't, thow perhaps they might bear you."

'" Can't be far out when I reach the New Road," he says.

'" Very well," says I. " We'll see arter the gun, *prowidin' you make me free of the old weapon.*"

'" Sartainly, bor—sartainly," says he ; " only *mind* ! she's a bit stubbin' *when* she like."

'Well, I see him get to the New Road, stumblin' and blunderin' along, and then loses him in a fall of snow. It was comin' on towards closin'-in time, so I turned in, not seein' much to shoot at, but was up afore daylight next mornin' ; and when peepin' over the wall what should I see but a bunch of fowl in a bit of open water, with a fairly straight wake leadin' from the sluice. The wind wos a bit easier and the tide jist about on the turn, and quiet.

'So I hops indoors, puts on a white jumper over me, fetches the big gun, which was loaden, and a tidy weight she was ; then, stoopin' low, I slips over the wall, and quietly drops her in the " knee ", bolting her all serene, and shoves the punt out. I didn't stop to clear the snow out of her, but lay down to the gun, and with the quantin'-pole pushed her quietly forrid, my heart palpertatin' nineteen to the dozen. Them wigeon was *smee-ouin* to one another ; no doubt they was chatterin' over the bit o' luck in findin' a patch o' wigeon-grass free of ice. You may guess I laid low, and how my finger itched to let go the quant and pull trigger. " Here goes," thinks I.

'Presently I'd got my range, and pulled, and knocks out eight of the eleven, and one or two bein' crippled, but not capable of divin' ; if they had bin, I shouldn't hev got 'em. I picks up all my birds and shoves back to the wall, mighty well pleased with myself, and as warm as toast, to see Thacker and a pal clamberin' on top the wall.

'"Good shot, my boy," says he. "Good as I could hev done it myself. Hull 'em up to me; I'll diwide them smee up."

'Thinks I to myself, "He'll take the lot of 'em," but he proved square and jannick. He says. "Two for me (layin' 'em on one side), two for you (shovin' 'em towards his pal), and the t'other four for you, Fred," he says; "an' how's *thet*?"

'"Quite all right," says I. "I'm satisfied." And that's how I got a hankerin' after a big gun, and it worn't many months afore I speckerlated in a punt and gun and took up the wildfowling business—first as a side-show, as you might

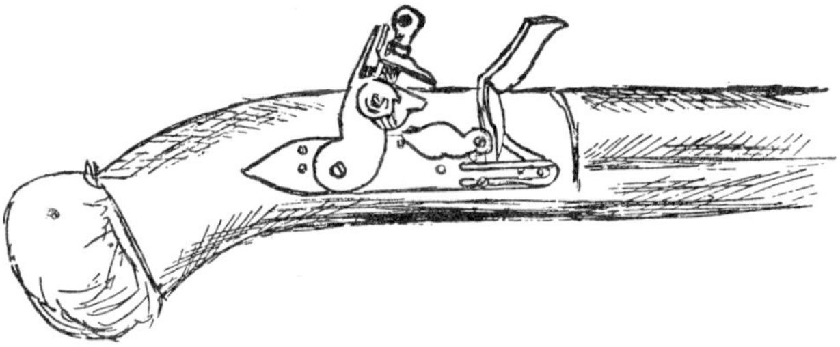

THE OLD FLINT DUCK-GUN

say, to the millwrightin'; and what's more, I enjoyed it, and when I'd built my first old house-boat, and drove in the stakes to hold her at the end of Duffel's Rond, I wouldn't hev changed top-hats with the King of Spain. And as for company—well, I was allers happier without any."

For many years Fred Clarke devoted his time to fowling, save in the slower days, after spring migration had slackened down; in wintry days he was mostly afloat. When fowl were scarce he could fall back upon his tool-chest and mill-work. When eels were moving he stabbed the flats and drains with his eel-pick. He occasionally helped with the smelters' nets. In summer and winter his little one-cabined house-boat was his home.

In one slack season he was mending some of the slats on a mill sail, close to the ground, his tool-bag between his feet, when a labourer inside the mill, forgetting Fred's position, started the sail revolving. Fred hung on, shouting to his fellow to stop her. Before this could be done Clarke was hanging to the sail high in air in an inverted position, his tools fallen to the ground and sundry things from his pockets. The motion was stopped, and Fred carefully made his way down again until he reached the platform going round the mill, and there landed, too scared for words. This was not the only awkward situation that Fred had experienced. Once when working at haysel he observed smoke rising from the house-boat, and on rushing back to it found it on fire. Without hesitation he dashed into the cabin, snatched out a large tin of powder, and thus saved an explosion. The tide was out and the drain empty, but he put out the blaze by smothering the cabin walls with wet mud.

Fred's first gun-punt turn-out was very like the clumsy old scows described by Richard Lubbock (*Fauna of Norfolk*) in the 'forties—' Flat-bottomed, upright-sided, and very narrow . . . very much resembling the Grede Vrouw in which Knicker-bocker tells us the first Low Dutch colonists rolled forth to take possession of America . . . perched on a transverse beam, was the swivel-gun.' Fred seemed to favour the decoys as an attraction to fowl to the neighbourhood, having in mind that Fritton decoy lay but a mile or so off, in a direct line with Breydon, which the flighting fowl, coming in from the sea, usually passed over. Old Skelton, the noted decoyman, stated to a certain naturalist that ' the mallard, pintail, and teal frequent rich flooded lands, *swittering with their nebs in the soil* and sucking out its strength ; but the wigeon feeds quite differently, being an *amazing fowl to graze—a strange eater of grass* '. He gave them grass sods around the decoys, ' on which they like to graze '. On Breydon, in its heyday, the *thousands* of wigeon that feasted on the succulent *Zostera* stems disdained all other provender. Occasionally, when the tide is off the flats, small parties of wigeon may be seen walking about when feeding on the ooze, even in midday. The following adventure, related to me by the chief actor in it, is a good example of the risks run by enthusiasts in pursuit of fowl.

My friend, A. B——, who was one of the youngest of the gentlemen gunners in my early days, may be said to be almost the only survivor of these devotees of Breydon who shot for sport only, and ' kept his henchman ', until misfortunes led to clearing out his punt-gun and paraphernalia. His reminis-cences of Breydon display great powers of observation and a relish for adventure. He began :

' It was in the hard winter of 1890, when the snow-covered ice-floes, formed on Breydon, floated on the tides—filling up the gradually widening ' wakes ', or drifting out again, as the ebb or flow was running. I was hanging about the Channel in my punt when I observed no end of pochards and coots swimming about in the biggest of the wakes in the ice. We—that's Billy Thacker and I—thought we'd have a try at them, if possible. The wind was favourable from the north-east. "Let's up-sail," said Billy, and we up-sailed. A host of huge floes floated about upon the tide, and they persisted in getting in our way, but we got "way-on", and charged each one that threatened our progress by both of us shifting well aft at a crucial moment, tipping up the boat's nose, when the impetus of the wind drove us on, and occasionally quite over into clear water, to be met again almost at once by another obstructive lump. Sometimes we did not succeed, and drove well up on a refractory floe, and had to use the ice-pick—something like a short-poled boat-hook, you know. To get right over, or to get off again, meant a bit of hard work. So we kept on until we got within three hundred yards of the fowl, when the wary pochards took fright and flew off; the coots, less alert, bunched together like a lot of sheep. We got one shoot, securing twenty-eight coots; the cripples, poor rogues, were ungetatable, and most of them fell, in the long run, to the hooded crows.

'This was the big frost—then breaking up for a bit—when the ice, reaching across the Waveney and the Yare entrances, was strong enough to bear a tumbril-load of swedes being driven from Berney Arms to Burgh Castle.

'Well, that shoot at the coots was a memorable one, for several damaged ones managed to get to the uncovered flats beyond the ice. Thacker and I were out early next morning to find that a big tide had brought up from the fish-wharf a lot of condemned, dilapidated swills, and left them stranded on the flats. It was so deuced cold that by sitting around we got quite chilled by the piercing wind. Thacker suggested we ought to light a fire with one or two of the drier baskets, and warm ourselves; and with that intent he stepped out of the punt on to the mud, in his water-boots; and to his surprise, on turning over the nearest swill, out bolted a coot—wounded, of course. I'd got the cripple-stopper in my hand, and settled number one—at a safe distance, of course, from Thacker. Another swill was kicked over, and out of it fluttered another coot! I downed that; and so coot after coot bolted from these hiding-places, until eleven birds were secured, and all brought back into the punt. Several poor rogues, I have no doubt, perished between the ice-floes, and others were demolished by the crows.'

Billy Thacker was highly pleased, as the Thackers esteemed the coot above all ' poultry ' on their own tables.

' Harry G—— for a short space,' continued B——, ' tried his hand at a bit of winter shooting. One cold day when near the George's dyke, that runs past the Lock-gate sluice, a wigeon fell wounded to his gun, and dropped on the ice that spread well over the flats opposite our house-boats. His dog was sent after it, but after nervously floundering upon the soft ooze, and baffled by the jagged edges of the ice-floes, it came back again, tail down. I offered G—— eighteen-pence for his chances of retrieving his victim, and he laughingly took it.

GOLDEN-EYE (HARD-WEATHER FOWL)

Now, after weighing things over, I had made up my mind that I would wait for the tide to lift, so that the floes might loosen and drift somewhat apart, at least sufficiently for me to push my punt's nose in between them. G——'s house-boat was in close proximity, so he went back to it, filled his pipe, and sat watching events through the window. Presently two keen-eyed hooded crows came along, and alighting near the fowl started to tear it to pieces, scattering the feathers like thistle-down. I myself had bolted into my cabin, and so had been unobserved by the crows; and when at the height of their jubilation I gave them a double shot through my boat window, downing both of them. Later came another; he too bit the—ice. A fourth bird, with a fifth behind him, also came to share in the devoted wigeon, and were likewise dropped. Such a massacre would have delighted that good sportsman Colonel Hawker.'

'Why Colonel Hawker?' I asked, 'or even Fielding Harmer?'

'Who loves a bird-murderer!' said B——, who continued:

'An amateur punter, one Garson Blake, who had speculated lavishly in an excellent punt and turn-out that would have astonished Colonel Hawker, had been spending a "perishing" night in his house-boat, in spite of rugs and fuel. He was glad to be early astir, and had gone in his punt after three wigeon in a wake not far distant; he killed two outright, wounding the third, that gave him the slip after nearly seizing it; and on stepping into the boat he made a slip himself and went up to his waist in icy water.

'I helped him to scramble out, and saw him into his cabin, where he was glad to have a change of clothing; then I awaited events that might lead me to securing that fowl. A big grey gull, hungry as a Russian wolf, who had seen the fowl drop, flew towards it, wheeled round it once or twice, and then dropped upon the ice, seizing the wigeon by the neck, and rose upon the wing with it, and after getting away a short distance let it fall on the ice. He repeated this manœuvre four or five times, endeavouring to get right away with it, when I up gun and killed the rascal.'

'"That jolly well sarve him right!" ejaculated my man Friday—Thacker forgetful of his own lust for prey. The fowl I afterwards secured.'

No gunner or fowler has a word to say in favour of the hooded crow, for on the lowlands and the mudflats it is as great a pest to the wildfowl shooter as it makes itself to the moorland keepers, whose grouse eggs it hunts for and appropriates wholesale. This crow has not even the virtue of being fit for the table of even a poor man, although, queerly enough, I have met with here and there an individual who professed to esteem its flesh superior to wildfowl; and I do not see why, with the rich assortment of its diet, which consists mostly of carrion, it should not possess a distinctive flavour of its own. In hard weather this bird patrols the marshlands, searches the flotsam flung to the walls by the tides, when wounded wigeon and putrid gull are equally welcome finds; failing these, the hairless carcase of a drowned dog or hog suits its appetite equally as well. This crow on discovering a meal almost invariably utters its hoarse 'Krae!' but whether from elation or as an invitation to its kindred is hard to decide. These birds watch each other, and judge matters by the actions of individuals; hence in a twinkling a parcel of crows arrive upon the spot. When hungry, and a carcase falls to its lot, the crow loses scant time in dissecting it, and defies all comers except the great black-backed gulls, for whom it makes way promptly.

But for all I have said against this predatory fellow I like him; his presence adds life to solitary places, and his voice breaks a silence that is sometimes oppressive.

The allurements of wintry weather punt-gunning not only lie in the hazards of the pursuit, but in the probabilities of remunerative shots. There is, too, the tantalizing likelihood of fowl escaping wounded on the ice, or floating into gaps in the broken ice-floes, where recovery is often next to impossible.

Two or three of us were discussing this matter.

'Some fifty year ago,' said Quinton, at one time bird-catcher, gunner, and factotum for gentlemen gunners, and by profession a shoemaker, and by instinct a philosopher, like many men of sedentary occupations, 'Old Stork Thacker was a bit pinched for a bob or two; there was such a frost as you never scarce see, and Breydon hed bin blocked—fairly paved with ice; the punters couldn't find a gap to push a boat's nose in, and as for wakes—well, you couldn't see a crack within a mile. Then it "gave" a little, and a biggish tide sagged and cracked the ice near the lower runs, and Old Stork starts choppin' a wake into a drain leading into the main channel. The ice in places was nigh a foot thick; but once opened a bit, the tide done a little more to it. Anyway, the pokers and smee and mallard what hed bin hangin' around all day, as if they expected a change comin', dropped into the widest gap in the wake. It was a bit of hard work cuttin' in, that would hev made sand-cartin' off the beach look a soft job. You see, the ice bore him, and the loose ice chunks a bit higher up began to drift and come down, to bump into each other, turnin' and cracklin'; that made it too risky to start shovin' a gun-punt into the wake. So he run'd back to the boat-shed and nailed some boards together, with a little help from Ben Harwood; then put a sort of swivel chock on to it, and laid the little old punt-gun to it, droppin' the iron peg in a hole what Ben had drilled. I wouldn't hev fired it for a pension. When the tide made up a bit again Thacker towed the little sorter raft up, and got it on to the ice and shoved it along. Two or three punts hed follered up to see what was goin' to happen and to tow old Stork's body home if so be he got busted up.

'His first shot told suffin' fearful, and scores of the fowl what rose in a body, like a small cloud, was killed, and it fared as if as many more was wounded. He collected 144' (said Quinton, pencilling the figures down on a piece of paper to tabulate the total). 'Potot Mesham gathered up seven of 'em with broken wings, and I picked up seven. Later on, I found fourteen more dead of wounds. Let me see : 14 an' 7 is 20—no, 21. Put another 7—that's 28 ; add that to Stork's 144. What do that come to ? That's 172. Reckon it up yourself. The biggest shot I ever know'd. And, mind you, several doove badly hurt under the ice what never come up no more, and no doubt drifted down with the ice to sea. Some we recovered after days in a woeful condition. Two or three got well away on the ice, but didn't go very far before the old hoodie crows was sune on their track.'

'Those hooded crows,' said Bellin, 'were jolly well hard up with the continued frost ; they watched from the walls and stiles all the gunners who dared the ice-floes, and flew around after the sound of a discharge, ready to nip up any small fowl ere the gunner could retrieve it. They seem more like hawks than *corvines*, for they lay hold of birds with their feet ; as you know, their toes are more hawk-like than a rook's, and the more curved claws help them to carry their prey. And so are the carrion crow's. Fred Clarke shot three or four mallard and duck one morning, firing from near the wall ; one duck flew over wounded, and fell on the marsh ; three or four Kentishmen hurried up and attacked it. I was watching from my house-boat ; one old crow dug its bill into the fowl's back, then another had a go, and they kept yapping as if encouraging each other. I saw one actually start to dig in at the breast while the duck was yet alive. Fred, by a bit of manœuvring, crept to the top of the wall, and let drive with his cripple-stopper, killing with the two barrels all the crows, and the wretched duck as well.

'I remember Fielding Harmer coming up George's dyke one morning and letting go at three geese, knocked out one, and pretty well defeathering the other two. The wounded one managed to get about a hundred and fifty yards from the wall, when away went a Kentishman after it, and started calling three of his chums to share in. Neither of us could reach the goose with the gun, nor dare try to wade and slide after it. Those four crows very soon flensed that wretched goose, and did not leave a great deal of picking for any others who might discover the remains. You see, a punt is so small, we never take a dog with us, and besides, if we could, a sloppy wet and muddy dog would be a nuisance.

'Those two fellows,' continued Bellin, 'viz. Mr. Dignity Fielding Harmer and Mr. Impudence Charlie Thacker thoroughly understood each other. The Tudor lord, as you choose to call him, quietly put up with the whimsical and unconsciously humorous little gunner; and Thacker, whilst

HUNGRY HOODIES

somewhat awed by the sober mien and aristocratic manner of his employer, took liberties that would never have occurred in a more refined and educated manservant. In an interval, the two oddly-matched men had drawn to the wall, in order to step ashore for a little exercise, and to discuss certain refreshments. Thacker kept on the alert, and stumped a sort of sentry-go, while pegging away at the large sausage roll—his favourite joint. A certain gunner walking the walls made as if to approach Harmer, when Thacker stepped between, and stopped him, remarking, "Can't you see, bor, the guv'nor is a-havin' his lunch? For Gawd sake don't you disturb him."

'The couple were on another occasion walking and stumping at the back of the Breydon wall; it was during that fearful cold spell of the '90–'91 winter. A big bird—a goose—flew over them, and pitched down into a bed of prostrate *Zostera*, out of gunshot, and began feeding and walking towards the wall. The ice of the previous week had broken up and floated away, but another stretch of icy-cold weather was on the way. It began to snow so that visibility became somewhat obscured. Presently up flew the goose, and Harmer shot at it with the shoulder-gun as it lifted itself over Fred Clarke's house-boat on the rond, and badly peppered it The stricken bird with here and there a broken primary, alighted in Dan Banham's marsh farmyard, and the owner of it, observing its condition, recognized it as one of his flock of forty, all of which wandered about and fed upon the mudflats when they felt so disposed.

'Old Dan had heard the shot, and, putting two and two together, strode down the wall to the gunmen.

'"I suppose you know what you hev done, Mr. Harmer ? demanded Banham.

'"I told yer, sir, you'd bin an' done a nice job!" said Thacker to Harmer, who declared that he had mistaken it for a wild goose.

'"Dear me! What shall we do about it?" queried Harmer.

'"Leastest said, sunest mended," replied Banham. "I shall want half a quid for this job, if the goose peg out; and I'll take five bob on account, ready money; and if it don't peg out we'll cry quits, and I'll keep the five bob for damages. Thet's fair, ain't it?"

'Fielding Harmer was glad to square the job so easily.'

. . . . .

Three Breydonians met (no matter where, but we were snugly roofed in, while the blast roared great guns outside). The trio included my friend Bellin, Little Charlie Thacker, his old-time factotum, and myself. One yarn led to another, mostly of a winterly sort, for the day was cold and darkening for snow. Bellin waxed reminiscent:

'What a day for Breydon!' said he. 'Lor', how I used to pray, almost, for such a day as this. I recall to mind—it might be—I think it was, in January 1906, when there promised to be a spell of exceedingly bad weather, just such weather as would have chipped up an old-time wild-fowler.

The wind had got into the south-east'ard, and was blowin' half a gale, freezing, and terribly cold. Breydon flats were hard and fast with ice, and there was left but one long, tortuous wake in the main channel to gun in, if anyone would be fool enough to try it ; the crooked lane of black water stole away between jagged ice up to Stone Corner. There were few fowl about as yet, but a fair lot of coots, with plenty of loose ice to negotiate to get a shot at them. There were also several pokers ; but the job was to get at them. At last, after a lot of muddling about, Charlie Thacker, who was with me, for I never went alone on such expeditions, proposed to sail over the sheet ice, and so get at them. Ice-sailing was a fad with Little Charlie, wasn't it old boy ? ' (handing him his tobacco-pouch), ' and his equally little old punt, which seemed to enter into the sport of it.

' " We'll try it," I said ; " mine's a bigger boat than yours, and there's two of us to manage her." So the big gun was taken out of the swivel chock, and laid well aft, the sail was hoisted, and we screwed ourselves together at the stern of the punt, her bows cocking up three or four inches above the level of the surface of the ice. Billy hauled in the sheet, and with a rush we charged the ice. Our stem seemed a yard out of the water before she levelled herself ; but the great difficulty we found was to steer her, for we had no runners under her nor anything answering to them, save the oar, and that was very little more use than a mop-stick. However, after a deal of trouble we got to the most open part of the wake and plumped in. Down came our sail, the gun was reshipped, and we started to scull towards the coots. They had paid little heed to us, and were undoubtedly desperately hungry ; and as they started to swim away they dragged fronds of the wigeon-grass behind them, which they were devouring with evident gusto. We got one shot at them, securing about a dozen, and eight or nine pochards and tufties that had put off their exit a little too long. That was all right.

' But the job was now to get back again, with wind and tide against us, not forgetting the cakes of ice slithering around us ; but we managed to haul the boat upon the ice again, having first laid the big gun on Billy's oilskin. It took us two solid hours to get her over a huge ice-field into open water in the channel, and I can tell you it was terrible hard work, and we were glad enough when we reached the boat-shed as darkness set in.'

' We don't fare to get sich hard winters now, bor,' remarked

Charlie; 'we fared to get more on 'em in the 'seventies. D'ye mind that flare-up we had just afore Chris'mas—let me see: must ha' bin in eighty-suffin'; I can't 'member like I useter.'

Charlie, who was getting a bit drowsy, reloaded his pipe and introspectively shut his eyes.

'I remember,' said Bellin, 'and I ought to have kept a log of my sporting days; but never mind, we'll put it at '84 which is near enough. You and I, Charlie, went up channel as far as the good ship *Agnes*. It wasn't daylight when we hitched our painters on the rusty chain-plates.

'There were several little lots of mallard and duck in the north-east drain, where Barber's old wherry is sunk, you know. We went after them as day broke and had very little trouble to get them together We got one shot, stopping nine fowl—six mallard and three ducks. I well remember how poor they were, with breasts shrunken and breast-bones like the keel of a yacht. The flats were smothered with ice that was exceedingly thick and hard in places. After the shot we went to our old station, but hadn't been there long when, on looking round, I thought I could see clear water over by the wall, and said so to Charlie.

'That's right, so ye did,' corroborated the little fellow, 'an' I said, "Yes, bor, but all the ice on the flats is comin' away, and we shell jolly well sune hev to get out of this 'ere".'

'We managed,' went on Bellin, 'to get round to the back of the ice, as far as our house-boat in the Lock-gate sluice corner. From there we saw that all the ice, lifted on the top of the flood, and now floating on the beginning of the ebb, was moving in one great body; and when it came in contact with the stakes in the channel, one after another went down like ninepins. But the most interesting sight, and more terrible, was when the jumbled mass of drift-ice struck the old *Agnes*. It piled up at her side I should think ten feet high, rushed and roared over her deck into the Ship drain; the noise of it I shall never forget. Old Charlie laughed and said we ought to have been there now—if we had been, our number would have been up. Isn't that so, Thacker?'

'You ain't far out. I can see now that white, grindin' mass of ice-chunks when I think on it. I wouldn't hev bin there for all I can see.'

'Well, after the tide had gone off the flats we found the drains all blocked, and that it was quite impossible to get away home the way we came; so our only chance—and a mere chance it was, goodness only knows—was to get the punt on the now greatly bared mudflats and tow her into the channel. Charlie said ," We was takin' suffin' on, don't blow me tight ! " '

' I *did,*' edged in the aged fowler.

' Anyhow, we set about it. Charlie took the fore-painter and I shoved at the stern. I certainly thought we were beaten when we got half-way, but we gallantly kept at it, not relishing the idea of emulating the unfortunate Captain Franklin. At length, utterly knocked up, we got to the open channel. At one halt, when nearly out of our bother, there was a shout from Charlie—" Look out ! "—and when I looked I saw a duck and drake nearly overhead ; on which I snatched out my double and made one of the prettiest right and left shots I ever made ; and the incident seemed to put new life into us. Charlie was very fond of talking about " that theer day ", as he called it.'

Bessey the elder, of whom I do not recall any personal recollections, was remembered as a famous fowler who 'gunned' as late as the early 'seventies, and had passed over to the Happy Hunting Grounds before I seriously took to Breydon myself. There was one outstanding incident of his prowess which lingered in the memory of comrades he left behind him, and was related to me as follows :

' In the terrible hard winter of 1870–1, Breydon was froze over hard and deep, and when the ebbs followed the floods the whole sheet settled down again, and friz up the cracks in it, as if winter hed come to stay for good, as you might say. You must know that when the ice settle on the wigeon-grass it often gets anchored down by it ; and when a extra big tide come up with a foot or more of water the sunk ice'll rise with the roots an' crabs an' the dowse know what. Thet's what we call stock-ice, what some people think was froze under-water.

' Well, theer was plenty of fowl kep' going over from sea to the Fritton decoys, where, you know, the decoy-men broke the ice to harbour 'em. Poor devils, they was between the devil, as the sayin' is, an' the deep sea ; and our chaps bein' onable to get uppards took theer shoulder-guns on the meshes, what was under snow, an' got behind the wall, gettin' a few low-flyin' passin' mallard and sich-like—enough for 'bacca and theer own dinners ; but the fowl got so poor folks worn't over-eager to buy 'em. Anyway we got a bit of grub for the wimmen an' kiddies, if it worn't over-nourishin' ; and little rents had to wait. Some on 'em got jobs at icing, and they hedn't far to go up-river to fetch it ; and when the ice-housen got filled, which worn't long a-doin', they wos down on their uppers agin.

'Bessey got the fare sick waitin' for a break in the weather what might mean a break-up on Breydon. Howsumdever, he worn't altogether a mug, an', bein' handy with his tools, he built a sorter carriage, an' fitted it with little wheels, and raised a kind of arm to mount the swivel o' the gun in ; then he got it round as near to the ice as possible, by towin' the truck behind the gun-punt in another boat, and looked around till he see a narrow wake where he shoved in and made fast to the ice, by hammerin' a iron stake in for a moorin'-post. He got the carriage on the ice, an' his gun on to it. Several of us wos argerin' an' discussin' this fool of a job, from the 'Bowlin' Green' Corner, and reckoned he'd do some mischief.

'Then the old chap altered his mind ; the whole job looked a bit too risky. He then carted truck an' gun athort the frozen meshes by way of the New Road, and landed 'em near his house-boat, jist beyond the big rond. Then, arming hisself with a hatchet and a ice-hook, he walked athort the ice, and started to hack out a longish broken wake, chuckin' the broken ice on the surrounding ice-field. Goin' back to the house-boat, he fixes up his artillery weapon, while in rushed ducks eager for a rinse an' a drink o' fresh water, and of course a bit of grub off the "garden" (*Zostera*), anyway. They was mostly hard-fowl—golden-eyes, tufties, and sich-like, besides a lot of scaups, and smee, what you call wigeon. He quietly shoved to within range and fired, makin' fearful havoc. We all speckerlated about his luck, and wondered. Of them as was killed he collected pretty nigh a hundred, and hung 'em on poles near the house-boat ; then he hunted arter the cripples. Many on 'em got away, soon to be picked up by walkin' gunners, who skidded around on the ice arter 'em as they tried to get to the walls for a hide. Crows an' gulls got their share too, among the farthest ones ; some deeved under the ice and got drowned, and arter the break-up of the ice you'd see, now an' agin, a draggled dead fowl among the broken ice goin' downstream to the sea. It wos a terrible slaughter. No doubt old Bessey got his idea from old Squire Berney, who once rigged up a sorter field-piece on wheels, for pigeon-killin', and dressin' it up an' ornamentin' it with tree-boughs, reeds, and other greenery.'

The winter of 1891 was an exceedingly hard one. There were more fowl seen upon Breydon than had been known to visit the place for many years; indeed, the surviving gunners avowed they had never seen anything like it in their day. Parties of swans were seen by day, and heard also at night; and to be able to boast of a successful shot at a party, or even one of them, was something to boast about until they retired from the cult. The wind had been blowing stiffly from the north-west, and the tides had somewhat broken up the coating of ice, most of it being swept down-channel to the sea. Eleven swans were seen to settle in the open water, where patches of ice, easily negotiated, were still to be seen. Two hard-up eel-pickers were at work on certain of the flats, where, even so recently as 1891, some of the mudflats did not run wholly dry

CHARLIE THACKER'S SWANS

at low water. Charlie Thacker saw the swans settle to feed, when he pushed his punt in their direction, and after some manœuvring pulled at them, just as they were uttering a warning '*Honk-honk*', and lifting themselves to wing. He brought down four—two dead, one badly winged, whilst the fourth began to swim away. Charlie, stupidly enough, left this bird to itself whilst he recovered the winged bird, after some little trouble. Presently the other bird rose upon the wing, but had evidently got a disabling shot, for it made upwards as if in an effort to top the walls, which was too much for it. It went, however, towards Berney Arms, where several Berney Arms and Burgh men, hiding behind the wall, poured one shot after another into it, killing it; whereupon a lively argument and considerable disagreement took place as to who was the right man to lay claim to it.

When Charlie rowed to the house-boat, where Bellin had been watching him, he was offered a pound for his bag of swans; but Charlie thought he could do better with them in the town. He sold one and brought the other two to my friend's house and said he'd altered his mind.

'Swans,' he said, 'aren't fetchin' much. I'll take a dollar each for 'em'; and was glad to accept even a slightly lower offer.

Albert Beckett was out in his punt with a friend one bitter January morning. There had been an extremely rapid thaw, and Breydon had fairly well cleared itself of ice; but a fiercely cold wind setting in from the north began to cover the whole Estuary with a thin but rapidly increasing coat of ice. It was in that condition known as 'window-pane' ice, or glass-ice, when a punt under sail would cut through it as a ploughshare slices moist earth; and the scattered pieces were flung on either side like broken earthenware. Beckett foolishly had come away without screwing his ice-plates on either side of the fore-end of the punt, where her broadening beam gave most resistance. These plates were of thin brass or copper, between two and three feet in length and four inches wide, and were easily screwed on or off. A rime frost set in rapidly, thickening the atmosphere. Some pochards flew by like the wind, too close even for a shoulder-shot. Just then Beckett noticed that the punt was taking in water somewhat freely, both sides having been scored by the ice, as by a chisel, at the water-line. On realizing the situation, and on seeing the pochards coming nearer again, he promptly fired, knocking out two. Quickly retrieving them, both the men went aft, thus tilting the boat's nose out of the water, helped by the added weight of the gun which they had snatched out of the swivel-rest, and made back hurriedly to their boat-shed. The scorings of the punt's sides were found to be deep and ragged; however, after being dried, sand-papered, and puttied, the wounds were made so well healed and obliterated that no one besides themselves would have suspected what had happened.

My friend B——, who used Breydon as a youthful gentleman gunner, and is an excellent ornithologist, had a worse experience some years since. He had started out early one December morning at three o'clock in his gun-punt after wigeon, rowing away gaily under a clear sky, guided by the town lights, for the five-stake drain, with a view to reaching the North Wall, and creeping round as far as his house-boat, near the Lock-gate Farm. He had scarcely entered this winding drain, that was easy of threading when the shore and bridge lights still shone upon the dark waters, when suddenly fine snow began to fall, pushed along by a wind that rose behind it with increasing force. Snow soon came down in real earnest, covering the fore-deck and smothering himself and gun. He made desperate efforts to feel his way along, but the swirling tide and the eddying flakes baffled him, increasingly so as the wind shifted now to the north-east, now to the north-west, and back again. At length he had to drive his oars deeply into the mud and lash-to, and there remain until just before daybreak, when a railway train, rushing past towards the town, gave him his bearings. He had pushed to within a few feet of the grim flint walls, but happily had staked down before reaching and dashing upon them. Having found his whereabouts, and cleared off some of the snow, he was very glad to do some stiff rowing in order to bring warmth back into his aching limbs, and make his way downstream to the boat-shed, and vowing seriously never to attempt a winter expedition at so early an hour again.

'We wos havin' a terrible spell of winter, in '95, I think it wos,' said my little friend Thacker, or as the fraternity more affectionately termed him 'Young Stork', a few short months before he joined his old mates, Pintail and Snicker, across the Jordan. 'We wos hard-up—stony-broke, as you might say—and Breydon worn't scarce safe to chance it, but we wos forced to do suffin'. . . .

'"Let's chance it," says Pero. "We might as well be froze to dead as starved tu it. An' 'bacca all done, and wuss, not even a rotten half-pint mug to dip a nose in! I've got a flask o' powder I ha' borrowed, an' some shot. Let's shove your old punt out and take a risk." So we wropped up as warm as we could an' shoved out. As we turned the Half-mile Point we could see the channel was froze over agin the Mile Point, and all the way beyind; and great chunks of ice wos floatin' around, makin' bad passage-way for us. I rowed, and Pero sits forrid with the ice-hook, shovin' 'em off. It wor showin' up rimy, too, as we gets into a wake in the ice. "Shull we chuck it?" I axes Pero.

'"Chuck it be d——d," says he, for he'd got a forcibler gift o' the gab 'an I hed.

'"I'd chuck parson's language," says I. "It might go agin our luck. Still, better chow that than *mockmoorins*."

'"Mop that onlucky word out!" says he; "it's d——d unlucky to bring that rotten word in."

'"D'ye hear that?" I axes Pero; "sounds like duck an' mallard."

'"I see 'em," he says; "kin jist make 'em out. Why the dowse don't they fly; sure-*ly* they must see us."

'"I'll bet you my Sunday trousers they're fast in the ice!" says I, "an' can't fly away. I hev seen two o' them loons, an' more 'an one old coot froze in, in my time. But how are we to get to 'em; the tide's shovin' ice afront of us, an' no punt 'ud stand gettin' jammed in that raffle of ice-chunks. They're two hundred yards off, if they're a inch!'

'So we argered things over; and Pero suddenly says, "I've got it! Let's row back to the shud, an' you wait while I run to Bob Guyton's the tailor's for a pair o' shears."

'Well, we done so, havin' a nice hard pull back amon' floatin' chunks what scraped the paint off us when Pero hap'd to miss the hook into 'em. He come back to the boat-shud with a pair o' bright steel clippers, like you shear sheep with. "That'll settle 'em," he says.

'We rowed back with some borther to the edge of the ice, but was more 'an two hundred yards off now; but Pero says, "Shove her snout into the corner o' the drain, an' I'll get out an' walk." I shoved in an' held on, while he was scrunchin' through the uneven sludge of ooze and broken ice in shallow water, an' gets to 'em, all a-quackin' and a-flutterin', like stuck chickens hung on a back door. Lor', didn't them poor devils take on! Pero made quick work on 'em, brakin' theer necks one at a time with his hard thumb, same as the 'coymen do, and snippin' through the legs and hullin' 'em on the ice. It fared more murder 'an sport, but you ain't goin' to tell me it's a bit wickeder than cuttin' their throats as you might a lamb's. Breydon, bor, was *our* farmyard. I hulled Pero a skep, and he put the dozen or so—I forget how many exactly there wor—into it, leavin' the feet still stuck in the ice. Some people I told about it made a laugh on it, but any old Breydoner'll tell you they ha' seen fowl held to the ice. Ours must ha' settled on the ice to rest an' sleep, and the next tide riz afore the ice lifted, and then flowed over their feet while they was unawares.

'We took 'em up to Billy Durrant's game-stall next day.

'"Well," says he, shootin' the lot on the stall, "what's

this ? Why, they're a nice little lot of cripples." He fared stemmed.

'" Yes," says Pero, " I'll allow they are, but people don't eat duck's feet, more 'an they do rabbits'. Have 'em or leave 'em, Billy ; an' if you *du* want them feet you'll hev to go up Breydon arter 'em. We had quite enough borther gettin' the bodies off 'em." Billy Durrant bought 'em.'

Waterfowl, poor rogues, do not lead an untroubled life when pikes and hawks deplete their numbers ; scarcity of food occurs in times of drought, and in severe winters gunners everywhere are after them with evil intent. It has been shown that the wounded are often drowned when diving among the ice-floes, and accidents like the freezing-in do happen, although not commonly, and would occur when it is difficult to make observations. I have known a wretched kingfisher unable to fly, its tail feathers having become caked with ice, in all probability due to the congealing of drops of water upon it.

Mr. W. H. Robinson, in April 1925, in a bird letter, wrote me thus : ' Yes ! I have seen duck frozen in the Orkneys and the Hebrides, but never in any number.' Oliver Ready, in his charming *Life and Sport on the Norfolk Broads*, refers also to this subject : ' In long, severe winters, ice on the Broads would sometimes be a foot thick . . . frozen out elsewhere, coots and wildfowl would by night join the swans in these wakes, and, from one cause and another, in the morning a good number of them would at times be found frozen fast into the newly formed ice, from which, however, the swans were strong enough to extricate themselves. . . . I saw a young farmer secure a score of mallard, pochard, and coots by means of his dog.'

One other outstanding record dates back to 1811, and is equally to be depended upon. In Howitt's *Book of the Seasons* he makes reference to a severe frost in which great numbers of birds were caught, amongst them several bustards, their wings being glazed to their sides and their feet to the ground. Such disasters may well be caused by rain freezing as it falls, or following a rapid thaw by as sudden a re-freezing, and thus covering ice and ground with a sheath of glassy ice.

CHAPTER VIII

AMONG THE GOSSIPS

'A few minutes' conversation with this interesting group will give us information which would otherwise take a stranger some days to collect by himself . . . the tides, the sports, present and to come . . . boats on the water and the boats that have gone . . . which is at all times interesting and instructive.'

—NICHOLAS EVERITT

AT the extreme end of the River Bure stood a huddle of picturesque water-side buildings and boat-sheds, including an ancient lime-kiln, a Dutch-like and ugly residence where generations of lime-burners had lived, and at the north-west corner a storage shed for piles of chalk, its outside old wall shutting in the whole kiln establishment from the up-river view. Above that shed had been built a workshop whose northern windows looked upon a quay-side dotted with wherries, the Suspension Bridge, the ancient North-west Tower; and beyond an area of tree-studded market gardens that spread over several acres—since razed, and now covered with barrack-like streets of houses. That old tree-sprinkled area held most of the romance of my early boyhood, where I watched fieldfares and redwings fluttering around the snow-topped hawthorns, woodcocks springing from among the cabbages, kingfishers streaking along the ditches like living emeralds. On walking back from the tower to the lime-kiln corner you would have seen, in their idling hours, gun-punts and eel-scows resting on either side the river, some still carrying weapons of offence against eel and mallard, all ready for action when the tide served, and were fairly safe, for the Malt-house Corner and the quay-sides were rarely clear of the watchful eyes of gossiping Breydoners. A shrimp-boat here and there lay-to, with wherries loading and being unloaded; a moiety of nine dozen wherries and timber-carrying keels made a gallant show, which was intensified by the clink of pawls, and the hoisting of sails and bellying ahead. The carpenter's shop above the chalk-shed was lighted, too, on the westward side, and through the windows privileged gossips viewed their Promised Land, which, even in those decades that reached to the 'nineties flowed, if not with milk and honey, with salt tides that provided them with fish and fowl for their living. Two or three generations at least told or listened to tales and yarns of prowess, of slaughter, of noteworthy hauls, of sunshine and storm, and days and nights of stress and adventure, most of them now lost to us as the story of Garienis Ostium.

Against that crumbling old wall fathers and grandsires of a less virile race leant in their idling hours of their day, and in their declining years of manhood told the story of Breydon to the shore-combers and out-of-works that listened to them, emphasizing their deeds of valour among storm-driven fowl with pointing sticks, that had supplanted 'cripple-stoppers' and eel-spears. In my youth many of the now departed Breydon men were sturdy and capable and in the heyday of life, and idled there when not afloat, or were seated in their favourite taverns—Snicker Larn, Short'un Page, Mouldy Piller, Scrumps Allen, Silky Watson, Billy Thacker, Charlie Harwood (amateur punter and philosopher in a small way), Gaby Thomas, and many another; and the ancients of their day hobbled thither also, for their beloved Breydon was only round the corner of the wall, and the river joined it thereat. They waved good luck to a younger chum going out, and hailed another returning with the query, 'What luck, boy?' and re-aired many an old grievance. Is not this the way with aged men who have plied the oar and hoisted sail, that stemmed the tides with vigour and hopeful expectancy? To-day but a remnant of that crumbling wall remains standing, and that on municipal sufference.

Little Billy Harrod, short, stuggy, and brimming with good humour and practical jokes, was tenant of that old carpenter's shop. All the idlers found their way there in turn, and standing among the shavings exchanged gossips. Billy was a famous boat-mender and designer and a maker of coffins. These old Breydon folk were always ready to assist at funerals for a small reward as bearers or mutes, at the obsequies of the river-side and neighbouring poor; they added to their dignity on such occasions by wearing a *crêpe* bow and streamers on a borrowed top-hat, known as a 'long-sleever'; now and then one appeared in a long-tailed coat, a palpable misfit made the more apparent by a portion of his blue guernsey showing for want of a button. With due solemnity each bearer carried a sprig of rosemary, or southernwood, held in his offside hand, that showed in strong contrast to the black kid glove that half covered the horny fist.

Little Billy Harrod had an inventive mind, and thought of many a little design or spree, carrying it out with an assumed innocence, to the merriment of the crowd. He was, one afternoon, at work on a coffin, which was still awaiting the usual decorations. One of the old fellows, who chance-time figured among the bearers, having imbibed somewhat too freely after a successful day with the nets, stumbled up into the workshop, presumably to ‘ mardle ’, but shortly fell off to sleep. At dusk the carpenter, who had not disturbed the snoring waterman, cajoled two companion gossips into lifting the old chap and depositing him, water-boots and all, into the grim structure, and there left him to sleep off his stupor. Early in the morning the unwitting tenant awoke ; he sat up in the coffin, and having gathered his wits together a bit began thus to soliloquize :

‘ Well, if this ain't a b—— rummon ! How the dowse cum I inside this b—— box ? Thort I wos in the old punt. Darned if—well ! So help me ! ’

Harrod, and another or two early risers, had quietly ascended the steps, and had overheard the old chap. They slipped in stealthily.

‘ Slept well, old man ? ’ asked the carpenter.

‘ Pritty cumfitable, Billy,’ he replied ; ‘ but theer ain't much rume to turn round.’ When they got him out, and he had taken a full view of his box, he weighed up the situation with : ‘ Well, I'll be —— ! I might well feel round for a pair of oars ! ’

Harrod went rarely afloat, and then only as a sort of supernumerary or passenger. He preferred building a punt to sailing one. At one period the local curates were inclined somewhat more to manly exercises than spiritual penances ; they instituted a rowing-club, and secured very fair replicas of the Thames outriggers. An annual water-frolic, which lasted for three or four years, was exceedingly popular both with the Breydon and river-side brotherhood. One popular event was a punt-race, into which were usually entered a score or more boats. Among the crowd always figured an optimistic gentleman, tall and lithy as a willow, who not only esteemed himself an expert rower but was generally accepted as such. To give him a name I shall refer to him as ‘ Ulysses Minor ’. In the dinner-hour—racing commenced at two—Billy Harrod and two others hauled out the champion's punt, tilted her up, and screwed a cleat nearly diagonally upon the bottom, and refloated her. On the up tide the owner rowed slowly, reserving his powers. When this particular race started Ulysses was still full of vaunting, but soon found the boat a little awkward to manage, and he had constantly to pull stronger upon his left oar to square her. News very soon spread around that some one had tampered with the punt, and there was noisy, hilarious cheering. The unlucky rower was highly irate and was obliged to submit to much chaff. The next year he kept a watch upon the punt, but while at dinner his deputy watcher had been bribed to secrecy ; and little Billy quickly managed with a hammer and two stout tacks, and a couple of bits of string, to fasten underneath the boat an open sack that became saturated and filled by the time Ulysses came back. This competitor found his troubles commencing as soon as the race started, but although suspecting trickery, kept on, to reach the buoy by the time the others had rounded it and arrived home. The onlookers, fully expecting this fiasco, thoroughly enjoyed it.

Marine regattas with yawl- and yacht-racing, water-frolics with wherry and punt, and shrimp-boat sailing on Breydonian waterways, have been relegated to the limbo of the past. Local as well as other youth now leave the science of movement to the two-dozen acrobats who kick leather balls about, shouting themselves hoarse without the least competition or exertion on their own part.

One little incident wherein Old Stork, Ulysses, and Little Billy figured, caused considerable fun among the water-side folk. Billy, who was exceedingly deft with his tools, carved an excellent model of a wild-duck out of the short end of a log, as much to satisfy himself that he possessed the cunning of his craft as to play a joke on Old Thacker, whose fiery temper was an outstanding characteristic. There were three or four ' in the know ', who watched the final touches to the bird's colouration with some interest, and with many a sally of Breydonian wit—its green-painted head greatly tickling them. A screw eye turned into the breast, and a long length of twine completed the outfit. Circumstances favourably combined to carry out this original joke, which to the chief actors was a wholly unexpected one. One fine evening it was known that Thacker was Breydon-bound for a shot at some fowl that had been reported to him as just then frequenting the Channel, hard by the Ship drain. The sun was well down behind the rising purple night-cloud when the old gunner was observed to set out from the Malt-house Corner ; the carpenter and a couple of chums were already rowing hurriedly in the direction of the Half-mile Point as he rounded the Knowl. The jokers dropped in the wooden fowl, and put Billy ashore holding the end of its tether, and slipping behind the wall he laid wait for his victim, the other two boatmen rowing slowly back.

On passing Thacker one made remark: 'Hurry up, Stork; there's a fowl—a mallard—this side the Half-mile Point; you'll get him with the shoulder-gun—believe he's just slightly crippled; he paid no heed to us.'

Off rowed Old Stork, and presently sighted the duck bobbing upon the slight ripple that ruffled the surface of the water; he could be seen to lay low and point his fowling-piece in readiness. The duck immediately began to swim towards the wall, which confirmed the old chap's belief in its being an easy prey. He was pushing the gun-barrel over the rail when the duck twisted round and began to progress backwards, a manœuvre he had rarely witnessed in a wounded bird; he followed—the duck righted itself and sprinted rapidly towards the wall again. Thacker, somewhat disconcerted, fired, the duck tumbling over to the shots which he heard strike it. But it still retreated—now sideways, and all ways, as Billy Harrod accelerated the pace. A loud laugh behind him exploded the joke, and a fine display of Thackerian pyrotechnics was loosened on the jokers from the highly incensed fowler.

The fiasco was to have a supplement to it. As the trio of conspirators were now reassembled in the rowing-boat Thacker angrily passed them by with a threat of revenge as he made upstream. Making for the 'Bowling Green', who should they recognize but Ulysses Minor hastening up in his punt. He, too, had been informed of a vagrant mallard playing near the point, and had set out intent upon its destruction. Billy persuaded his chums to put back again and assist him in carrying out similar tactics. The oncoming punter, rowing with his back to them, had not noticed this manœuvre. To cut this story short: the duck was replanted and held in leash, and Billy took his station behind the wall again; and very soon the same display of retreat, pursuit, astonishment, and defeat was witnessed; but in this instance good-fellowship was quickly established, the four of them adjourning to the 'Bowling Green' bar-parlour. Ulysses Minor, who was not so good with his linguistics as the hardened old professional, found that discretion was the better part of valour. The story became well broadcast all round the Estuary, and many a 'chip' was made of the wooden painted mallard.

. . . . .

One bright afternoon in August, soon after that month had become tacked on to the close season, when no man was expected to seek rare birds, or common ones, of the wading classes, although they might raise their hands and guns against flappers and wild-ducks generally that often dared to leave their native broadlands, whereat they were now fair game to riparian owners—one bright afternoon, I say, found the Breydon men here and there, in gardens and allotments, where worms abounded, and where also they had liberty to search for them, digging or wriggling for lobworms for the manufacture of their 'babs'. With an excellent forethought, severely taught by their experience, that earthworms tunnelled deeply in the soil in droughty periods, most of the men scrupulously economized in worm-bait, and kept a surplus of it in some deep old pan or bath tin, among moist earth, for drawing upon from time to time. One method of worm-catching took them often on a dark warm night to some friendly lawn, with candle-lantern and tin, to gather the sprawling *Lumbricidæ* that had come up for dewy refreshment and their queer hermaphroditic carrying out of the Great Demand to 'be fruitful and multiply'. The men did not like the larger 'ringed' worms, which were too easily pulled to pieces by the biting eels, preferring medium-sized creatures which they knew as 'maiden dew-worms', that became less brittle when tutored and toughened by keeping a day or so in almost dry mould. Better still, they liked a worm which they designated the 'black-nosed'. Another process of capture—for digging they heartily disliked in the warmer months—was to 'wriggle' for them. A long, slender crowbar was gradually thrust deep into the soil and wriggled about as it went deeper and deeper, which much alarmed the worms, that hurriedly came to the surface, to be tenderly but quickly caught between finger and thumb and dropped into a tin of mould awaiting them.

Later on that same afternoon found little Billy Thacker, during the tea-time hour, sitting on a garden seat beside the 'Bowling Green' parapet, behind which spread out his Breydon. A half-empty pewter stood by his side.

'Getting ready again, Billy?'

'Yes, Master Patt'son, yes. This orter be a good night for eels: I done pritty well last night; got a good lot up theer in the "Fleet"—more than I'd like all the chaps to know. I sold two stone this mornin' to old Bessey, gettin' riddy money at sixpence a pound; so one good night's work, you see, 'll give me a good start for the week's earnin's.' Billy drained his pewter and lit his pipe, then set to work making a necklace of protesting worms—brutal but necessary, for eel-men must live.

'I'm duberous of one or two river mouchers. There's Cadger Brown—never know when he's around or'll turn up; A and B, two others what's pritty light-fingered—you know what they are to be trusted. My new eel-trunk ain't bin tampered with *yet*; and theer's a stone and a half of eels in it, if a pound.'

'Many an angler would envy you your dew-worms.'

'An' sure they would,' said Billy; 'but for all theer lively ways, give me a tough old black-noser, what's born tough, so to spake, and keep so. I usually go to Yarmouth Market for *them*, when the land is over-dry.'

'Whoever sells them, Billy? Surely country-folk don't bring them up for you?' I ventured to say.

'No, bor, no. I'll tell you, if you really don't know. It's like this. You know the Market is paved with cobble-stones all over its two and a half acres; you'll see grass-tufts growin' between 'em, till the Corporation send two or tree old wimmen with hassocks and stumpy little knives to root 'em out. I, myself, like to see the grass growin', and what harm do it du? Well, theer's thousands of worms livin' below—look, an' you can see their holes all about. So I—and so do others short o' bait—take up a bucket or tew of salt-water from the river, by daylight, and pour it carefully into the holes, and it will fetch 'em up in a hurry to see what it's all about. Then you nab 'em gently, same as you would golden harf-sov'rin's. We rinse the salt water off 'em and put 'em into the mould-tin.'

[To-day Yarmouth Market-place is paved with close-fitting Yorkshire granite-sets.]

Just then his brother Charlie drew up and leant upon the low wall-top, pulling at his little black pipe. 'Lovely weather!' said he. 'The river fare full o' whitebait. Look at the little warmin flingin' theerselves over floatin' rubbidge, bits o' raffle and weeds; one now jumped over a bit o' cork. Some people say they're little herrin's, and blest if I don't think so too; leastwise, I'm sure, because I've seen 'em pulled in on the mudflats amon' the smelts, of all sizes right up to yawlers, like what you get amon' the Soufwold sprats late in the sprattin' season—over a span long. Sprats you kin tell by bein' a bit stumpier and deeper; and if you drew theer belly athort your cheek you'd wish you hadn't—they're reg'lar saw-bellied. What time d'ye start, Billy? They all fare gettin' ready, smelters an' all.'

'You go and fetch me my frail basket; my missus'll hev it riddy with a bottle of cold tea and the shortcake, and get a ounce of 'bacca as you come by the 'bacca shop.'

'I was tellin' you about the worms,' said Billy. 'Worms don't fare to like a baitin' needle t'rust clean through 'em,' he half apologized; 'but it ha' got to be done. People must get a livin' somehow or another; and worms ain't much use for nothin' else 'cept mowls an' chickens an' peeweeps. But it's sune over: sune as you've drawed the shewmaker's hemp—doubled—through the whole length on 'em, they fare dazed.'

It might be policy to agree with him and to praise his deftness, for in a remarkably short time he had threaded about three yards of tough, well-trained black-nosers, each going through the ordeal tail first, which seems really to stupefy them, for a prick at the nose end is followed by a variety of painful contortions until the complete perforation of the poor creature has been performed.

Thacker was loud in praise of rain that fell yesterday, for he declared 'It brung the worms up to drink; and last night they was layin' by thousands smudderin' Mr. Gibson's close-cropped lawn. If you don't catch 'em exactly right they shoot down the cellar like lightnin'. Eels' (he continued) 'is wery partickler; stale baits chuck 'em off—they 'on't even smell on 'em; and if the slightest bit o' cotton-waste touch agin' 'em, you might as well chuck up an' go home.'

We sauntered together to the popular old pub, and round to the punt-shed, where Thacker had the boat ready upon the rollers: a shove, and Breydon would be under it. He had, of course, had his glass of ale at the bar as we went by.

'August ain't no use to us much,' said he; 'we don't get much only young stuff round—sea-swallers feedin' their young 'uns, young stints and dotterels, swarms of young and old kitties, and a few cur-lew; the blowflies get to 'em and maggot 'em afore you can sell 'em, and there's very little sale for 'em at all. And what's the use of goin' arter the odd flappers the gents on the private broads let escape?'

Just then Pero Pestell sauntered by, carrying a short flick of larchwood in one hand and a hammer in the other. 'Just come a minute, Billy,' ordered the dogmatic boat-builder, 'and hold a hammer for me; I want to mend a strake on old Ribbons's smelt-boat. Cuss them old copper-fastened boats; they'll get half stove-in afore they'll shift a rube or two off theer nails and let the water in. It don't pay to repair 'em, though I'll allow a quart-pot job is better 'an none at all.'

The twain hurried off to the ' Bowling Green ' staithe, where a broken strake needed repair, and the lusty old boat-jobber's tinkering up badly. The two walked back to the tap-room, for Pero had insisted on the small payment being promptly made, and his standard pint pot, the froth running over, which he felt was necessary after so severe a task. Thacker left Pero with his pewter, and walking back to the boat-shed found his frail basket aboard his punt and his brother Charles preparing to launch his punt and join the little fleet of eel-babbers already going up on the tide.

. . . . .

For many decades there stood what was known as the ' Old Black Boards ' on the eastern side of the River Bure, hard by the stile that pedestrians use to this day who would walk the Bure-side wall that trends away—as a tow-path—to several of the river-side villages. Why these dry, tarred boards were erected it is difficult to say, but in years gone by its southern broadside sheltered halting fowlers, if they wished to rest a while or to gossip, and from the snow-flakes that a wintry north wind spitefully flung around them. A rail or two would have answered the purpose as well, if they had been merely intended to keep cattle from straying ; it is true that a deep pool-like end of a wide ditch just behind it entered the river through an archway under the road. These Black Boards, however, stood in the line of flight of wildfowl that had spent their day upon the sea, and at nightfall were speeding to the deeper filled marsh ditches of long ago, or to Breydon, and incidentally were making for Fritton decoy. Hiding behind these Boards at night might have been found Billy Sampson, a lame fowler of some notoriety, lusty George Blake, and certain other gunmen who frequently brought down fowl without seeing them, locating their position by the sound of their flight. In this neighbourhood, too, were often scattered in October evenings the shoulder-gunners, who crouched behind the wall awaiting plover-flight, as the lapwings came from the far-away drier uplands to feed upon the marshes across the river. I myself wandered that way many a time, more for the romance of the night than from a lust of slaughter ; and when the hoar frost hardened the muddy wall the solitude and flat-land scenery were equally alluring. As for the fowl and plovers—well, if I did not get a shot at one I was equally gratified at seeing it.

As the eventide fell, and the noctule bats were flitting around audibly scrunching their hard-cased beetles, one after another of these gunmen and lads drew to the Old Black Boards, to linger with emotions they did not or could not express, to recount their small adventures of the flighting and the number of their peewits slain—which were rarely very startling—and to spin yarns of past exploits and to dream of more. Seldom did a walking gunner venture to stroll on the opposite side of the river, save here and there a puntsman, who rowed up and left his craft safely moored at a spot easily indicated. Snipe, golden plovers, and lapwings, and odd fowl preferred that side for its quieter pasturage. Twice had I to run at my utmost speed across these marshes—on one occasion when a savage bull ran out from his harem and gave me the sprint of my life as he lessened the distance between us, for he jumped the ditches with less care than I, and was within a length or two of me as I sprang into my punt and shoved out into the stream.

'Talk of bull-chasings,' said Feek, one of the gossips. 'Toby Blake, when out on the south Breydon marshes, was splouncing a dyke, with his lamb-net set at the far end of it late one evening, when Long's brown bull gave him an awful chase; and he only reached a ligger and shot across it to the next marsh in the nick of time. Fortunately for him it didn't attempt to cross the narrow plank too, and boggled at the width of the dyke.'

'I reckon a man chased by a bull,' put in Ben Dye, 'if he's not on private land, have a perfect right to shoot it to save his own life.'

'Bulls are too loosely guarded on the marshes very often,' said I, 'partly, perhaps, because of marsh farmers' dislike to prowling gunners trespassing, and, indeed, too often allow them to wander upon public rights-o'-way. Did you ever hear of my old friend Billy Brand's narrow escape from a bull?'

'Suffin',' said one, 'but t'others might like to hear it.'

'Well,' I went on, 'fortunately I was not there to see, but you shall have it as told me by Billy himself.

'"The worst fright I ever had in my life was when I and a chum were stumping along Paddy's Lane, a public pack-way leading from the New Road across the marshes. There had been a lot of rain, and the roadway had been made exceedingly bad by the tread of many cows, while big stretches of flooded marsh were being used by golden plovers and peewits and hundreds of kitties, for drowned worms laid right thick around the edges of the pools. We'd got well towards the Cow Farm when we noticed the cow-keeper waving his hands. Stupid-like, we didn't attach any importance to his antics, and merely waved back to say all right and serene. The farther we proceeded the more he jumped about, as if in a terrible hurry; when, just as we were nearing a gateway which had obscured our view, up jumped the most vicious bull I ever saw and started to make for us, head down and tail up, with lightning speed. It then entered our minds what the cow-keeper meant; he had been signalling us to be off, and not come that way, but we hadn't understood him because his voice couldn't reach us.

'" Now, you know I'm handicapped with a lame leg and a crutch, although I can hop round pretty fast with it—from long use and companionship. We were at the moment some eighty yards from the bull when he started to run; and had a hundred or more yards spin to do before we could get back to the nearest marsh-gate that way. I had never spun my old top before at the mileage I was makin'. My chum had a loaded gun, and I begged him as we ran to shoot the beast in the face; but we kept on, the perspiration streaming down me like the basting of a roast duck. The bull had got to within a few yards of us when my companion gave him a shot which made the fur fly off the top of his head. That stopped him to ponder a moment or so, of which we took due advantage; then on he came again roarin' and thunderin' on the cow-trodden corrugated sort of marsh road—you know the rucks they make in them. My chum's gun still retained the second cartridge, but as we were getting pretty near to the gate he hesitated to fire.

'" 'Blind him! blind him!' I yelled, panting and puffing, and fit to drop with the fearful exertion. So he put another dose of shot straight in the bull's face, which caused the bull to stagger and fall; but before he could get upon his feet again we were climbing the gate—a difficult job for me, being lame and exhausted; but I was clear over the gate, and so was my chum, when the bull, half-blinded and bleeding, thundered into it.

'" We heard afterwards that the bull belonged to a marsh farmer a mile away across the river; and having heard the call of a heifer had swam the river and found his way across marshes and ditches to where we had seen him waiting. He was got back somehow across the river again, but when reaching Caister, he was so maddened that he had to be shot dead!"'

Just as I had ended this yarn the '*whizz-whizz*' of a fowl was heard as it passed overhead, but owing to the creeping on of darkness it escaped scot-free.

Feek next jibed in with a yarn, the foundation of which had reference to an arrival of golden plover upon the marshes over the river. These birds fifty years since very frequently visited the marshlands in wet Octobers and Novembers, and were much sought after by all sorts and conditions of gunners. Let Feek proceed:

'I was up here after golden plovers, and was standing against the Skeleton mill, some fifty yards away from where we are now standing, and which tumbled down from old age and neglect, when I spotted Sergeant Crowther walking the South Wall across the river on the same lay—after golden plovers. As I hailed him, a whizzing sound, like a blast of wind forcing its way through the mill-sails, caught my ear, and which I somehow unconsciously mistook for it (other gunners have had the same experience); when on the instant a very large flock of golden plovers were speeding across the river. I fired, but by some bad luck never hit a bird; they were beyond gunshot before it occurred to me to fire the second barrel. Nearly all old gunners know that after a first shot is fired golden plovers have a way of dropping a little, thus often giving a good chance with a second pull.

'I hailed Crowther, who had fired as they went over him, but he, too, missed, although an excellent shot. Crowther was walking along the bank top; he hailed me back, and suddenly started to quicken his pace. What happened I'll tell you in his own words as he told the story to me.

'"Old Jack Gibbs is as selfish as they make 'em. On Breydon he's always getting into trouble with other gunners for shooting in his wrong turn and sometimes retrieving a bird he hasn't himself shot. If a fowl, as you know, gets away wounded, and a nearby gunner with a second shot kills it, it is only common courtesy to hand it over to the first shooter, if seen by him and asked for. A similar trick may be expected if the case is reversed. One day Gibbs got a shot at three or four hundred fowl, knocking out only four birds. Two were wounded and got away; these I picked up, when Jack immediately rowed over to me, very peremptorily demanding them. I gave them back, and he might have said 'Thank you'.

'"One day I wounded a swan, which got away across the flats and Channel; Gibbs, who was making for home, saw the bird fall to my gun, but killed it before I could get round by the Ship drain. However, I overtook him and demanded the bird, according to custom. But he with impudence refused, argument and threat having no effect upon him ; he'd killed the bird, and he should stick to it.

' " ' All right,' thought I, ' I'll have *you* first chance.' As soon as I got ashore I went to the police station and made complaint.

' " I saw the policeman in charge, and told him of the little trick, but he put it pretty plainly to me that Breydon jobs scarcely came under their jurisdiction ; besides, he argued, Gibbs didn't take the swan out of my boat, or off my premises—that, indeed, I had never had it in my possession. How could it be a theft ? I had never, he went on, bred the bird, bought the bird, or ever handled it.

' " So I left it at that. I could see his reasoning was moderately tangible, but I vowed I'd make Gibbs whistle for it before I had done with him—if it took me twenty years. I could easily have knocked spots off him, but what was the use of knocking a man down that couldn't stand up to it ? Some fellows, like old Fiddler Goodens or Lucky Bob, would have measured distances and peppered him with shot, and said it was an accident, or blowed the bows out of his punt.

' " One day when I was going up the Bure walls after a big bunch of golden plover that used the marshes a mile or so up, I espied a nearly new short ladder stranded on a rond after the last night's high tide. I drew the ladder up and laid it on the grass on the inner side of the wall, intending to take it home after I'd had a shot or two at the birds. When I was resting against the Black Mill I espied old Gibbs coming up the wall, with his gun on his shoulder, to try his hand on the plovers ; but coming to the ladder he hesitated, looked around to see if there was anyone in view, then lifted the ladder on to his shoulder, and with the gun under his left arm started for home, considering its value no doubt would cover the loss of his prospective game, on the old principle of ' A bird in the hand . . .' Highly elated, Gibbs took the nearest marshes, and trudged away homewards. I hurried up to within a hundred or so yards of him, and kept behind him all the way to the town ; he was pretty warm, I can tell you, by the time he got into George Street, when I tapped him on the shoulder and thanked him for the trouble he had taken to save me the hard labour of taking it home myself. He turned round savagely at me and said that he had found it stranded, and having brought it home it was his. This little argument happened very near my own back-door, so I politely took it away from him with profuse thanks, and opening my door stood it up against the wall and turned the lock on him. He was exceedingly angry, and was glad to cool his hands and temper with a refreshing wash.

' " Meanwhile, I had started out for the police station to report my finding of the ladder, which had certain marks upon it, and on giving the constable in charge a fuller description of it he at once said that it answered to the description of one lost from a foreign ship in the harbour, the captain of which was willing to give five shillings reward to any finder. Perhaps the captain would send one of his sailors to the house for the ladder. I left the police station, and observed poor old Gibbs coming along the quay towards the place I had just left, evidently with the intention of reporting the find himself. He did not see me. I heard afterwards that Gibbs was very angry on finding that it had already been reported, and that the policeman to whom I had told the yarn told him to shut up and take himself off. The next time I met Gibbs I informed him that, in my opinion, ladders were as good as swans, and sometimes a good deal better " '.

. . . . .

In the palmy days of Breydon the slopes around its southern entrance were dotted with boat- and yacht-sheds—none too many for the great demand for them. Some of the poorer punters were perforce content with mere declivities of the several boat-yards for storing their punts, covering them in with light hatches, to keep pilfering hands and rain-storms from their weapons and their tools ; whilst a flotilla of them lay afloat on the Bure moored to staging and quay-side. Some of the gentlemen gunners took pride in their little establishments, some of which boasted an ante-room to the actual boat-house, wherein they had sundry cupboards, a table and chairs, gun-racks, not forgetting drawers for ammunition and lockers for liquors of their own personal choice ; a window or two (with strong shutters), a stove, and even carpets and rugs, which made an hour of leisure and yarning a delight and a luxury. The punts rested on rollers in the boat-house and were tethered with four painters, so as to keep the craft from injury when a high tide and a rough swell obtained, that made them prance like live things, but in safety. A rollered slide ran from the outside door right down to low-water mark. As a rule the big gun was lifted on to one of the racks protruding from the walls; on others were suspended eel-picks, oars, light spars, etc.

It goes almost without saying that many a jolly company, gathered in one or another sanctum, spent a lively time over cards and gossip. Many a yarn of adventure on the old Estuary was spun while the elements raged outside, many a discussion on guns and fowls and waders, and on the idiosyncrasies of other sportsmen.

There met one night in Jimmy Hurr's little cabin a party of gossips who had dropped in to spend an hour so in a friendly mardle and a game of cards. Among the gang were Little Stork, Ben Harwood, and two or three others. Jimmy had seen three of the wall-gunners that morning justify their claims to being excellent shots, as indeed they were, for in those days they had plenty of practice at snipe-shooting on the upper and wetter marshes. Said he:

'They were old Whiley, Little Billy Maystone, and Strike Sharman, all crack shots. They'd come down the South Wall from the early flighting, when, on reaching the yacht-sheds, two very superior persons—swell gunners, you know—made rather light of mouching amateurs in words that were evidently intended to reach their ears.

'"You hull a penny up in the air," says Billy, "and you'll never see it again"; and taking his gun off his shoulder put a cartridge in one barrel. One of them readily enough spun a coin in the air, and Billy fired, and sent the penny to Jericho. The gent said it was more by luck than wit that he hit it. A second penny was hulled up, and Whiley sent it to the same old city, but it dropped into Breydon, half-way; then Strike showed 'em the same little trick.

'"Not bad shooting for bloomin' amateurs!" said the other gent; and it didn't take much kidding to persuade the two swell gunners to speckerlate a shillin'.

'"Another go!" axes Whiley.

'"No. We've no more coppers; but we're very well satisfied that you are better sportsmen than you look".'

'Cadger Brown made a better shot than them three moskyteers did,' said Charlie Thacker. 'He once told me his old woman had a bare cupboard jist afore one Chrissmas; so she ordered him to go up the meshes and shoot a hare for the Chrissmas dinner, or live on his knuckles till she got hold of some money somewheer. Well, he told me when he got on Squire B——'s mesh he see a hare, what see him, and riz on its hind-legs to reckynarter. He fired at it, but at the identrickle moment a pheasant shot up, and afore it was three futt up in the air he swung the gun round and killed the hare, and the pheasant, with *half a shot each* ! He swore it was the truth.'

'You can reckon Cadger Brown told you an outrageous lie, then ! ' was Bellin's comment, ' for no gun ever shot round the corner.' To which they all agreed.

The first game of penny nap finished, they lighted their pipes to make an atmosphere so beloved of sportsmen. In a lull of the conversation the cries of a flock of curlews were heard overhead in the darkness.

'Look like a shot in the mornin',' remarked Thacker, looking at Bellin, who rose and opened the door to listen, and to make comment as he closed it ; ' and we look like having some worse weather by the cackling of a party of geese making for the marshes.'

Before settling to another hand at cards the conversation turned upon the marsh geese, which forty and fifty years ago were by no means so frequently seen as they are to-day, and then but in small numbers.

'I was spending a week at the house-boat,' said Bellin, 'up there on the little rond next the sluice-gate ; and had made up my mind to get a big old bean gander that had been hanging about the flats for two or three weeks ; he had got a taste of the wigeon-grass, and very much fancied it. When flowed off the flats he took to the rond, but was so wary that all efforts to get a shot at him had so far failed.

'One day came along a peregrine falcon, when the gander was feeding at very low water. As the tide began to make up, I stepped out of the house-boat to see how my punt stood, that is to say, theboat being moored at the staithe might need shoving from under the plankway. The old gander instantly spotted the hawk and began to cackle excitedly ; then took to wing, and made for Rotten Eye Corner, the bird of prey circling in order to get a swoop. At length the peregrine swooped and struck the gander, which scrambled into the drain, and began shooting under-water and splashing at a furious rate, not being disabled wholly. Four times the hawk swept round, but made no strike, as the gander splashed and baffled it ; and at length the hawk, on seeing me getting into the boat and shoving off, made away. The old gander clambered on to the flat and shook himself, feeling very sick, it was evident ; it then hunched itself as if feeling very miserable.

'Just at shutting-in time I was enabled to get within range

of the gander with the shoulder-gun and killed it. On examining the bird, I found a hole the size of a crown piece through which I could see into the body. The peregrine, instead of breaking the gander's neck, had struck at the back, hitting a fleshy part, and it was evident that a hook-like claw had torn away the flesh. If not shot the bird must have succumbed.'

'Peregrines,' continued Bellin, 'seem to come from nowhere, so suddenly do they loom into view, although their screaming may catch the ear at times, while yet a good way off. I remember when young Smith, at the Lock-gate Farm, kept a fine lot of homing pigeons. They were out flying one day, when all on a sudden they rushed home, hiding in the first shelter that offered—in a shed, under a lean-to, and under a cart. But one of them, the most valuable bird of the lot, was knocked out by the falcon before it could get under cover ; it fell stunned, and feathers from the back lay scattered round it. The peregrine on spotting Smith and myself flew off in a hurry. I picked the pigeon up, and Smith said he was afraid it was done for, but I told him the raw spot on the back would soon heal, and it did ; and he had several excellent youngsters afterwards owning its parentage.'

The audience was so interested in Bellin's narratives that pipes were relit and a bottle of excellent stuff left its companion in the cupboard. Asked if he (Bellin) had ever seen the white-tailed eagle on Breydon, he assured them that in his recollection he had never seen more than two, and these were on stormy days, when they were flying in airy circles overhead ; but he had never seen one alight. Walter Lowne, the stuffer, had preserved one that had been attracted by the fowl on the Fritton decoys a short way from the top-end of Breydon, on December 9th 1882. It may be interesting to add that another was shot when passing over Breydon on May 2nd 1892. This species has never been met with in eastern Norfolk in the adult plumage.

'As to sparrow-hawks,' resumed Bellin, 'they might be termed the peregrine's understudy, for they are equally as quick and sharp in their movements. I once saw a sparrow-hawk circling overhead above a peewit, screaming as it gyrated around, and then with a dash killed the plover. I also once saw one manœuvring above a snipe, paying little heed to me ; and for all the little bird's trying to get away, he had it. Very shortly after I went to the spot where he was having his dinner ; he flew off with a screech, leaving behind him but the scattered feathers and a clean-picked breast-bone.'

Thacker now jibed in with a quaint little story. 'Well,' said he, 'one of the funniest things I ever see—and I hev seen a few—wor a hawk, what I reckon wos one o' them pennygrins, and a ring-dow sittin' togither on a tree-bough. The hawk wor a-bangin' the pigeon with his wing, jist as the turkle-dow'll do if you disturb it; but for a time it would not budge, in spite of the tother's tryin' to get it on the wing. Suddenly, kinder unawares, that ring-dow dashed away, and down'ard and plungin' in a hazel clump, escaped the inemy. That's as sure as you're alive.' It was thought by the company that the hawk was a peregrine, and gave his would-be victim the chance to fly, not from any 'sporty' impulse, but from its natural desire to kill its quarry on the wing.

Jimmy Hurr reverted to the goose question. 'Some one told me that old Blunderfield in the marsh-house, half-way to Burgh, had shot a white-fronted goose. As I wanted a specimen, I thought I'd trot up the walls and see what he'd done with it.

'"I hear you've got a goose—one o' them white-fronts—and if you ain't made off with it I should very much like to have it."

'"Well, Jimmy, me boy," says he, "I did shoot one, but we've jist had it for dinner, and jolly good eatin' it was!"

'"You're sure it *was* a white-front, Blunderfield?"

'"Oh, yes, he was white nearly all over; but I thowt it was a funny kind of a beak for a goose, and the legs fared rather long. Stop a bit, Jimmy. Come out along o' me an' you'll p'r'aps tell me if I made a mistake." He took me to the muck-heap, and there I found the beak and head of a spoonbill, and the two legs as well.

'"Well, bor, you ha' done me. I sart'nly thowt it was a white-fronted goose, but though you swear it's a spunebill, I'll never want a better jint on the table".'

'What a silly old fule Blunderfield must ha' bin!' commented Thacker.

Snipe and woodcocks were among the subjects discussed; lucky shots, queer hiding-places, and unexpected appearances of woodcocks freely spiced the conversation.

'One October day,' ventured Bellin, 'when I was walking through the little St. George's Park, I espied a woodcock pottering about in broad daylight under a large spreading euonymus shrub, where the soil was still damp. I watched him for a moment or two probing the earth, and suddenly the desire to catch that woodcock possessed me. I immediately bolted off to an old net-braiding fellow who lived not very far away, and catching the old chap at home, I asked him to lend me a length of herring-net, which he did. I rushed back, and seeing that the bird was still under the shrub, I got a boy to help me surround it. I then carefully tucked in the net below, but did not notice a small hole in it about the size of a child's hand. I started the woodcock, hoping he would bag himself in the net, as I have known a bird to do ; but in a few moments he discovered the rent and went through the hole like a rat. I hadn't the slightest idea a woodcock could see so well in broad daylight. Much taken aback, I watched the direction the bird went in, and raced after it, and when near the " Saxon " public-house I observed it drop and scuttle into the bar. In a moment or two I was behind the bird and slammed-to the door ; believing it must have run into a quiet corner, I searched under one of the benches. The landlord, who was very much surprised, asked what it was all about, and I showed him the bird, telling him it was a woodcock. He said that he had never tasted woodcock, but had heard they were very good eating. I told him the usual price of the bird was half a crown, and as he very much desired to have it we amicably split the difference.'

Ben Harwood, who, with his usual quiet manners, had been enjoying the conversation, touched Charlie with his elbow and asked him which he liked better, baked woodcock or fried sausages ?

'Why, sausages ! ' snapped Charlie.

'What's that I've heard about you and sausages ? ' asked Hurr. Thacker hesitated a bit.

'Well,' said the little chap. 'I s'pose you 'on't be satisfied unless I tell ye. It's like this. I'm particklar fond o' fried sausages. I'd give up any day a mutton chop, a rump steak, or a turkey, if I had one, for a pan o' fried pork sausages. One night they got up a party, five or six on 'em, in Jack Boning's shud, t'other side the " Bowling Green " wall. They said it was got up in honour o' my shootin' a swan, what they'd got on the table for the supper. Jack says to me, " What'll ye hev—swan or *sausages*, because we've got some hot in the oven, thinking you'd like them best ? " Of course I said sausages. So they brung me four on a hot plate, and piled on the taters and Brussels sprouts by the side on 'em. So without any grace we all started to tuck in. I got half-way through one, an' I'm blessed if my mouth worn't sune all on fire and my innerds was bilin' hot, like a railway engine gettin' steam up. I thowt the bottom of the pepper-box must ha' fell out. Howesomever, I got outside one sausage an' some o' the greens, and laid the knife an' fork down, and begins to sweat. The tothers were settin' their eyes up at me, and beggin' on me to go on, and was gigglin' innerdly fit to bust at me. So I fared to smell a rat. "Look here," I says, "four sausages is generally my cut; one'll do for me to-night. I fare to ha' lost my appetite. Hand me that bottle o' stout; I'll finish up on that!"'

'What the devil was the matter with the sausages?' asked Jimmy.

'Well,' replied Thacker, 'they was home-made 'uns got up special for me—so they told me arterwards. Jack Boning had got his cook to make up them sausages with sawdust, a few crumbs, a lump o' pork lard, and a lot o' cayenne pepper; so now you know. I fare hot to-day when I think on 'em.' Turning to Harwood: 'Now you tell us about them godwicks.' Ben hesitated, and Bellin stepped in:

'Our old friend Ben,' said he, 'never loses his temper; but once he did get a little below the level. He passed me up the Ship drain in pursuit of some godwits he had espied; and after a lot of patience and effort got his punt-gun to within range of quite a hundred godwits. He pulled trigger, but did not hit a single bird. I had followed him up, and turning to me all he said was, "*That's a curiosity!* How in the world I came to miss I don't know." We went to the spot just vacated by the birds, and could not find a single streak of a slithering shot in the mud.

'"Well, that's a curiosity!" he repeated; but it gradually dawned upon him as he rowed home beside me that, having put in the powder, something had attracted his attention, and he forgot to put in the shot!'

'That's quite correct,' assented Harwood.

Between the shuffling of the cards and the relighting of pipes other items of common interest were discussed. At this juncture the 'Admiral' and Pero stepped into the shed and drew up to the fire, when the former asked what was the chief topic of conversation.

'All sorts of curiosities,' jibed in Ben, 'and the last one, barring mine, was of Thacker's sausage proclivities.'

'A good word,' said Gooch, 'and most of us know the story, whilst Charlie never forgets it. I am very particular as to what sort of game I put between my mandibles. Some people are not. Old Pintail once went deep-sea trawling, and told me how tired he got of the continual and monotonous meals of long-salted sow, and doubtful beef equally as briny. He much preferred to have game of his own catching, and nothing he liked better than the black-headed kitties and the young herring gulls for the stew-pot. His skipper, so he said, carried his gun to sea with him, and allowed old Thomas to get pot-shots at ducks; albeit these, such as scoters and scaups, were of no great acquisition for the dinner-table.

' " When I went to sea," said little Pintail, " we sometimes snared them old gants by tyin' a dade herrin' on a osier ped-lid, and castin' it adrift with a string fast to it. 'Tworn't long afore the gulls was round, and now and agin an old gant come to look at it. Presently one of 'em, high up, would turn his eye on the floatin' bait and come down like a stone, its bill and hid goin' through the ped-lid, and breakin' his neck. All we hed to do was to haul him in and hull him to the cook.

' " Talkin' about herrin' baits an' that,' went on Thomas, " herrin's what dropped out o' the nets, and didn't sink at fust, but jist swum anyhow atop, we called 'sick herrin's'. The gulls an' gants sune snap them up; if they didn't the dorgs pretty quickly did " (of course Pintail meant dogfish). " We used to see a body o' Tom Taylors [storm petrels]; they'd swarm around the boats when the grease was heaved over the side out o' the great fryin'-pan; they reg'lar skum it off the water—thet's what they fare to live on. We see plenty o' cormorants an' shags, and called 'em 'Cobblers'—why, I can't say—and we never ate 'em; p'r'aps they tasted like cobbler's wax, and so got the name for it."

'I must tell you one other little yarn perwidin' you can stomach it'; to which all assented. ' " One day," said Thomas, " we thort, as we'd got short o' meat, we'd get Dutchman—one o' the crew—to catch a gant for dinner, so we opened a small whitin', and stuck inside it a piece o' cork, jist sufficient to float it. A bit o' wire, part of a knittin'-needle, was put in the fire and bent into a hook, and a long string was tied to a looped end. He hove the bait out—he called it a 'hake' (eyke), and it worn't long afore a old gant swooped down an' took it. It was hauled in, knocked on the hid, and skun. Made into a sea-pie, it was cooked. One or two hands thowt it was middlin', or said they did. I hed a taste, but it was too much like —— old stinkin' fish for my likin'! and I wouldn't hev no more on it".'

'Captain B——' put in Jimmy—'p'r'aps you remember him—was a great snipe-shooter in the late 'sixties. He very rarely missed his bird, but if he did it was either his " blissed beard " or the powder, or the wind, or the fault o' some other thing. One day he shot a fat shelduck, whose diet of shellfish made it too rank for my likin' as a tenant for the oven. He demanded of me to know if it was edible. " It might be," I replied, but didn't let him know that one I sat down to turned me up. So his fowl was duly prepared, and when well baked, was brought from the kitchen by the cook, the smell of it preceding her. The Captain's face blossomed up strawberry colour. " What the —— —— have you got here, stinking out the place ? " demanded he.

' " The duck, sir," meekly replied the cook.

' " Then fling the —— fowl, dish and all, into the —— dustbin ; the smell's enough without dissecting it ! " '

' I remember,' said Admiral Gooch, as he stood his wineglass on the table, ' Lowne having a supper off some doubtful game, although he never knew it himself. His assistant birdstuffer was starting to skin a couple of moor-hens when Lowne handed him the bodies of a couple of owls to deposit in the rubbish-box, and left him, as he was then off to the train to go to a fishing-match. " When you've skinned those two moorhens," said he, stopping at the door a moment, " take them to the kitchen and ask them to cook them for my supper." The assistant said " All right," but whether from the spirit of mischief or experiment he handed in the two owls' bodies instead. They were served up at supper for the angler, who had won another cup on the broads, and he ate them in all innocence, and enjoyed them."

So they chatted on and on, as is the fashion of all sportsmen, till the late hours suggested a respectable dispersal.

CHAPTER IX

DIAMOND CUT DIAMOND

'He was a curio enthusiast himself, and he knew both from experience and observation that strange madness may at any moment affect the collector, blotting out morality and the nice distinction between *meum* and *tuum* as with a sponge . . . collectors who would not steal a loaf if they were starving, might, and did, fall before the temptation of a coveted curio.'

—P. G. WODEHOUSE

ONE is inclined, very strongly, to believe that there is not a hobby existing, save horse-racing, that has given rise to more sharp dealing, often bordering on sophistry and deception, than that pursued by the—now happily lessening—specimen-hunting bird collector. The petty acts of guile and unfairness would be matters for contempt were they not so whimsical and diverting to an outsider, and withal are so unsportsmanlike. Sharp dealing exists in many walks of life ; and to put a rival to some disadvantage may be business-like but is certainly not straight.

A mild case of outwitment among Breydon-side folks bearing somewhat on this manœuvring is interesting, as showing that cautiousness, in some cases, is strategy. It was rumoured around among the birdy people in the early 'eighties that Pintail Thomas had eluded the Breydon Watcher and had got safely home with a very desirable bird an avocet. Certain collectors and dealers were quickly on his track ; but little Johnny was by no means a smart business man, leaving financial aspects to his much larger mate ; so the bird rivals began to badger the more business-like lady to sell the bird, or even allow them to look at it. The self-conscious gunner wisely, or otherwise, had ambled off to the 'Staff of Life' for a drink, as the fraternity said, 'to lean upon', and brag of his prowess and valour. Walter Lowne, whose bird-stuffing establishment was situated lower down the 'hill', was early at the Thomases' little shop prepared to do immediate business. Thomas, in spite of its being close season, was evidently making no secret of his exploit.

'You've got an avocet, I hear,' began the bird-stuffer, who was gifted with more persistence than persuasiveness.

'Who told you that fairy story, pray ? '

'Well,' said Lowne, 'these little things will leak out.'

'Well, and what if I *have* ?' she demanded, with her usual toss of her head; 'and are you fule enough to suppose it'll come your way?'

'I don't see why it shouldn't,' said the taxidermist. 'I suppose it is for sale, and I don't suppose you're going to eat it.'

'Then what are you prepared to give for it?' she snapped.

'Well, at the most,' spreading one of the bird's wings, 'I'll give you two pounds for it,' showing her two golden coins.

'I thought that was about your figure, Mr. Lowne,' returned the lady with a grin, 'but it ain't *your* bird!'

It usually answered Mrs. Thomas's purpose to hold on a bird, and to set up a little spell of competitive rivalry, for securing rare species in close seasons was not an everyday occurrence; so that eager collectors ran up against each other, literally and figuratively, to obtain them. It might almost be suggested that Mrs. Thomas was a kind of auctioneer acting without a licence. What was known as 'hawking' a bird round from collector to collector with a view to a constant rise in its value, and in the end a *top price*, became a commonplace that led to much jealousy and unpleasantness. Dallying over a bargain in mild and bad-keeping weather led occasionally to the bird being spoiled for stuffing. Alfred Isaac Harvey, son of old Isaac, referred to by the Pagets in their wonderful little book on the Natural History of Yarmouth, was an exceedingly artistic and clever bird-stuffer, which business he pursued when not measuring timber trees landed upon the quays. He mostly took their attitudes and positions from the engravings in Yarrell's book; he purchased up-to-date books upon the subject of birds, and a number of these were kept, unbound, in a big sea-chest. He was never slow to show the plates to persons who brought him birds, either for sale or for preservation. Even the roughest old gunners were delighted when allowed to peer at them, always confining their interest to the waders and swimmers, many of which they were familiar with. They began to examine more carefully all strange birds that came into their hands. They were most enthusiastic with Morris's *British Birds*, and Bree's *Birds of Europe*; they troubled little about the somewhat weak descriptions and worse sentences, but the coloured illustrations charmed them. Morris's plate of the kingfisher, that had been painted with a yellow breast and abdomen in the popular edition startled them, as they could see at once it was not dressed like the little bird they had so often seen flying along the marsh ditches; but once in a while Harvey's copy of Bree's *Birds* settled the identity of some exceedingly rare or difficult visitor. George Smith, who had always a list of specimens ' wanted ' to the order of well-to-do collectors, gave Harvey preferential treatment, yet the whole of these dealers and bird-collectors were out for advancing, or cutting the prices.

One particular gunner, when out shooting by the seashore, brought down a little bird with what he thought an abnormally long tail. He took no one into his confidence, believing it to be a species that had never been before met with, but went by an early train to Norwich, taking the bird with him, to one of our leading ornithologists for his inspection. The great bird-man, somewhat amused, took down a book of foreign birds, and pointed out a coloured plate of the species, which was a

LAND DOTTEREL

shaft-tailed whydah, as English dealers name it, but known to science as *Fringilla paradisea,* an African finch, and an undoubted escape. . . .

Mrs. Pintail Thomas, already referred to, was a shrewd, hard-bargaining lady. All the fraternity declared she had her ' eye-teeth cut '—and always one eye upon the look-out for the ' main chance '. On one occasion, at the request of the late Henry Scherren, I took him to see the redoubtable ' Johnny ' at his little home in the Fishermen's Hospital, as this naturalist had been greatly impressed with Breydon and my yarns of the gunners that I had narrated to him. He had very much wanted to see a notable Breydoner. We found Thomas sitting up in bed, groaning over his gout and rheumatism, a sorry wreck of a man. We chatted to the old fellow of spoonbills and avocets, and of some interesting waders that we had seen, trying to draw him out into a bit of reminiscence, but he was too uneasy to respond. As we rose to go I gave Scherren a hint to give the little fellow a tip; on which he put his hand into his pocket and drew out some mixed coins, and, dropping them into the hand of the vigilant Mrs. Thomas, he made remark to her, 'Get the old boy a bottle of brandy'. Before I had lifted the latch of the door to go out, Mrs. T. remarked, 'Just a minute, sir,' and counted the money, and then said with a decided snap, 'I thank ye, sir; but you'll excuse me, there ain't quite enough—it wants another ha'penny.' . . .

The elder George Smith was well advanced in years when I first came into contact with him; he was stout, and rolled in his gait; and was a moderate gardener, and acted as warehouseman to a gun-loving pawnbroker. His buxom old lady and a masculine-like daughter kept a rabbit stall in the market, more than making up by the sale of rabbits for the ancient's scanty earnings. His favourite occupation was rambling upon the then extensive sand-dunes with its acres of furze bushes and marrams, which were popularly known as 'The Common', a kind of everyman's land, where geese rambled in crowds and beach donkeys spent their spare time in the lodging season. Adult and juvenile gunners there sought rabbits, stock doves, and even partridges, that often nested there; bird-catchers by the score at a time set their nets for linnets, snow buntings, and even rarer birds. In September, chance time, a solitary snipe could be flushed from the sand-hills; woodcocks were frequently met with in their season. In 1863 the irruption of the sand-grouse tempted every rambling gunner from thenceforth to patrol the dunes on the look-out for a bird, commonly valued at three guineas at that time. Smith was one of the greatest of these enthusiasts. At that period the abundant seaweeds strewn at the tide-mark were a great feature of the seashore adjoining the sand-dunes. The hordes of sand-hoppers, that frisked all summer long, attracted many shore-birds—some that had been flooded off Breydon by the rise of the tide, and others that were lured ashore when skirting the coast. The stretch of pebbly ground lying mile after mile just between the tide-mark and the base of the dunes was much used by ringed plovers for a nesting-ground; in winter the snow-buntings and ‘ Laplanders ’ searched the sand-drift for the seeds of the marram and sand-sedge. The land-dotterel now and again visited this spot on its migration northward in spring, and Smith took exceeding great interest in them, especially after he had, on one great day, rounded up and shot a party of nine of these fast-disappearing, simple birds. Smith had evidently read an old author, who thus described the land-dotterel: ‘ It is a foolish bird, but excellent meat. . . . It is taken in the night-time by the light of a candle, by imitating the gestures of a fowler ; for if he stretches out an arm, it also stretches out a wing ; if he a foot, it likewise a foot ; in brief, whatever the fowler doth, the same doth the bird ; and so being intent upon men's gestures, it is deceived, and covered with a net. . . . We call a foolish, dull person a *Dotterel*.’ Whether Smith pursued these methods I know not ; for he tolerated no onlookers and wanted no company. His son, who was known as ‘ Hoppy ’, from an unfortunate limp acquired in a serious illness, followed the old man to his haunts, and conceived a strong liking for the company of fowler and gunner ; to become greatly enamoured also of ornithology—at first for its own sake, and eventually as a matter of business. In the heyday of his manhood he showed extreme enthusiasm, which was his habit, even as he in his youth, when a Methodist, esteemed himself a missionary among a different type of individuals. He raced to and fro among Broadmen, Breydoners, and all the outdoor characters who sported a fowling-piece, or rifled a nest, or pulled over a bird-net. It must be remembered that in the earlier half, and even the latter half, of the nineteenth century the shooting of rare birds, and the preservation of their skins as specimens, were thought to be the essence of sporting, and the ideal hobby of a gentleman. Observation of a bird's life and habits, and the study of its migrations, were esteemed the whim of a few. It was even thought necessary to slay a rare avine visitor to prove that it had lived—and here was the genuine creature's skin, stiffly posed, with glassen eyes, in the lucky collector's possession ! If one collector boasted a unique example, every other one envied him, and endeavoured when a second bird of its species was in the market to outdo or outbid the fraternity to secure it. Herein was the cause of so much eagerness to kill every rarity met with.

Our energetic ornithologist-dealer collected birds' eggs, and in time became a dealer in birds ‘ in the flesh ’ ; and in bird skins so prepared as to be amenable to the skilled hand of the taxidermist. For their retention he had many drawers, wherein he displayed them ; his walls and tables had much the appearance of a small bird museum. Several Broadmen prior to the conversion of the broads into bird-sanctuaries, whose forefathers had done the same before them without let or hindrance, were much addicted to egg-hunting and the slaying of rare species of birds ; they were supplied with receptacles and labels for the reception and sending of these to Smith. Bearded tits, and their young and eggs especially, suffered from these activities, for there was a great demand

GREAT CRESTED GREBES

for them among collectors all over the country ; and for this decimation our bird-dealer was described by prominent Norfolk ornithologists as a great bird-vandal. But it was the unscrupulous bird-collector who tempted and forced his hand.

Our indefatigable bird-man Smith for many years paid frequent visits—in the shooting season they were daily—to the homes and resorts of the Breydon men, bird-catchers, game-dealers, and others, whose interests took them among the desired birds, securing many coveted species. Several good examples went to Norwich Museum, to the Gurneys, Connop, Rev. C. J. Lucas, Stevenson, Lord Lilford, Robert Chase, and many others who very largely collected. Harvey,

Walter Lowne, Benjamin Dye, as well as his—Smith's—sons, made up his 'skins'. As characteristic of Smith's temperament, the following story may be interesting: Ben Dye, who was a self-taught taxidermist, took in birds for preservation in the spare hours between his bakings, and prepared the 'skins' in an excellent manner for cabinets. Smith, who had somewhat tired of Walter Lowne's work, left certain birds with Dye to be made into skins. On taking them to 'Larus House' (George Smith's residence), the skins were laid upon the table to be inspected. Smith was delighted, and vowed that Lowne had never turned out such work in his life. 'I'll show you what I think of your work and Lowne's,' said he to Ben, and pulling out a drawer he filled his arms with Lowne's work, strode to the fire-place, and cremated the lot. Some cases of interesting birds set up by Smith's sons are in the Yarmouth Tolhouse Museum. One of the cases contains a considerable number of Lapland buntings, only one of them showing any sign of mature plumage. Bird-loving visitors to the Museum have been known to remark what a pitiful waste of bird-life. This species had been considered a very rare visitor until the beginning of the 'nineties, when a considerable number were identified in company with snow-buntings by the bird-catchers, then a numerous fraternity, who caught an unusual number. In October and November 1892 a surprising quantity were seen, over sixty being shot or captured.

Among the rare birds that came into Smith's hands, the following were new to Norfolk: tawny pipit, white wagtail, Iceland gull, greater shearwater, and the Mediterranean black-headed gull. His most notable bird was the Mediterranean gull, which, unnoticed by the gunners, visited Breydon in 1886, and that was to create great excitement amongst the fraternity, more especially in Smith, who became its owner.

It appears that on Boxing Day 1886 two amateur fowlers—Tom Reed and Charlie Harwood—had gone up Breydon for a bit of shooting, and having spent some hours without a shot they determined on reaching the Knowl, a hundred yards from the 'Bowling Green', to 'pop at any old gull that came by', as they discovered that a cartridge had become jammed. It happened that *Larus melanocephalus*, being mistaken for a mere common black-headed gull, became the victim as it was passing overhead. On landing at the staithe, it occurred to Harwood that the bird did not seem to 'tally' with the appearance of the commoner gull (*L. ridibundus*). It was shown first to Pintail Thomas, who promptly declared it to be 'only a d——d old sprat-mow! ' The common gull (*L. canus*) is a bird with a bluish leg, and is known on the coast as a 'sprat-mow'; and so pronounced a difference did no credit to Johnny's eyesight or his intelligence.

Quinton happened to come to the 'Green' at a crucial moment, and was shown it, and he, although not observing its definite individuality, declared that it was so great a stranger that he at once volunteered to find up 'Hoppy'. The bird-dealer was quickly on the spot, brimful of eagerness as was his wont, and with his usual 'Well, boys, what have you got?' asked to see the bird. He immediately observed that the bird's primaries were white, and knew it for a stranger, but, making an effort to hide his excitement, offered five shillings for it; this they accepted.

He failed to find a description of the bird in Yarrell's *British Birds*, so he immediately submitted it to Messrs. Gurney and Southwell and other expert ornithologists, who all agreed as to its identity—as *Larus melanocephalus*, and was believed to be the first authenticated occurrence in the British Islands; although it was also believed that an immature bird had been shot in January 1866 on the Thames, but which had not been correctly identified until examined by Mr. Howard Saunders. All doubts aside, its characteristics were described in Yarrell's fourth edition, with the result that the identification of the Breydon bird was established. Hoppy had it made into a skin, and a neat glass-lidded box, which all of us named 'the coffin', was also made, and lined with cotton-wool for its reception. A common black-headed gull was also stuffed and laid in a corresponding casket; and strict orders were issued that only *this* bird was to be shown to any inquisitive person who might call at the house in his absence.

George Smith talked of this bird and dreamt of it, becoming absolutely obsessed by it; and wrote letters making offers, or asking them, to ornithologists far and wide, endeavouring to secure a fancy price for it. He offered it to the late John Henry Gurney, who was quite willing to give a very fair price for it; but Smith threw up his hands and vehemently exclaimed:

'*What!* I have asked you for bread, and you have offered me a stone!'

Connop was asked £100 for *Larus*, but the offer was not entertained; but, contrary to the usual order of lowering a demand on refusal, it was reversed; with every refusal he added to its price. Quinton assured me that, in poor Smith's penurious days, he had seen a letter from the late Lord Lilford offering him £300 for the bird ; but he went still higher, and the bird remained on his hands. Eventually he offered it to a rich titled Jewish banker at, I believe, a still more advanced figure, but that gentleman, in answering the latter, naïvely made remark that 'Such a rare bird ought never to leave its own adopted country ! '—a very neat and ingenious form of refusal. The remainder of the story may be told in a few words. It passed out of Smith's possession, much to his regret, and was sold to Robert Chase of Birmingham for two figures, and added to his great collection.

It was not to be wondered at that, with all the discussions about the bird dealer and the gull, in the 'Lord Nelson' and other debating places of that ilk, reports of these negotiations should become known to the two gunners, nor was it surprising that their cupidity was aroused. To use the local parlance, 'That there five bob stuck in their throats'. But they went the wrong way to work to get an increase ; they somewhat abusively demanded some extra money. Hoppy, as might be expected of him, resented their badgering and stoutly refused to give them more ; for which they never forgave him, and none more exulted over the fate that later befell the gull than they.

After the death of Smith several of his treasured birds and a few ornithological works were sent to an auction sale-room ; the auctioneer was a little the worse for drink at the time of the sale, and very few bidders attended. There were no bird-collectors or dealers present and but one representative from a museum, notably from Norwich, who had been commissioned to secure, if possible, the Iceland gull. For some minutes not a bid was offered, but I stepped in, hoping to stir up competition, and made a bid of a shilling, which was somewhat resented by two or three of Smith's friends present. I had taken my cue from the ridiculous prices realized for some other odd lots. The Castle Museum authorities secured this first Norfolk example for the sum of ten shillings, case included. . . .

'Is this 'ere a proper titlark ? ' asked 'Jibro' Jessop, a cute bird-catcher, of Jack Quinton, on meeting him in the street.

'No,' replied Quinton, the doyen of local bird-catchers, and a remarkably entertaining teller of Breydonian stories. 'No, it's a tree-pipit. Take it to old Hoppy ; he'll give you thrippence for it.'

FRED CLARKE TO-DAY

LAST OF THE PROFESSIONAL PUNT-GUNNERS

JACK QUINTON — SHOULDER-GUNNER

BEN DYE — THE BLIND ORNITHOLOGIST

'Then you might as well give me the thrippence for it yerself,' said Jibro, 'and let Hoppy hev it as you go past his house.'

Quinton purchased the pipit, and on being invited into the bird-dealer's sanctum was met with raised eyebrows, and the usual inquiry, 'Got something good to show me ?'

'See for yourself,' replied Q., who possessed a knowledge of the smaller land-birds that was exceptional.

'Richard's pipit, begad !' exclaimed the impulsive dealer ; and without more ado handed Q. half a crown ; he pocketed it and said a prompt 'Good morning'.

'You see, Patt'son,' said the wily bird-catcher to me, 'I hadn't told him it *was* a Richard's pipit—he said so without asking ; and if he was fule enough to throw good money away like that it worn't my concern, and place, to tell him he shouldn't.'

Unfortunately for Smith's prestige, and his pride as a bird expert, he packed up the bird quickly without due examination, and dispatched it to a wealthy collector. He received a quick acknowledgment in the shape of a telegram, which read as follows : 'I am really surprised . . . that you have sent me this worthless tree-pipit !'

Away at once ran Hoppy to Q., and was soon at his door, demanding to know 'Why he had let him in over a mucky little tit-lark, making him look such a fool.' He also demanded back the half-crown.

'Look 'ere, you damn fule,' laughed Q., 'afore I could say anything, you jumped, and swore it *wos* a Richard's pipit ; and it worn't for sich as me to contradict you. If you had said it was a bloomin' elephant I shouldn't a-argered you that it was otherwise—'tain't so jolly well likely ?'

'These here bird-stuffers and bird blokes,' said Quinton to me, when chatting over my poor old friend Smith's little vagaries, 'they all fare very knowin', but they don't know everything. Why, I once took Walter Lowne four woodlarks, and *he* didn't know 'em till he took down his bird book.'

A noted bird-collector was greatly in want of a couple of 'red' knots, and had commissioned Smith to obtained them for him. The season had passed for really good-coloured birds, which of late years had been coming in far less numbers than formerly. Quinton was earnestly requested by Smith to secure them, if possible, and there would be no quibbling over the prices. Q. will tell the story :

'Hoppy comes to see me, all in a hot hurry, on the first of August, the close season havin' ended the day afore ; that was before the extra month was took in. Of course, everybody what had a gun was rousing around, eager to get a crack at anything—terns, stints, curlews, flappers, or anything else as flew. I left my snobbin' bench and put off in the punt, hardly expectin' to get what Smith so badly wanted. Howsumever, I did fall in with two knots feedin' on the edge of a drain, some distance apart from each other; the nearest one worn't a bad bird at all, bein' pinky, more 'an a brick-red. The other was well on the change, though, bein' potterin' about in a rather bad light, it might turn out better than it seemed. I aimed at the pinky one, and as I pulled trigger the other flew up. I killed my bird, and afore I could shove up to retrieve it, the other come flyin' round the dead 'un, as knots always do, and I downed *him*.

'There didn't fare much else worth waitin' about for, so I rowed home, and took 'em round to Hoppy's house, and offered him the two for four shillings. He offered me three bob, but after a bit of argument I said he might have 'em for three-and-six. No, he wouldn't pay a farthin' more than three shillings. After a lot more jaw, he says, "Let's go to the 'Admiral Seymour' and have a drink". Thet was his way of softenin' people down, but it didn't often wash with me. Well, he got reg'lar excited, and meant havin' his way, if he could.

'"Two glasses of whisky!" says he to the landlord, and hands me one of 'em; then he gets goin' all round the candlestick, about spunebills, fulmar petrels, black terns, and of course about his Mediterranean gull—*thet* made him worse. "Have another glass, Quinton," he says; and I had thet. He still kept on argerin'; then calls for two more whiskies. By this time we was gettin' both our fiddles well tuned up, and my eyes fared gettin' a bit dim.

'"I think we've had quite enough!' says Hoppy, handin' me the three bob, which I slips in my pocket, without counting; and then he adds, "We've had enough, old Wire, of bargaining and whisky, and I've got *my* way!" Them birds cost him enough, or I'm a Dutchman, seein' as six drinks and six sixpences was added to my three bob! It didn't fare to me as if he'd got the best of the bargain after all.'

Mr. Booth of Brighton, who was a keen observer as well as a gunner, when shooting on Breydon in the 'seventies, did not fail to notice the knot's friendly habit of showing concern for fallen and wounded comrades; how survivors make not the slightest attempt to escape, but after having seen companions dropped wholesale, time after time, still persist in wheeling around the wounded and dead, loudly twittering to them, as if trying to persuade them to rejoin them upon the wing, failing which they settle again, only to be slaughtered in their turn. Quinton seemed unconsciously to emphasize this fatal habit. He continued :

'We had lots of knots come to Breydon in them years gone by, as you've seen yourself. Well, one day I was on there when there was a big bunch of 'em around. Charlie Harwood and a swell gunner chap was staked aginst the Ham drain side, so I passed them, and staked down myself in a little off-drain a hundred yards higher up. A bunch of seventy or eighty knots come flyin' past me and alighted on the mud about twenty yards off, among 'em one good red 'un at the extreme end of 'em, what fared extra shy. They rose again before I could get a clip at 'em, and went round Harwood's boat, when they got a shot each, droppin' a score or more. The remainder flew round me again as I whistled 'em, the red 'un among 'em. I had a try at him alone, but missed him. Round Harwood's boat they went again, and they emptied four barrels into 'em, another score droppin' out ; but the red 'un was still goin' strong. Once more they come my way, and again I fired at the red 'un, some fifty yards off ; but they hadn't got as far as Charlie's boat when I see my partickler bird fall into the water, as dead as a stone.

'As I rowed to pick the bird up, they had another bang at the flock, droppin' a few more. Why the dowse do knots, more 'an all tame waders, fare so concerned about theer dead mates instead of sheerin' off, licks me. However, that's their consarn ; but old Breydoners allers called 'em " fat an' fulish ", which they are. The gent in Charlie's boat called me to him ; well, when I drawed up, I never see such a spread of dead knots in all my life. They'd got some afore I went up ; they'd got more 'an eighty, and not a red bird among 'em.

'" How many have *you* got ? " axed the gent. I lifted up my red 'un and said, " Only that one, but I think, sir, he's worth all your lot put togither "—that was as a specimen fit for stuffin'. He said how badly he'd wanted to shoot that very bird hisself.

'" Have a glass of beer ? " he axes, to which I didn't say no ! Nor yet to another question, " Have a bit o' cold chicken ? " You guess I took 'em ; and when I'd scoffed 'em, he axes the same two questions again. I ginerally know when I'm full enough, so I says " No " to the third servin' ; " But I'll take a bit home to the missus, if you don't mind," I says

Blest if he didn't axe me to take the remainders of the cold chicken. I could see what was his drift.

'"What'll you take for the red bird?" he presently wants to know.

'"Four shillings," says I. He hands over the four bob and told me that it was a bird he had very badly wanted for his collection; and, turnin' to Charlie, he says, pointing to the grey 'uns, "You may have the lot of 'em, Charles." They fetched him a good day's work.'

Most sportsmen of epicurean tastes esteemed knots extremely good eating. In Sir Thomas Browne's day knots were plentifully captured alive on the Norfolk coast. Says he: 'Gnatts or Knots a small bird which taken with netts grow excessively fatt. It being mewed & fed with corne a candle lighted in the roome they feed day & night, & when they are at their hight in fattnesse they beginne to grow lame & are then killed or as at their prime & apt to decline.' In the le Strange *Household Book* knots are mentioned, with other wading-birds: 'Itm pd to hym for a curlewe, a dosyn Knotts, a dosyn redschanks and stynts, ijs . . .'; and again: 'Itm pd to the fowler for ijj dosyn and di [half] of Knotts, iiijs.—jd.' The following item is from the Northumberland *Household Book*: 'Itm Knottes for my Lord at Principall Feestes and no other tyme, and at a jd a pece, except my Lordes commandment be otherwise.'

Fred Clarke, hale, hearty, and nearly eighty, was sitting by his fireside reading a magazine when I dropped in upon him with a few others to read (1927). Some rare bird I told him of greatly interested him and made him open out at once, to tell me a story of a rare adventure which befell him in connection with a 'spunebill', which he had been commissioned by Hoppy Smith to shoot if possible. It had always been a difficult matter for me to get Fred to yarn reminiscently, except by guile.

'It's like this 'ere,' he began. 'Hoppy comes to me late one Saturday night, all in a kinder sweat, as he usually did when he'd got some little scheme of mischief up his sleeve.

'"Fred," says he, "there's a nice spunebill up a' Breydon——"

'"Well, what o' that?" I axes. "As much right to be theer as you, ain't it? Perhaps a jolly sight more."

'"I've got an order for one for Captain Blake, and I partickler want you to go arter it; and theer's your money on the nail, if you cop it."

'"Well for you," says I; "but goin' to bed is more in my line at ten o'clock on a Saturday night. I only bolted home this arternune from the house-boat for some fresh grub and water."

'"Oh, well, be off arter it right early in the morning, afore the crowd get afloat."

'You know as well as I do that I don't care for Sunday shootin'; I allers leave that to chaps as is at work all the week ashore, and them d—— amateurs as break the Sabbath promiscuss-like, frightenin' every blessed thing off the place.

'Smith fared abserlutely determined about it; and thinking as I could do with a few shillings, I told him that if he didn't make a song of it, bein' close time, I'd have a look round. So I got up on the Sunday mornin' at two o'clock, afore any of the others was astir, and makes straight up the Channel t'words the Dickey-Works, and catches sight of my nibbs, at the top end o' Breydon, standin' thigh-deep in a drain, 'longer two old harnsers, towards the north side. When the harnsers got up and made toward the big mill the spunebill followed 'em. There was plenty o' water, so I slips round by the mill and works my way towards Banham's place, stoppin' there a bit to progue [prick] out the nipple of the gun; and stealthily slippin' into Dan's mill-house, begged of him a little fresh powder. He lent me a flask full.

'The spunebill fared wonderfully tame—they mostly are, till they hev bin harassed a bit; go to sleep even, trustin' to the old harnsers or the gulls to keep an eye around; and them old warmin allers give 'em due warnin' when they think it best to make off. As I lay a-watchin' spuney, I says to myself, "Old chap, you're in danger!" He was cleanin' himself after a bit o' shrimpin' on the ooze. He didn't rise when the harnsers cleared out this time; I reckon he thought he know'd as much as they did. Thet's where he was wrong. To cut the story short, I quietly sculled towards him, laid the gun, and pulled the trigger, and bowled him over; and picks him up as nice and clean a bird as you ever saw, though he'd got five shots in his constertution. I puts a little waddin' in his mouth, closes his wings, and lays him in my coat on the floor of the punt, coverin' him up carefully, and starts to row downstream, leisurely, like as if nothin' had ever happened. I had great hopes as Joe Buddery wasn't around just then; probably he was still snorin' in bed. I landed at the "Bowling Green", where I found Hoppy waitin' for me, all eager and tip-toein'.

'"Got him?" axes Hoppy, almost in a whisper, and dry-washin' his hands.

' " Got him wropt here all nice and serene," says I.

' " Blimy ! " says Smith, " that's all right ; come on out sharp, and make a nice little parcel of him in this clean sack, and come home with me to the house," which was in Harley Road on the North Denes, you know. I leaves my gun in the house at Runham Vauxhall, and we crosses the Suspension Bridge, athort the Quay, and slips up the " White Horse " row.

' " You step on ahead," says Hoppy, " well in front." And it was a jolly good job that I did ; for, blow me ! if I didn't pass Joe, the self-appointed Watcher. We only nodded ; and when I'd got a goodish way on, I turns to see if Hoppy was behind ; and he was a goodish way too—actually talkin' to Joe Buddery ! Joe was all likely to be suspicioning Hoppy—perhaps hesitating afore turning to come back and overhaul me. Down Ramp Row I hopped, turned the old North Tower, and went up the river walls as far as the tar works, then shot round, passing where the destructor now stands, and got to Smith's house, where his gal let me in. Hoppy comes sweatin' along, and presently he walks in, in great jubilation, praisin' his own cuteness, and all that sort o' slops.

' " Diamond cuttin' diamond ! " says he.

' " More by luck than wit," says I. " Suppose we hurry up an' settle, and let me go."

' " Righto ! " says Hoppy, offerin' me half a sovereign for my share of the job.

' " Why only ten bob ? " I axes sharply.

' " Well," says he, " I think ten bob is a very fair day's pay for four or five hours' work. But for me you wouldn't have earnt that, or got the bird."

' " And but for me," says I, " you wouldn't have had the bird ; besides, if Joe Buddery had suspicioned me, and had collared the spuney, the fine of a quid, and costs, and my time lost, would have fallen on me. And where'd I ha' bin ? You took good care not to carry it ; and you hadn't the pluck to shoot it. You'll get three pounds for your specimen, and I want half that or none." Hoppy fenced and argered, but hed to give in at the finish.'

For several years in succession there came to Breydon a keen Italian sportsman, who was more in quest of recreation ; that recreation was the killing of birds, albeit he held strong opinions against wholesale slaughter, and would only aim at a single bird at a time. He spent hours daily in Quinton's punt moored beside a mudflat ; taking aim at every bird that came along—turnstone, grey plover, swallow, tern, or skylark. He very rarely missed; he set no store by his little victims, which were always handed over to his boatman at the close of the day. One of the rarest of these was a white-winged black tern; this he handed over to Quinton, who was allowed to dispose of it.

'B. D—— was soon on my track,' said Quinton to me, 'and offers me a quid for it; and a taxidermist hearin' of it, came almost as quick, and offers thirty shillin's. B. D—— was informed of this rise in value, and at once sprung to thirty-five. The bird-stuffer riz to two pounds, and vowed he'd go no higher. Why-a, I worn't satisfied as yet, so I told him that it wouldn't be *his* bird if he didn't spring a bit more.

'"What's the stuffer offerin'?" axes B. D——.

'"Why-a, he's goin' no higher, he says, than two pounds; and it's up to you if it's goin' to be his bird."'

B. D—— had been thinking furiously, and at once prepared to come to terms, if possible.

'"I'll give you fifty shillings for it, if it proves to be only a young bird in the change of plumage; if a two-year old one, fifty-five shillings; if adult, three pounds."' Quinton agreed to that, and the taxidermist, who had promptly made a skin of it, was asked to send it to Mr. J. H. Gurney for judgment. The following is Mr. Gurney's report:

'*August 12th*, 1895. Wind: N.W. in the morning. A *White-winged* tern shot on Breydon Broad: this bird, which was exhibited at the Naturalists' meeting, and is now in the collection of B—— D——, is an old male passing from its summer to its winter plumage, the nape and occiput being mottled with black, and the grey feathers of the back blotched with new black ones. The White-winged Tern, which one is tempted to think might, like the spoonbill, establish itself with protection, is not, oddly enough, included in Gatke's *Birds of Heligoland*.'

The bird-stuffers, naturally enough, chaffed the successful competitor, who was already annoyed with Mr. Gurney's decision, and angrily suggested that the great ornithologist had made a mistake; and when argued out of that position, insisted that 'there had been an error in the printing!' He paid Quinton his price somewhat grudgingly, for he had prided himself on having a specimen rarely met with in that particular condition of plumage.

The white-winged black tern was first recorded for Norfolk on May 17th, 1853, when some fifteen or more were observed on Horsey Mere, one being killed. Booth of Brighton, on a tempestuous day in May 1871, shot into a flock of five birds, killing four, subsequently killing seven others on the broads. This tern's visits to Norfolk have been very uncertain, and well for it, as its reception when recognized has been an exceedingly warm one.

An old fowler of my acquaintance, when discussing this question of bird-killing, on being asked who ought to be blamed for such wanton slaughter of rare and beautiful birds, thus made prompt reply :

'Well, sir,' said he, scratching his grey head, 'I reckon as how the fault kin be laid to these 'ere speckylative collectors. Would you, if *you* was like *me*, and in my old water-butes, sit around, cold and perished, and see two years' back rent fly past yer, without hevin' a shot at it ? So, as you *may* say, sir, it *did* go past—*but not werry far* ! '

Durrant, the game-dealer, was well liked by all who knew or dealt with him. He dealt fairly with the gunners ; but was too easygoing with his customers, many of whom 'ran accounts' with him, and some were very slow to pay. In the end, in his old age, he became an honourable bankrupt ; and much sympathy was shown him. Wildfowl and game appealed to him more than rare birds ; over the latter he sometimes lost, and more rarely made a satisfactory profit. He dealt largely in pheasants and other game, and occasionally had set-backs in this direction, as cold storage had not yet come into being. His stalls—facing each other—in Yarmouth Market were, in the shooting season, besieged by collectors, bird-stuffers, walking gunners, punters ; on Saturdays by country sportsmen, who were usually poachers in a small way, for they brought up hares and longtails of their own or others' getting. Transactions were carried out usually behind the stalls with all the secrecy of bookmakers' touts at the street corners. Many a small canvas bag went away empty in coat-tail pockets. Saturdays were a great delight to me, and others, who kept a keen eye on the geese, swans, ducks, waders that hung in rows or in bunches on one stall ; hares and pheasants on the other. He sometimes offered fixed prices for snipe when orders were many ; at other times for plovers, wood-pigeons, and so on. When snipe were exceptionally abundant prices were low ; after protracted frosts, lower still. On one particular occasion so many snipes were brought to him that, after giving three-ha'pence apiece for them, he lost on his deals. When these birds were scarce, and orders came in for them, it is more than probable that 'stints' (dunlins), whose standard price was a penny each to the gunners, found their way upon the tables of snipe-lovers.

Durrant had an order come in for a number of wood-pigeons for an official dinner, and was somewhat anxiously awaiting arrivals, for very few pigeons had come in. At a critical hour Whiley, the gull-shooting shoemaker, obliged him most unexpectedly. To use the cobbler's own words:

'It was blowin' a half-gale from the nor'ard; the gulls had all taken to the meshes, and water was breakin' in sheets of spray over the South Breydon Wall, which I had to dodge as best I could—just the weather, though, for suffin' unexpected turnin' up. I had my old double gun, and was makin' poor headway towards the Stone corner, when I suddenly see a vast number of pigeons comin' athort the meshes and Breydon, a reglar cloud on 'em—them old rough-feathered Norwegians. They cum straight for me, so I dodged down behind the wall and lay for 'em. It ain't often you meet with a big flock like that, though I hev seen 'em so thick and extensive that they cast a big shadow on the ground. I got a shot with each barrel into the thick of 'em, and down dropped eight; I oughter got a skepful. The old dog had a risky time retrievin' them, it bein' so rough.

'Thinks I, that ain't so bad; it means at least four shillin's —earnt afore breakfast. So off I went with 'em to Bob Durrant, quite satisfied if he offered me sixpence a-piece.

'"Here, Durrant," I says to him, "can you do with a few wood-pigeons?"

'"Ah! that I can," says he. "I've got an order on for some, and badly wanted a few more to make up the complement."

'So I handed 'em, one by one, out of my pockets, a bit ruffled, but that didn't matter; he was rather busy at the time, but snatched 'em each by a wing and threw 'em on the stall.

'"Well, what are they worth?" I axes him.

'"Well, they feel fairly heavy birds; I'll give you eightpence apiece," says he, and handed me the money over. I reckon that them pigeons must have come along the coast-line, hevin' landed perhaps on the Yorkshire or Lincolnshire fields. You may be sure that the next lot of pigeons I could lay hold of I took up to Durrant's stall.

' " Well, Whiley, I don't want any more pigeons just yet," says he. " Them birds you brought me the other day were all *horse-beans* ! "

' Them warmin no doubt had bin hevin' a bean-feast on their way south,' added Whiley, ' and there was hundreds and hundreds in that flock.' . . .

It was usually an amusing experience to be in the company of bird-folk when a rare visitor was laid out for inspection—dealers, would-be purchasers, and those who were interested in, or indifferent as to, results of negotiations. Some would praise a specimen, others belittle it ; and their opinions upon an accomplished deal were worth hearing. When Breydon folk were interested in the matter it was usual for a bargain-maker to treat his partner in the deal, and sometimes all the onlookers. A certain keen collector wasted considerable time in pointing out defects in a bird, however badly in his own mind he wanted it. If this did not answer, he would haggle over the value of it—to him.

As an example : Whiley, who keenly studied the various gulls, now and then dropped upon a rarity. He shot a little gull, and took it to B—— D—— asking two shillings for it. B—— referred to two examples which he already possessed ; and with his usual diplomacy talked of various other birds, evidently with a view of tiring the shooter out, who might be solicitous of closing the deal. B—— D—— should have been a shunter in a signal-box, as he was always very keen on side-issues. Whiley was becoming bored—a shilling, fifteen-pence were refused.

' I'll give you eighteen-pence for it,' at length conceded B——.

' I'll chuck it away first afore you'll hev it for that ! ' said W——.

B—— went on with his haggling, and in the midst of it I came on the scene, when Whiley, turning to me, informed me how long they had been arguing over the bird, and for nearly an hour over a paltry sixpence. Knowing B——'s idiosyncrasies and methods, I inquired :

' What do you really want for it ? '

' Two shillin's,' replied Whiley, ' and well worth it too, takin' into consideration shew-leather, powder and shot, loss o' time (includin' argiments), and a two-mile walk to the pier-head, and back.'

' Quite right, too,' I replied, and although it was farthest from my desire to possess the bird, I put my hand in my pocket

THE NOTED GAME STALL

DURRANT: 'A NICE WEIGHTY FOWL, MY BOY!'

remarking :

'Let me have it, and here's the two bob.'

'Oh, no, you won't ! ' snapped B——, who snatched at the gull, laying two very warm shillings, which he had been holding all the while, on the counter. B—— very much disliked a rival.

The Breydon fraternity were an exclusive and conservative lot, and greatly averse to the incoming of any new gunning recruits, more especially if they were not of the sort that needed pilots and henchmen. They tacitly claimed lordship—individually—over the mudflats, even among themselves, and they browbeat, questioned, and occasionally threatened new-comers into their domains. The Italian already referred to was intensely disliked, as he would employ no other puntsman but Quinton, who cared not the snap of a finger for any or all of them. The Italian's favourite resort was the Ship drain, near the then respectable hulk the good ship *Agnes*. He was a deliberate butcher, and very rarely failed to kill ; indeed, Quinton insists that he never knew him to once miss, so sure was his aim. His pilot found this method extremely provoking, and which was against all precedent. He once even ventured to ask him to shoot at a bunch of sleeping curlew-sandpipers. The Italian became argumentative, and was annoyed, but for once shot to please Quinton, killing eleven birds, and with a double shot following, killed the four wounded ones. Quinton sculled to the flat, and on returning with the slain made remark :

'That's suffin' *like*, sir ! '

'Abominable ! ' said the Italian. 'It's wholesale murder ! ' and was within an ace of throwing up the contract. His boatman, becoming somewhat alarmed, for his master was a very payable guest, apologized, and hoped that he would overlook his—Quinton's—little whim, which he reluctantly did.

'He was the masterpiece shot I ever see,' said Quinton ; 'why-a, one year he brought down from London a thousand cartridges, and fired seven hundred and twenty-seven shots—all at single birds, *and never once missed*.' When narrating these facts to me, as we sat chatting in his little allotment-holding, this sturdy old bird-catcher volunteered a description of some of his best birds, slain by his *own* gun.

'I ha' killed in my time eighteen black-tailed godwits, and many a curlew-sandpiper ; and allers got half a crown apiece for 'em off collectors. I once put up four good grey plovers in a bunch, and with a good shoulder-gun killed all four. I ha' got several Kentish plovers at different times—nobby little things they are too. Once old " Brusher " Broom passed my punt, hevin' got his eye on two spotted shanks [very rare visitors to Breydon], but he dallied too long, and up they got, and was makin' off when my Italian killed 'em both at one shot, one bird passing the other as he pulled the trigger. He didn't want 'em ; but I'd much rather have shot *them* myself.'

Quinton and a certain bird-dealer figured in quite a series of lively incidents ; one of these, showing the human tendency to a peculiar elasticity of conscience, when opportunity offered. As the aggrieved party, let Quinton relate the story himself :

' I was working a few years ago on my allotment, when I chanced to spot a woodchat shrike on the may-trees [hawthorns]. I'd got the bird well in my eye from looking in the dealer's bird-books. I know'd and had shot red-backed shrikes and grey shrikes, but never before see a woodchat. The bird-dealer, who was in the garden with me chatting, when I pointed it out to him, also reckernized it. I kept a gun allers handy in the shed in them days, and loaden ; so I got a pop at the bird afore it had decided we was dangerous. I hit it, too, but it dropped wounded in the rough stuff below, and got into a quickset hedge ; but when I reached the spot it had vanished, and for a blessed hour we hunted for it. Mr. Bird-man was nosin' around, but said very little—keepin' what you may say his own counsel. At last I gave it up, but he said as he'd try *his* luck a bit longer ; he comes back later sayin' the bird must hev got clean away—said it quiet-like, as if it didn't much matter. When I groused a bit, he put on a show of bein' as vexed as I was. But I very much suspicioned him.'

Some years after this little episode, when chatting with Quinton, whom the since-deceased dealer had instructed to burn all his papers and private books, he—Quinton—pointed out to me an entry in a sort of diary which read :

' One woodchat shrike. Gardens. Yarmo'. 17th May, 1885.'

It leaked out some years later, from a reliable source, that after a long search the dead bird was discovered. It was seen by this individual, and later a note to the effect that the bird had changed hands for five pounds. Quinton related the incident with perfect good-humour.

Very few Norfolk collections appear to have possessed a woodchat shrike ; among the several collections sold in recent years I have traced but two. At Mr. Masters' sale in Norwich, in 1886, a grey shrike, a woodchat (not authenticated), and a number of tits (all in one case) realized twenty-seven shillings and sixpence ; in 1891, at Frere's sale at Burston, two red-backed shrikes, a grey shrike, and a woodchat (in one case) made three guineas.

Norfolk is not accredited with many of this species, which may be briefly mentioned as follows: a somewhat doubtful record is given of a pair having nested and reared young ones at Beachemwell, near Swaffham, a fairly likely place. Mr. J. D. Hoy reported a Swaffham example as being in the collection of the Rev. Robert Hamond, with three others, his communication being dated March 16th 1831. The Pagets give one example as killed at Bradwell, near Yarmouth, in April 1829; and Mr. J. H. Gurney is accredited with possessing another in his collection, shot near Yarmouth in April 1859. The latest record of one is dated in 1885, undoubtedly the woodchat that passed through our bird-dealer's hands. I am not quite sure, but believe this bird was purchased by Mr. Gurney. . . .

Local bird-stuffers, in years gone by, had remarkable opportunities put in their way by the far greater quantities of birds frequenting the neighbourhood, and by overhauling the two or three game-dealers' stalls which then obtained, and also by handling the birds brought to their own establishments by illiterate gunners who had, in an indifferent manner, observed something dissimilar in the plumage, or the length, or the peculiarity of its extremities, in some fowl or small wader taken among the common herd. It was to their advantage to appear indifferent and apathetic; to belittle the fowler's anticipations by offering a paltry sum, although weighing up in their own minds its potential worth to a likely customer. If an amateur gunner called and produced a bird whose species, or value he did not know, it was not, as a rule, readily named for him, nor did the stuffer 'jump to' at once, but would cautiously make an offer for it, and not infrequently secure a prize by a little roundabout circumvention. Wodehouse was quite within the truth when he said that 'collectors who would not steal a loaf if they were starving might, and did, fall before the temptation of a coveted curio'. The game-dealers, who set greater store upon their hares, pheasants, and partridges, rarely troubled to identify unusual specimens: a bittern, a Bewick's swan, or a peregrine was showier, and saleable on sight. I myself have observed the spotted shank, the black-tailed godwit, and other interesting birds tied by the neck with a bit of coarse string among a bunch of grey plovers, or another of knots and redshanks among which a rare sandpiper was suspended. The loose lots shot out of wild-fowlers' handkerchiefs, e.g. stints and dotterels, were carefully rummaged on Saturday mornings, or any day of the week in severe frosty weather, by Harvey, Carter, George Smith, Dye, Lowne, and others; and in the decades before these an older school of bird-men turned over the exhibits of Watson, of Fuller's Hill, Alfred Harvey's forebears and others, including Girdlestone, Lilly Wigg, Youell, and their contemporaries, whose names appear in Stevenson's *Birds of Norfolk.* The dealers in rare birds were no worse than speculators who haunt auction-rooms for antiques and for bargains; indeed, they were by no means so well versed in deception and knavery, and whose clients were many degrees simpler.

As an illustration of the above remarks, the following may be of interest: a certain taxidermist, long since gone to his reward, had an excellent specimen of the little tern taken to him for preservation. The shooter had set his heart upon encasing this bird, and to make sure of its identity had clipped off the extreme end of a certain toe. On calling for the bird again, the stuffer stood on the counter before him a far less perfect specimen.

'That's not my bird!' declared H——, and refused to accept it. This seemed to upset the stuffer, who began to resent the tone of the other's remarks. Said he:

'It's yours, and if you won't take it, or pay for it, I'll sue you for the work done.' The customer insisted on the stuffer having another look round his workshop, but without result; so he somewhat meekly offered him two stuffed crested grebes, that had been left on his hands, to make up for the other's disappointment.

'Very well, then,' said H——. 'I'll take the tern; and trot round with it to some of the bird people, *and show you up*!' On so saying, he made to grab it, but the astonished stuffer was a little too quick for him; and to save further complication asked H—— to put his value on the lost bird, which H—— did, with a little interest added. More than one bird have I known, or suspected, get into the wrong but wealthier hands, to be reported missing—mice, and the cat in particular, being blamed for the 'mishaps'.

Dan —— was a rough old marshman who, whenever he went to town, liked to indulge in a comfortable sleep, and allow his horse to find its way home along the marsh roads without any assistance on his part, to wake up when he arrived at his own door. He also made a dead set against all mushroom collectors, at least off *his* marshes. He was somewhat addicted to shooting fowl that were a little too venturesome for their own safety. One day he slew a beautiful avocet, and was persuaded to have it preserved. It was sent some distance to be set up. For a long time he was unable to get the bird back home—for years, in fact, and had at length given up all hope of ever seeing it again. The excuse given was that it had been accidentally destroyed ; and he had been too indolent to county court the taxidermist for the value of the bird. One day, in a certain town was opened an exhibition under the auspices of east coast nabobs ; a section of it was devoted to the stuffer's art. Ben Dye and I were inspecting the show when he suddenly stopped in front of an excellently preserved avocet, and made remark :

'I know that bird,' and making reference to a distinctive identity mark, and knowing the circumstances of its shooting, and subsequent trouble, added, 'That's Dan's bird.' He later saw the old marshman, and persuaded him to visit the exhibition ; Dan walked straight to the taxidermical exhibits, and having closely inspected it, seized the case, and putting it under his arm walked out. Dan was challenged by the stuffer and door-keeper, but held his own.

'Send your bill in if you like, but the bard's mine, and I'm goin' to hev it ; you'll know my face if you look straight into it.' Anyone who had once seen Dan's hairy face when he was angry would not be likely soon to forget him. . . .

On May 3rd 1887 five avocets, daintiest of our wading birds, visited Breydon, putting all the gunmen of every degree into a state of great excitation. Before nightfall it was rumoured abroad that Pintail Thomas and Jimmy Hurr had secured one. My old chum Ben Dye and myself were early afloat on the following morning, by sunrise, in spite of its being the close season, and to the great perturbation of Joseph Buddery, the pseudo Bird Watcher, who was keenly on the alert ; he was in a measure self-appointed for the duty, and was usually dodging about the walls endeavouring to obtain a 'case'. The fraternity stoutly alleged that he was awarded a commission on any 'case' he obtained. Dye and myself were by no means 'gentlemen gunners' ; our outfit was, in the Breydon man's estimation, 'no great shakes'. As we shoved off in the dilapidated old punt we agreed to share and share alike—in kind or in values, having regard to the avocets in question. On rounding the Half-mile Point, two Breydoners in a gun-punt could be seen skulking around the five-stake 'lumps', a stretch of mud slightly higher than the surrounding flats, a favourite resort both of birds and fowlers near the top of the tide when the lower muds were covered. We took no notice of the fowlers, as the avocets could be seen in closer proximity to them than ourselves; so we rowed up-channel to the Ship drain, and hitched our painters to the rusty chain-plates on the side of the old ship *Agnes*, and lay-to for concealment, as many an ancient Breydoner in the 'seventies had done before us. At that time the hulk loomed up like a rock among the mudflats, forming an excellent hiding-place for those who moored to it. It might have remained intact to this day but for the saws and hatchets used upon her when driftwood was scarce.

The loud boom of a punt-gun disturbed the quietude, as well as the gulls that had not yet been a-wing for their breakfast foraging. Redshanks and curlews clamoured in affright. A puff of white smoke hung around the punt of Pintail.

'Look out, Ben!' said I. 'Lay low—here comes a parcel of oyster-catchers straight for us,' an excusable blunder to make at first glance. As they came nearer, 'No!' cried Ben, 'they're avocets!'

It was but the matter of a few moments ere they had flown within range of our guns. I fired, and down dropped the leading bird into the drain, and began to float upwards on the tide. Ben was so excited on sight of the approaching birds that he forgot to try his hand at the others, but put the gun across my shoulder, and promptly settled the poor wounded thing. He evidently meant making sure of one bird, and to this day claims the *honour* of killing it: to that he is perfectly welcome. The explosion from his gun badly hurt the drum of my right ear, which was out of action for several days after.

We recovered the beautiful corpse, and having lifted it by the bill, and shaken the water off its plumage, laid it on the fore-deck to admire it. Ben begrudgingly acknowledged I had had first shot, but insisted that he really must have it for his small collection.

'It's my bird,' said I, 'according to the rules of war. I'd like to have it stuffed.'

'But you don't collect,' he insisted, 'and I do.'

'Very well,' I acquiesced, 'what's it worth?' He replied that it was worth thirty shillings; Ben never bid extravagantly at any time for specimens, but would argue and barter for over an hour on occasion when it suited him for a bird worth a shilling.

'We had better toss up for it,' said I. 'Here's a button—

fifteen shillings or the bird; concave side has it.' Ben's excitement grew as we tossed for possession, and he won the bird. He had scarcely finished wrapping it up in wadding and a newspaper, and pushed it under the fore-deck for safety, when a boat, which we had not noticed approaching us, sharply bumped into ours, and the high tenor voice of Jimmy Hurr informed us tartly:

'That's our bird—and we'll be very pleased if you'll fork it out!'

'You'll have no bird of ours!' responded Ben. 'If it's yours, why didn't you kill it when you fired in the five-stake drain at the flock of four? Your old gas-pipe won't kill at half a mile distance!'

High words followed between Ben, Pintail, and Jimmy, in arguing the rights of ownership, each glaring defiance. I sat, half-amused, with one hand in my pocket, jinking the six half-crowns, wondering why they left me out of the question. Jimmy Hurr, who was the most aggressive, rose in his punt, and with a Breydonian epithet, threatened to take the avocet. Ben also rose with every feather up, seized an oar, and promised to bring it down on top of Jimmy's head. He also prepared to bayonet Pintail Thomas with it if he made any move towards piracy. There seemed to have arisen a great peace, negotiations having come to a standstill.

'Now, look here,' I said, intervening, 'let's sort the little matter over quietly; what sized shots did you put in your cannon?'

'Fours,' both of them promptly responded.

'Very well, then,' said I, 'we are using fives. You shall see the bird skinned in Ben's bake-office, and we'll all abide by the result.' This bit of Solomonizing slightly mollified them. So it happened that in the evening, when Ben skinned the poor thing, for he stuffed his own birds, nothing but number five shot were picked out by the skinning-knife. Even then the two old Breydoners groused and grumbled about young fellows coming up there and taking the bread out of other people's mouths.

The visits to Breydon by avocets to-day are extremely rare; occasionally a year passes without seeing one. R. Fielding Harmer thus records the fate of these 1887 avocets: 'Five is the greatest number of avocets seen at one time here. . . . Four of them were shot in three discharges. These birds are seen in pairs or singly; whilst spoonbills are generally found singly.' On May 5th 1895 there were no less than sixteen spoonbills feeding together upon the mudflats, at a very short distance from my punt: in June 1905 I took poor old Ben with me in the punt to see nine avocets feeding upon the mud near the edge of the Channel, until they were floated off by the tide; whereupon they swam away most gracefully in line over a gently undulating tide. A certain gunner—one who had classed himself as a 'gentleman gunner'—in my hearing, and that of Jary the Bird Watcher, whose punt was lying near mine, offered him a sovereign to clear out. I promptly settled the argument by rowing close up to the birds and putting them to flight. I instantly said to Ben, who at that period was fast becoming blind, 'Look up at the lowering sun and you'll see something!' He did, and immediately said, 'I now saw some spots going over it.' They were the avocets. It may be interesting to add that this delightful species at one time regularly bred in Norfolk, particularly at Salthouse and Horsey, where they nested until 1818. They also nested as near Yarmouth as the Seven Mile House on the Bure marshes; these are so dry to-day that lapwings, once so common there, do not now nest thereabouts.

A characteristic story of Breydonian jealousy may be cited.

During a sharp spell of frost in the winter of 1891 a parcel of some twenty pochards dropped into a wake in the ice on Breydon. There were two patches of particularly luxuriant *Zostera* where these birds were usually looked for when driven into the neighbourhood by stress of weather: one patch was near the Upper Stile, a landmark on the North Wall; the other nearer the big rond. Fred Clarke was at work upon the mill-sails at Banham's Mill—that most predominating Breydon landmark, and had seen the birds alight at the farther pool. He was quite aware that if disturbed thereat they would make for the wake, which happened to be open at the time. Fielding Harmer was doing his best to push his punt sufficiently near to the Upper Stile to get a shot. Clarke, in telling me the story, said that he was reported as having 'clumb down the mill-sails'. He had already got his punt and gun in readiness in case the pochards came to the second-named pool—which they did. He paddled off after them, and made a notable shot, killing and maiming some twenty of them. According to Clarke's story, Harmer, with his usually lordly impulses, and greatly annoyed at losing a shot, wrote to the late Sir ——, then owner of the mill and surrounding marshes, suggesting that Fred was wasting *his* time. Did he know it?

A reply came promptly to the effect that he (Sir ——) had

sent his agent down to inspect the work, which Clarke had done most satisfactorily, and well within the time agreed upon in the contract.

One other story may be added to this somewhat patchwork chapter ; its title, I think, justifies its insertion. My old chum Dye, who has shared so many of my earlier escapades, still possesses a small collection of choice Norfolk birds, among them the avocet, an historic stilt plover, adult spotted redshanks, Pallas's sand-grouse, white-winged black tern, and several others. Once in a while he manages to add a new bird ; he has been blind for several years, but lives among his birds and upon his memories of former days, by marsh and sand-dune and the mudflats of Breydon.

In the beginning of December, a few years ago, a smelt-catcher who was rowing downstream on the Bure observed a tall, dark bird pottering about at the muddy edge of the river. On reaching his landing place at Runham Vauxhall he informed a neighbour next-door, who carried a gun, that 'he had ketched sight of what had fared to him like an old cormorant'. This neighbour, who was a cowman, went along the bank up-river, the smelter returning by boat ; but before they could get near enough to the bird it flew up, and crossing the river, alighted on the other side in a turnip-grown marsh, just beyond the north wall of the Bure. The smelter put his friend over ; and this time the cowman made a successful shot. They at once decided it was not a cormorant, the beak and legs convincing them, a mistake made owing to the failing light.

It was taken to Lowne, the bird-stuffer, who, telling its owner that it was that bird which was usually described as the 'black curlew', offered him five shillings for it. Few usurers could have beaten a Yarmouth bird-man at a deal. The cowman demurred, and, scratching his head, said that he would have it stuffed ; he didn't see why he shouldn't have a stuffed bird like other men had.

The news of the stranger quickly got wind among the fraternity, and the dealers buttonholed the cowman, but for a long time to no purpose. My blind chum at length heard of it ; and, having ascertained where the cowman lived—at the far end of the River road—set off on his two-mile trudge on a dreary wet night, groping his way along the last half-mile with his left hand and stick tapping the walls and fences, the sullen Bure on his right being but a few yards away. Fumbling his way, down the back passage, he stopped to listen, when he heard familiar voices, and was speedily shown the door he wanted.

A very guarded conversation began on either side, the cowman being evasive, the bird-man cautious, and striking out upon various side-issues as usual. ‘ Now then, what's your business ? ’ he asked Ben, being a man of quick moods and direct action. Ben replied, ‘ I came to hear something about the glossy ibis that they told me you'd got.’

‘ Well,’ said the owner, ‘ I don't particularly want the bird myself, but I thought for once I'd have somethin' to show on the table. I know'd Lowne's offer of five bob worn't a very 'stravagant one ; but that fare his way. Still, what sort of walue do you put upon it ? ’ This brought Ben up to the scratch at once, and he endeavoured to keep himself in check and not to let the slayer of the ibis see his desire to have it. But Ben's tremor of voice belied him.

‘ Well,’ said Ben, ‘ I've only one price to offer you, so you'll know.’

‘ Go on,’ said the gunner coolly.

‘ That's all I'm prepared to give you for it,’ said Ben, producing two pounds, and dropping the gold chinking upon the table. ‘ Yes, or no ? ’

The cowman demurred for a few minutes, and then made remark, ‘ Very well, then. Them two bits of gold, as far as I can see, will look jist as nice in my pocket as yours. Come on ! But if I let you have it, you will have to pay for the stuffin'.’

‘ Oh, yes, certainly, I'll do *that* ; you make out a receipt, and here's a stamp.’ The bill was made out and receipted. ‘ I shall want you to go along o' me to-morrer mornmg to Mr. Lowne's.’ They went next morning to the bird-stuffer's and declared the deal, Ben making remark, ‘ You see the bird's mine, let me have it as soon as possible, and you'll have your money for your work.’

The taxidermist, who had been in high hopes of securing the specimen for himself, was greatly incensed, and never after forgave his rival for this little bit of sharp practice.

CHAPTER X

BREYDONIAN HUMOURS

' These enchantments are medicinal, they sober and heal us. These are plain pleasures, kindly and native to us. We come to our own, and make friends with matter, which the ambitious chatter of the schools would persuade us to despise. . . . Cities give not the human senses room enough.'

—R. W. EMERSON

NOTWITHSTANDING the fact that many of my old Breydon friends often stood upon the verge of poverty, and that the wild life they led was ever in the shadow of embarrassment, they, as a rule, kept a stiff lip ; they made light of misfortune and adversity, and did their best to keep clear of the relief authorities. Their means of livelihood, although so varied, were much affected by conditions of weather, the caprice of bird migrations, and the vagaries of fish life. Little shopkeepers who catered for them often allowed ' their little accounts ' to run in bad times, resting assured such debts would be liquidated when they met with ' a run o' luck ' : a spoonbill, a big slaughter of mallard and wigeon, a pectoral sandpiper, or a ' rattling good catch ' of smelts, would at once wipe off part—probably all—their debts. When a chum could help another who might be worse off than himself he willingly did so, if it meant only the loan of a pipeful of tobacco.

A gunner very rarely pawned his gun, and then must have been in deep distress to do so ; but many a beautifully made eel-spear, the pride of old Flaxman the blacksmith (and in odd cases never paid for by the eel-man for whom it was made), went to the sign of the three golden balls. Flaxman possessed a kind heart behind that frayed leather apron. ' He might cuss a bit,' said an aged eel-catcher, ' but he meant nothin' by it in partickler, though he said some *cruel* things ! '

One of the humours of the Breydon man was his great dislike to being overlooked at his work, or even when preparing for it ; and as to his success, he, as a rule, unless he had idled a little too long at the tap-room, kept that to himself. They watched each other, however ; and whenever a fellow eel-picker happened to bring to the scale a somewhat unexpected weight of eels, the rest of them were on the alert, for although there was a certain unwritten law of trespass, the mud and the water many of them considered the property of all, with regard to the fishes. One fellow who started to pick in the Channel, which was not at that time the practice, 'lit lucky'; another, on observing him remarkably busy, from his 'pitch' across the mudflats, drew his stakes, where he had been babbing, rowed round him to have a look, but the first-named immediately marked his spot and rowed away. It goes without saying that there was a spirit of badgering very prevalent, more especially when a crowd congregated in some favourite bar; this sometimes led to considerable argument and rivalry, and when tongues were loosened much boasting and vaunting ensued in enlarging upon personal prowess, while doughty deeds of fowl-slaughter and smelt-capture were subject to exaggeration. When drink was in wit was out; and an occasional rough and tumble fight was indulged in upon the Green, which ended up with black eyes and knuckles that needed strips of plaster. The landlord had his work cut out in endeavouring to bring peace to the excited, hilarious crowd. Lucky Bob met me one afternoon as I reached my boat-shed; he had just shut the door of the yacht-shed opposite. I looked at him; he returned the compliment as well as he was able to do.

'Good gracious!' said I, astonished at the two swollen and blackened eyes that he had but recently acquired, 'what in the world have you been up to?'

'Well, young Patt'son,' he said, puckering his swollen lips in a grim smile, 'old Fred Baldry [the last of the local professional yachtsmen] jist now gi' me 'em.'

'Tell us about it, old chap,' I asked.

'Well,' said he, 'Baldry an' me ain't hit it off werry well lately; he's a —— down-charger if he gets his knife into anybody—narkin' an' grinnin', till yer very flesh crawl. Then it come to a case for settlement, somehow. You can't summon a man for narkin', nor nothin' else, perwidin' you ain't got a witness.'

'But I always thought you were a bit of a bruiser?'

'Maybe,' he admitted; 'and when it comes to yer own size an' weight I think I can more 'an hold my own. But look at the length of his arm? I couldn't get one in nohow.'

Baldry was at the time over seventy years of age; in his prime he had stood over six feet, and had the physique of a guardsman. I have seen him carry a yacht's mast which took two men to lift it on his shoulder and walk away with it. For all that, the tussle in the yacht-shed, with its raffle of shavings, fish-trunks, spars, paint-tins, and other sundries scattered about the place, must have been a lively one indeed. These men usually settled a grievance with their ready, hard-knotted fists, and without the aid of lawyers or magistrates; and on finding himself a victor, the winner almost invariably bettered his position by taking the loser to the tap-room and treating him; if the remedy needed repetition, probably the pair of them would get perfectly fuddled and help each other home, to the great delight of those who had umpired or encouraged the fighters.

One of the outstanding characters who frequented the vicinity of Breydon and the Cobholm marshes was a gentleman known as 'Punt' Palmer; he was of medium height and of comfortable girth. He owned the finest punt in the county; it had been built by Albert Beckett on beautiful lines, and of the finest mahogany and other superior woods. His punt-gun was its equal for workmanship and value; he kept it more for show than use, and in all the years I knew him he very rarely used it on Breydon, nor did I ever hear much of his accomplishments as a shot, although he delighted to tell of his marksmanship among the brent geese in the Scottish lochs. 'Boy,' said he to me one day, 'never miss a shot at an old Scotch goose; it's the finest bird on the table.'

There are two opinions amongst gunners on that bird's good qualities. The boat- and yacht-sheds adjoining Breydon were built for him by Albert Beckett and my old Breydonian mentor, the pleasant little shoemaker and student of the classics, Ben Harwood. Ben much amused me, for when knocking in a nail he would be reciting how heroic Greeks and Romans fought and died. Between these sheds and the great Breydon bridge was a long row of landing-stages, recently destroyed. In the palmier days these sheds and stages were virtually scrambled for by local yachtsmen and punt-gunners; and from them the owner derived a comfortable revenue. The bridge entirely annihilated local yachting.

R. Fielding Harmer was an arresting personality. His Breydonian get-up, his sedate mien, and impressive airs made one take a second look at him as he strode like a Sir Walter Raleigh to his wet dock of a boat-house. Nicholas Everitt, in *Broadland Sport*, describes him as 'the present father of scientific puntsmen . . . an authority few would dare venture to contradict'. This was written in 1902. He was not held in great esteem by the professional punt-gunners; and over their mugs and pewters they not seldom ventured to discuss him, and that very freely. They resented what they thought his arrogance and authoritative mannerisms.

'They uster call him " Potty ",' said Little Stork Thacker, 'and he wanted to boss the whole of Breydon. Of course, it wos as much ours, and p'r'aps more 'an it wos his, for we come for a livin', and he come to play. Still, he wos all right to me; he liked me to see to the punt, and help him with the big gun, me bein' small, didn't take up much room in the boat, which worn't over big; besides, he used to like me yarnin' about the ice, and birds, and flightin', and that. But I'll own 'tworn't everybody as could stan' him, 'specially when he tried his best, sometimes, to shove in wheer another gunner orter bin let alone; and there wos *words*! They swore pritty promiscuss when he jined the Protection of Birds' Show—you know what I mean—when he started to harp on the close season business, jist arter he shot his t'ree (three) spunebills. They rounded on me in the " Bowlin' Green " pub, and says as how old Harvey orter hev stuffed *me*, and stuck me an' Harmer in the case with 'em—what's now in Yarmith Museum, with the date and Harmer's name to 'em. How could I help Harmer's ways? It wos my livin' partly seein' arter his boat an' gun. You orter heerd old Pero an' Ben Dye cussin' tremenjuss over it; they said as Harmer hed got all *he* wanted, and the poor man might go to the wall, or the devil, for all he cared! They all cheered old Pero, becos he opened his mouth widest; and he might hev swum in beer, arter he'd stowed away as much as his innerds would hold alriddy.

'I couldn't help laughin' inside, like,' went on Thacker, 'one day when we wos both out with the old gun. It was blowin' pritty nigh a gale from the nor'ard, and Breydon wos like a sea. So we drawed up the North Wall drain, round by the pump-mill corner and moored agin' the corner of Banham's rond. There wos a few fowl about, but terrible shy, and theer wos more 'an a brevell of water where we wos. As we sits a-chattin', and samplin' two kinds o' bottles, a big soft hat cum sailin' over the wall on the wind like a hin-harrier, and after topplin' over two or three times, dropped on the water like a basin, mouth up'ards.

'" What the dowse! " says I, and hed more 'an half a mind to take a shot at it, when, puffin' and blowin', up the wall clomb a mesh-chap—he was racin' arter his old hat.

'" Hullo, you chaps! " says he, spottin' us staked below the wall. " Now look sharp afore that d——d old hat o' mine's lost."

'"You might ha' said please," says I, and looks at Harmer, who didn't like no orders from nobody; and the old rag of a hat was sailin' away like a lugger afore a squall. Harmer says nothin', but hauls out the stakes, and away we goes arter the greasy old thing, what was gettin' a bit waterlogged; and jist afore we gets to Duffell's drain he grabs it, and bangs the wet off and out on it on the fore-deck. When we gets back to the wall, arter a terrible pull, Harmer hands up the hat to the mesh-chap, without a word; and we starts shovin' to our old spot.

'"Half a mo', guv'nor!" says the feller, fumblin' in his pocket. "Here," he says, "hold yer hat," and throws a penny what fell on the floor of the punt. "When you get ashore *get yourself a drink.*" Thet was the time when you could get a half-pint for a penny. Harmer laughed when the chap wos gone, and often told the yarn aginst hisself.'

Little Stork was gossiping with me against the Malthouse Corner, whereat, aforetime, several of the punts were berthed, the most notable of which were Pintail's and Silky Watson's.

'You mentioned Pero,' I made remark; 'he got drinks without asking for them.'

'Oh, yes,' went on Thacker, 'but he cadged one afore he gave that opinion' (above accredited to him). 'Nobody really thought much of poor old Pero; if theer was a crooky side, he fared mostly to find it. Couldn't help it—born in him; all we cared about him was his bein' allers riddy to patch up an old boat, perwidin' we paid for a drink fust, *and* last. Poor chap, he allers fared hard up. One May-time, in them years ago, when French petridges cum over from athort the sea—Mister Harmer allers said they didn't—he swore they got excited-like at the pairin' season, an' flew out seawards, an' then gettin' skeered, turned back; one May-time, as I was a-sayin', some on 'em came over an' got in a rare muddle.

'It fared that one of the shrimpers was out in the Roads, it bein' a bit hazy, when he see five o' these sort o' petridges fall all together, tired out, into the sea, and by a little artful sailin' got clost to 'em, and nabbed the lot as they tried to swim, breakin' theer necks. When he got to the "Bowlin' Green" staithe, where he allers moored, Pero was leanin' on the wall, and spots the petridges layin' dead in a sieve.

'"Hullo!" says he, "some rum shrimps, old Balls! Why, petridge-shootin's over long ago, and you ha' bin a-poarchin' in rum stubbles."

'"Yes, bor, yes," says the shrimper. "I hev," and told him the story.

'"Whatcher goin' to do with 'em?" Pero axes.

'"Take 'em home to the old woman, to cook," says Balls.

'"Look here, old chap," says Pero, "let me take 'em home; I'll pluck an' dress 'em for yer, and save you the trouble; an' 'on't charge yer nothin' if you let me hev the feathers—to put in a piller."

'The shrimper, like a fule, handed 'em up to Pero; he didn't know *him* as we chaps did; and that was the last he ever saw of 'em. Old "Peko" Balls dussent say much about the job to us chaps, or he'd have never have heerd the last of it. If you lost an oar or a shovin' pole, you'd only to tell him what you wanted; he'd scour the back-ways for a pole standin' idle, or an old smack's-boat's oar waitin' to be shortened, and you'd hev a new one arter breakfast next mornin'. By religgen he wos a Red Injin.'

To revert to Palmer and Harmer. There had long existed a feud between them; neither could say a good word for the other. One evening at closing-in time a large flock of wigeon had alighted in the main Channel near a flat, and were busily feeding upon the *Zostera* that grew even there in those days. Palmer was strolling beside the wall enjoying his pipe and the eventide when he discerned a punt-gunner, lying low in his boat, quietly sculling up to get within shot of the fowl. Mistaking the punter in the gloaming for Fielding Harmer an evil spirit entered the jovial Punt Palmer, and inspired him to trot off as fast as his legs would carry him, on the grassy wall-slope, to his shed. Seizing a double-barrelled gun, away he went back, with Jimmy Hurr some little way behind him. Jimmy, on peering over the wall, saw the blunder, but loving a rumpus, said nothing and laid low. Arrived at the Mile Point, exactly opposite to the now all-attentive puntsman, who was crouching for a 'pull', Palmer fired two shots in quick succession behind the wall; the birds rose in a body.

A volume of mixed broad Norfolk and choice tap-room linguistics rent the air, produced by the infuriated gunner. At this juncture Jimmy Hurr drew up to Palmer:

'Whatever have you been shooting at, sir?' he asked.

'Oh, I only fired at a hawk, Jimmy,' replied Palmer.

'What, at this time o' the evening, sir? Besides, your gun didn't bark as if you'd put shot into it,' said Jimmy.

'That scamp over there—Fielding Harmer,' snorted Punt Palmer, 'was laying at some fowl, and I've spoilt his shot for him. I've long waited to give him his deserts.'

'Why, sir,' expostulated Hurr, 'you've gone and done

suffin' for yerself, and done a poor man out of his children's dinner; why, it's old Fiddler Goodens (who was still busy coining fresh lurid phrases); you'll have to pay for this, sir.'

'Good gracious, Jimmy,' said Palmer, 'you run and shut the boat-house doors, and put the window shutters to; he'll go and blow the whole dam lot out!'

Goodens certainly was likely to take the law into his own hands, and get value for his lost 'gains' in mischief, unless matters could be comfortably adjusted. Jimmy was deputed to act as peacemaker, and to bring Goodens to Punt Palmer's fortress. Goodens came along, and had his say, spicing his indignation with his opinions on the subject of 'live and let live'. Palmer wanted to know how many ducks he—Fiddler—reckoned he had lost by the error and interruption—'half a dozen wigeon?'

'Half a dozen be ——!' said Fiddler; 'twenty is more the figure I lost; and at a shillin' a time, you can square it—not a farden less!' And Palmer squared it.

One of the readiest-witted Breydoners of my acquaintance, who, for a change, transferred his activities for some months to the Tyne, on returning to Yarmouth came across me, and told me a few of his experiences.

'You know,' said he, 'round about Newcastle you get some real good shrimping, and more eels in the pots than ever you can get here nowadays. Big steamers and sailing ships run in and out of the Tyne, some on 'em drawing in with muck stickin' to their bottoms arter long voyages in warm waters—weeds, barnacles, whiskers [zoophytes, etc.], and spongy things and worams. Big salmon, you know, come up there from the sea, and play and root about under them bottoms; you can see 'em work up'ards, and then flap and splash when they catch sight of yer. I had a longish bamboo pole with cod-hooks fastened on it, and useter hook 'em in the gills, or anywhere handy, as they come scuttering along. It was poachin', nothin' more nor less, but like all us old Breydoners, I was pretty artful, and never got copped by the police.

'While I was busy one day beside the big ship *Mauretania*—she was built and launched theer—and was doin' all right, I hears a voice from up'ards.

'"What are you up to?" shouts a leather-lunged gentleman; and on lookin' up I sees a brass-bound cap with the mate or skipper's face peepin' beneath it.

'"Nothin', sir. No harm," says I; "only a little bit o'

fishin', which I got leave from the pilot, if I didn't run foul of or shift yer moorin' ropes."

'"Don't you know," he axes, "I'm the captain of the *Mauretania* ?"

'"I *didn't* know, sir," says I, "but I can go one better 'an you, sir ; why, don't you know I'm the *owner* of this d——d little shrimp-boat ?"'

Continuing his yarn, my white-headed friend remarked : 'One August Sunday morning, when the salmon were still in season, I was out after a few. It happened, after the removal of the big ship from Armstrong's, they'd shifted the stages and left a great hole ; inter that hole crowded a reg'lar mass of salmon—after some kind o' mud-worm, no doubt. By keerful movin' around I hooked no less than twenty-three nice fish. I was fairly frightened at my luck. Well, I ranged 'em on the floor of the boat, coverin' 'em with nets an' old sails, and rowed back to a quiet part o' the quay ; and in spite of its bein' Sunday, and a pleeceman patrollin', I managed to box the lot an' send 'em to London. Salmon was fetchin' at Newcastle—let me see, I don't exackly remember, but anyhow, I only received ten-pence ha'penny a pound for 'em at Billingsgate, *no questions bein' asked*. They know'd me ; they'd hed some afore ; and they know'd I dussent arger the point.' . . .

Ulysses Minor, who is well into the seventies of his age, still drops his eel-lines in the finer days on Breydon. When a Government employee, all his mind and spare time were devoted to hobbies of a sporting character. Gunning and babbing, mulleting and angling, draw-netting and bird-catching were some of his diversions.

Ulysses had for some years a partner or shareholder in some of his adventures ; he was a knight of the tape-measure and needle, and I have named him Sartor. Ulysses had a great inspiration ; he had read somewhere about the planting and breeding of oysters ; imagining the conditions of Breydon most suitable for a trial, he repaired to the fish-wharf and brought home in a sack a number of coarse-shelled molluscs known to local fishmongers as 'smack-oysters'.

'Breydon !' said he, with great emphasis, to Sartor, 'there isn't a place on the east coast so suitable ; clean salt water, nice musselly bottom ; we'll give the Breydon chaps a show in a month or so after we've laid 'em. We'll get plenty of spat ; and they'll fatten like hogs in a stye.' They kept their oysters in the back-yard until that eventide, some fifty yards from the mooring-place of the punt. A sack of mussels, the pick of a local catch, were—with the oysters—secretly smuggled on board and covered up, ready for the night's expedition to the famous-to-be oyster scalps.

Sartor, much the wiser of the twain, begged of Ulysses to keep away from the pub that evening; or at least to keep the expedition absolutely secret, for the main mover of the enterprise was much given to loquacity and gasconading. He went, however, having promised the strictest secrecy. But the usual thing happened when the first glass or two of beer had vanished.

'I'll have a rare surprise for ye one o' these days,' said Ulysses, 'what'll make ye open yer eyes and yer mouths as well; reg'lar take ye by storm!' At least the head of the cat was out of the bag.

In the deepening dusk of the evening they presently saw the two punters turn the corner of the Knowl, and make for one of the nearer drains, when, steadying the boat, they lifted one of the bags and began throwing something into the shallow water that ran over a shelly bottom. They then passed over the same ground and emptied another sack. They then rowed home. There was little fear of anyone observing the shells of the oysters, for the dark waters of the sea effectually hid them; and the ebb-tide, drawing its water from the flats, muddied the stream, so that the silt held in solution made discovery even more remote.

Ulysses and his friend left the molluscs to their fate until the day came that was fixed for sampling them, and hearing nothing from the old Breydon folk thought their secret had been well kept. Then came the second great day of the adventure, in the evening of which the twain, armed with mussel-dredge, passed into the night on Breydon, and began to drag for their fattened oysters. Time after time they drifted over the same stretch of ground, but only dredged up a number of rusty tins and rubbish that had not been dreamt of. It was evident that some enemy had been sowing tares. Never a mussel or an oyster was brought to the surface, and then it dawned upon the twain that some unfair play had occurred.

Day after day in the interval between the sowing and the reaping certain of these Breydon jokers had been so busy with their dredges that they had left nothing behind them. . . .

Lushington Preston, who was of some legal standing in the town, was for some years an enthusiastic amateur punt-gunner, and like others of his kind found it more profitable and of less responsibility to hire a man and his gun and punt than running a gunning establishment of his own. The punt-gunners benefited too by this arrangement. 'Gutt' Thomas, who rejoiced also in a more euphonious nickname, had by some inadvertence greatly incensed the man of law, who resolved at the first opportunity to not only make a certain 'quittance' but lower the gunner's dignity in the eyes of the fraternity. L. P. hired the services of another wild-fowler, who was to row upstream at an opportune time, 'under the moon', when Thomas was known to be getting afloat and under weigh for the flighting. Eleven champagne bottles were to be attached to a line, and anchored by a flintstone in the tidal water running close to Duffell's rond, not far from the spot where L. P.'s house-boat was moored in a creek, or grup in the rond, with its expectant owner inside it remaining out of sight. The adventure happened to be well timed. The 'mine-layer' rowed to L. P.'s boat.

Upstream in the gloaming came Thomas, and dimly espying the bobbing, undulating line of bottles, now in echelon, and now a-twister, and being a little hard of hearing he did not notice anything in the nature of a tapping of bottles together, seems to have concluded that they were a flock of tufted ducks. He laid at them, and fired his gun, the report of it informing the hidden watchers that the ruse had succeeded. They chuckled as they dimly discerned him dodging about endeavouring to find dead birds or cripples, himself the while wondering why none were to be discovered, nor did any bob up at the surface. Ten bottles had been smashed, the eleventh he discovered still bobbing upon the ripples, and, following up its tether, presently brought up certain bottle-necks with jagged edges, and finally the anchor. In silence—for he could not discern anyone to anathematize—he pocketed the affront and went on homeward vowing vengeance.

A night or two after, under the 'full o' the moon', a number of genuine fowl could be heard babbling over the 'grass' not far from the house-boat referred to. Gutt had gone up, and had waited for the tide to lift, so as to get near enough for a shot, himself and boat being in the shadows. Shortly after away came Lushington. It should be mentioned that there were many slabs of ice floating around, and taking advantage of these as a sort of screen he felt his way towards the fowl, which were not very clearly discernible; but coming along, in the light of the moon, L. was visible to the lier-in-wait. Both gradually got to within shooting distance, and just as he saw his rival preparing to shoot, Gutt's gun roared into the night. Preston rowed to his house-boat in high dudgeon, while the punter collected his quarry, and having secured all the dead, and such as were badly wounded, he started to row home, first drawing into the light streaming from the house-boat, and, holding up a brace of tufties, assured the tenant that he'd 'got several more like 'em in the boat if he cared to see 'em.'

Fielding Harmer has related a capital story of two Breydoners who got to loggerheads over a matter of prestige. Another of the Thomases, known as 'Myhill' Thomas, had a grievance against an individual of the doubtful name of 'Tinkler'—a character whom I have been unable to trace—who had shot out of his turn, having left his berth and spoilt that of Myhill's. Myhill was a well-known gunner and a customary follower-up of the early morning and the evening flights. He was of an indolent disposition, and frequently had to take his berth in a position unfavourable to his sport. Myhill swore revenge, and adopted the same tactics as Lushington had done of substituting bottles for ducks. In this case they were square-faced Schnapps, three in number. What followed was extremely like the adventures already related of his near relative Gutt Thomas and the lawyer; but here a terrific fight upon one of the muddy ronds took place between the two gunners, who fought bootless and with little clothing to encumber them. Tinkler's eyes, nose, teeth, and lips had suffered; Myhill was as severely punished, and still they fought.

Fielding Harmer stayed to see the finish of the contest, to find that Myhill came off the victor; and when the matter leaked out upon the Green, and was supplemented by the condition of the two men, and the subsequent airs assumed by Myhill, the deepest of regrets were voiced by the whole brotherhood that they had not been there to see.

The river-side publicans, three or four of whom had been Breydoners themselves, entered greatly into the ideals and amusements of the fraternity. Harry Feek, an amateur gunner, some years since was landlord of the 'Norwich Arms', which overlooked the Bure; at the rear of his premises was a long room that in all probability had been a skittle alley, but was now used for parties, clubs, and not infrequently was held in it a mock parliament, wherein matters of Breydonian interest were discussed. The frolics, and yarns told after and during the session, would have made an exciting volume.

At one of their meetings it was decreed that strong measures should be taken to abate the shore-crab nuisance, these little wretches having taken possession of the lower reaches of the river, where they had become an intolerable nuisance to the salt-water anglers, who spent part of every Sunday during the finer months capturing flounders, eel-pouts, or any other species that could get a bite at the baits between the nibblings of the said crabs. The outcome of this important meeting was that, on the following Sunday, the greatest crab-catching match in all the history of Breydon should be held. It was decreed, amid deafening applause, that anglers could fish where and how they liked within the boundaries stipulated, namely, between the north-west tower on the river, down to the Knowl, and round the bend as far as the southern corner of the 'Bowling Green' wall. Anglers could use shrimp-boats, row-boats, punts, or fish from the river banks; they could use whatever baits they chose, big or little, but one only was to dangle from the end of each line. Crabs only were to be bagged; and numbers, not weights, were to count. Starting by pistol-fire at eleven, they were to down rods at one o'clock pistol-fire.

Sunday morning came in smiling; extra barrels of drink that had been laid in were early tapped; a huge crowd of sight-seers swarmed the quays and the 'Bowling Green' fore-front, and almost as numerous an army of anglers lined the quays, or sat expectant in the boats. Among the contestants figured wherrymen, smacksmen, gunners, poachers, smelters, and two or three score of landsmen.

At eleven every rod was out, the baits having already been attached. No sooner had these baits reached bottom than the crabs rushed at the lures. Up and down went the lines, the fishermen swinging them over the boats, or the boxes and buckets the quay-siders had provided as creels. As for the boats—the one-man crew troubled little about escapes, as the clustering crabs let go and fell safely on the floor-boards, to scuttle under them as they listed, or around the boat, looking for a loophole of escape, and finding none. The supply of victims seemed inexhaustible; ones and twos, fours and sevens, sometimes dozens at a haul on some of the larger baits were shaken off into the boats, whilst the shore anglers, jerking their victims upon the quay, were helped by numerous urchins to collect the runaway crabs.

As the easy-flowing flood tide meandered up-river the *scent* of the baits crossed the keen olfactory organs of crabs hundreds of feet upstream; the lower outsiders scuttling towards the baits, also attracted those above them, and the army of shellbacks followed them on into captivity. There was much loud chaffing, laughter, and cheering; and the excitement had reached its height when the stop-shot was fired. A short time was allowed to collect their captives—some clutching them by hand; others scooping them up in baler-scuppets; yet others using a dust-pan. The lively crabs caused much amusement by their endeavours, often successful, to escape; the quay-side was alive with those that managed to get out of boxes and buckets.

At one-thirty the competitors squared up on the open quay, keeping the crowd back, and making a space for the promoter, his officials, and umpires, and also for the quart, half-peck, and whole peck measures needed for the appraising of the chief catches. Shouts went up for the half-dozen winners, as the figures were read out; the first three prizes were given as follow: First prize, 1½ bushels of crabs, 3 bottles; second prize, 1 bushel, 2 bottles; third prize, 1½ pecks, 1 bottle. The other three prizes were of smaller moment.

Much laughter ensued when each lucky winner stepped forward, and mounted a fish-trunk, to exhibit his lucky bait. No. 1 exhibited a cow's udder which had formed so mighty and desirable a lure; the second winner displayed a still usable half bullock's-head; and the third a huge lump of bullock's tripe. What to do with the crabs was now the question; some of the less successful had turned their crabs adrift, to be rid of them, others had shot theirs back into the river, whither nearly all the rest instinctively shambled—save those which the boys were treating in no kindly manner. The 'Norwich Arms' was thronged for the rest of the day with excited debaters.

One of the most absurd and witless Breydonian jokes ever perpetrated dates back to the early 'eighties. Bob Flaxman the blacksmith had a great liking for monkeys; a deep-sea sailoring son had brought home, at various times, three or four of these animals. Old Jack, the hero of the punt-gun explosion, was long time his favourite—a badly-behaved, rascally Simian, without manners, good looks, and what was esteemed to be 'forecast', and was continually in trouble; an irresponsible, bad-tempered Bonnet macaque. From long usage of the warm cinders at the side of the forge fire, as cushion and couch, he was tousled and ragged of fur; he was allowed far too much liberty, and delighted the rough Breydoners with his uncouth mischiefs. Jacko one day sadly transgressed, and Flaxman was in two minds whether to drown the rascal in a sack or knock him on the head; but in the end gave him away to the landlord of the 'Apollo' tavern at the north end of the town, a house much favoured by greyhound owners, poachers, and shoulder-gunners.

Jack was chained to his tub, and kept in check, much to his dislike; but he gave as much amusement to the new circle of sportsmen as he had done to his former friends. It was not long before he had committed an almost unforgivable misdemeanour, and was relegated to the beer-barrel shed at the back, where he learned to relish the waste drippings from the tubs and pots, and drifted into very degraded habits. At length sickness overtook Jacko, and he died—like Napoleon at St. Helena, almost forgotten and unsung.

Now, Cadger Brown, who knew most of the members of sporting clubs and cliques beyond the Breydon pale, held confab. with the landlord, and for free drinks put him up to what he considered 'the greatest gag on record'. At this particular time there dwelt at the Workhouse an old Breydoner known as Jack, who had retired thither having finished his work on Breydon. Brown associated the two Jacks, and slyly gave it out that poor old Jack had pegged out, and he would let them know when the day came for the funeral. A waggish carpenter was taken into the beer-shed to measure the monkey for a little coffin, and when the receptacle was made laid the dead monkey, in its little white shirt, into it. Jack, in his new home, was carted up to a bedroom, and the blinds drawn 'out of respect'.

Cadger, the publican, and the carpenter kept their own counsel; and it was bruited abroad that the funeral of 'poor old Jack' would start from the 'Apollo' tavern, where, out of respect to a poor dead pal, he had been removed. Each mourner was to wear a top-hat, no matter how dilapidated, and as much black as he could manage to borrow. Around the hat was to be a band of *crêpe*, with a bow behind, and streamers to hang below it. At the time appointed there met outside and chatted sorrowfully a number of mourners, talking of Jack's exploits as a gunman and eel-catcher. Of course, a curious crowd collected to witness the funeral procession, not a very solemn assembly at that. The landlord called in all the principals, and treated them, helped by Cadger as a sort of waiter. The publican was very free with his beer, assuring them that he could not charge them *before the funeral*. They trooped in, and when they had imbibed as much as was discreet, or even a little indiscreet, the landlord asked if any of them would like to see the deceased brother before screwing him down. Most hesitated ; a bolder few went up and saw daubed in ink on a card :

BOB FLAXMAN'S MONKEY JACK

Two or three of the visitors laughed at the joke, but there was some terrible language distributed by the others—language not usually uttered at the obsequies of the departed. The joke got round among the company rapidly, and loud laughter greeted and followed the disgruntled mourners as they did their best to lose themselves ; and others who had taken undue advantage of the Freedom of the Barrels were helped into an oblivion that they did not much desire, but seemed too helpless to resist. It goes without saying that the publican had 'good houses' for the rest of the week.

My old Breydon friends, who spent their working hours in the slaughter of birds and the capture of fishes, naturally, like butchers who slay calves and lambs, became to an extent obtuse and indifferent to the sight of blood, although not necessarily relishing the taking of life wantonly. But their pleasures often reflected some indifference to pain and suffering that would be repellent to more sensitive natures. I have heard a sportsman describe how he had laughed at the antics of a poor wounded thing in its endeavours to escape, or to lift, itself normally again upon its little pinions. As an instance of this *numbness of heart* the following is an average example : some one in a Yarmouth row had reared seven tame ducks whose only bath seems to have been the puddles in the gutter hard by the pump.

Cadger Brown had ferreted up these wretched creatures when on his water-cress round, and had informed the landlord of the 'Bowling Green' that they were for sale. Jimmy Hurr and Cadger were commissioned to bring these unfortunates in a couple of hampers to the 'Green', where they were transferred to a chicken-run, and exhibited to the public. A brilliant idea had seized him—the landlord—who decided to get up a shooting-match on Breydon ; and competitors might enter for it by the payment of a shilling per shot. Cadger hunted up some flint stones for weights, and cut some lengths of cord for tethers. Quite a flotilla of punts and smelt-boats went up Breydon on the tide to the flats hard by the Big rond, when duck after duck was hauled out of the baskets, one end of a tether tied to its leg, the other being made fast to a stone for an anchor.

To find themselves to an extent free, the grubby-eyed, clung-feathered fowl were beside themselves with delight; they ducked, they flapped, they swam and shot about with great excitement, making but few attempts at flight, their dirty feathers becoming waterlogged from their water-frolics. The competitors were to shoot but one shot each at a bird, in rotation; any shoulder-gun was to be used, the distances to be at first sixty yards, and then at eighty yards. It took twenty-seven shots to settle the first five birds; and no less than sixteen shots to kill the sixth at a hundred yards; Quinton shot at the remaining bird, killing it. Quinton assured me that he had made up his mind to 'put the last one out of its misery'. He had watched the various shots, and found that the birds mostly ducked in the nick of time at the discharge of a gun. He had mentally judged the seconds between a dip and a rise, and also the direction in which the birds ducked and rose. The competitors seemed much to have enjoyed the sport; and the crowd that awaited them ashore gleefully discussed the sport and the narratives of prowess given by the slayers.

Now, with regard to the weight of lead spent in those forty-four shots, we shall find that, at an ounce and a half each charge, the sum total was 4 lbs. 2 oz. It would be absurd to even suggest the total weight of leaden shot dropped into Breydon during the past hundred years, but it must amount to many tons! Where they have gone, and whether they collect at a certain level, no one knows; but there must be a little 'gold-mine' of lead down deep in the ooze somewhere—so have said the old gunners to me.

The late Colonel Leathes, who at one time owned much of the land at Herringfleet, near Yarmouth, and who was exceedingly fond of wild-fowl- and snipe-shooting, on being questioned by a well-known sporting authority upon the subject of snipe-shooting, replied:

'You ask me about snipe. The best snipe-shooting manor I know of is "Whitecast", near Lowestoft, on Oulton Broad [the property of the late Mr. Nicholas Everitt]. Whitecast is only fifty acres—rather less, I think, but the marshes that go with it cover about a hundred and fifty acres.

'On Whitecast this bet has been won, namely, that in three square feet of ground, one spade deep (provided it is not on rotten land), you will find three ounces of shot, dig where you will. The fact is, fifty acres of this land has been shot over backwards and forwards for ages, and the whole surface of the ground is covered with shot. I know this bet was made and won.'

Before the building of the great railway bridge across the neck of Breydon, yacht sailing and racing was still a favourite pastime with some of the leisured townsfolk; and before the dolphins were erected on the Cobholm side of the water a row of stagings ran out from the wall, most of them forefronted by local yachts. When racing was on, a committee-boat was usually moored near the Half-mile Point; and excellent matches sailed over the miles of Breydon, making a gallant show. In the annual fixtures was given a place for a punt race; small prizes were given, mostly of a useful character, and were eagerly competed for by the puntsmen.

On one memorable occasion a crowd of nearly a score punts lay near the Knowl, within hail of the 'Bowling Green', their crews smoking and gossiping, awaiting the signal to run up sail. Cadger Brown, who had been idling on the Green with a few other sightseers, more particularly interested in the punt race, had an inspiration.

'Boy,' said he to a gunner, just over the wall, 'lend me yer—loaded gun! I'll show you and t'others suffin' funny—don't, I'm a fule.' A loaded gun was handed over, and Cadger made for a corner round the building that had a habit of producing very loud echoes; and some five or more minutes before the signal would be made to start the punt race, fired the gun. The noise of it was startling enough, but appeared to the competitors to have proceeded from the committee-boat.

Anyway, there was a terrible confloption among the men lolling in the punts, for no one was ready; a scramble was made to ship the little masts, to hoist sails, and away. But the boats were so intermixed in the hoisting of the sails, the swinging of the booms, and the muddling of the sheets that there was chaos for a few minutes; oars were thrust out to keep off other boats which were colliding and bumping, and supplemented by raucous oaths, made a perfect Babel. The farther boats drew away, the hindermost creeping after them. The committee-men on their boat were scandalized by the proceedings, and throwing up their arms, made violent signs for the men to stop, and to begin again at the proper time. These 'monkeyisms', as the Breydoners termed the movements on the starters' boats, were, so they said, mistaken for signs of encouragement. Finding it utterly useless to continue protesting, the committee wisely entered into the joke. When the leading punts came in matters were explained to them; but the suggestion of re-sailing the race met with no success; so to settle matters the committee accepted the situation.

Cock-fighting in this country at the present day is taboo; what little of it obtains is done on the quiet. It was undoubtedly a favourite sport all over our country, and was indulged in and encouraged even by royalty. Edward III winked at it, and Henry VIII, among certain additions to Whitehall, consented to the establishment of a cockpit. James I not only encouraged duck decoys, he delighted in two cock-fights weekly. Oliver Cromwell suppressed both kings and cock-fights. It became a favourite pastime for the lowest of characters, and no doubt led to many abuses. The breeding, feeding, training, and matching gave employment and diversion to many, and provided sport for a vastly greater crowd. In many Asiatic countries this ancient game still obtains: in South America even the clerics may be seen, to this day, parading the streets with a cock under each arm.

Norfolk had its cockpits, and its sporting circles. Even at Yarmouth we had cock-fights, at the 'Feathers Inn' the 'Duke's Head', and the old 'Dolphin', within a stone's throw of the 'Staff of Life', and the 'Lord Nelson'. In 1849 the law stepped in and made cock-fighting illegal. But it did not abolish the breed of fowl, nor wholly stamp out the sport, which continued to be indulged in occasionally, but clandestinely.

A virile old fellow-townsman, one Jack Thompson, in the 'sixties, was a grown man and a near neighbour of mine in the low back street then known as Charlotte Street; at the age of ninety-seven still remains one of my oldest friends. Until very recent years he was 'up to the neck' in pony racing, pigeon flying, and other forms of sport; he still loves to spin a yarn of his old fighting-cock days, when he bred some of the finest birds in the Eastern Counties. He assures me they had some rare fun on the Bowling Green, even after the law decreed cocking 'out of bounds', but the Green was so out of the way and sheltered, and the police of the past so few and friendly, that a case rarely came into public notice.

He has told me of a bird which he purchased off a country wheelwright at Hopton, just south of Gorleston, giving a shilling for it, that knocked out all comers in a stable situated within stone's throw of the parish church Thompson and several other sporting fellows were having a right royal time in his garden on one occasion when they were discovered by the police, but they had the ready wit to throw the birds over the wall to continue their scuffle in the next garden. Thompson's excuse was, when charged with the misdemeanour of ' practising cock-fighting ', that his bird had got out, and had flown over the wall to have a go at his neighbour's bird ; and so they decided to let them enjoy themselves and fight it out.

His confirmation of what I suspected allows the following cock-fighting story to be placed in the same sequestered spot on the Green, which was so snugly placed between walls and buildings and shaded by tall elms as to be practically ' police-proof '.

Sam W——y's hobby, and a paying one too, was the breeding and training of fighting cocks. He was, in my earlier days, a stout, pudding-faced old fellow, with a fringing of beard from ear to ear, that went under his chin like a strap of much-worn Palestine bearskin. He waddled in his walk, and had for his livelihood killed more calves than would fill a dozen railway brakes with veal, at the very lowest estimate. His blue butcher's apron he wore all day—probably slept under it at night ; I never saw him without it. Sam's pet hobby from childhood was the duck-wing grey strain of fowl. He managed to get his birds about, and travelling now and then beyond the county, to show the natives how the Yarmouth birds ' did it ', and his pets fought some noted battles. Sam was so jealous of his strain that he never sold a pure-bred egg, but ate those that were not used for sitting purposes ; he, however, crossed his game-birds with Dorkings, in order to provide himself with sitters, but sold their eggs freely enough. A certain doctor, who was great on the fowl fancy, hearing that Sammy possessed a magnificent bird, arranged with him (W——y) to pit his cock against that of a certain well-to-do sportsman's, the odds being a hundred pounds a side, W——y to be well paid in event of a win. The Diss man brought his birds—he brought two. On the day fixed Sam took his bird round in a sack, never once allowing it to be out of his sight, even when enjoying a superb lunch in Bessey's sanctum, which the doctor had provided.

An expert who was tending the Diss bird offered to fix the spurs on the other man's bird.

' No ! ' said our Sam, ' no man handles my fowl ', and taking the spurs out from his waistcoat pocket proceeded to fix them on his bird. The Diss bird was weighed against Sam's, just prior to this ; but when it was brought into the ring (it was

SAMMY'S FIGHTING COCK

hardly a pit) :

'Take that bird back ! ' said Sam, ' or no fight'll come off.' A larger and stronger bird had been substituted ; and Sam's practised eye had noticed the difference.

Matters being adjusted, the birds were placed in the area. The feints, dodges, and cunning of the fowls to get a first blow in, to the crowd were exceedingly funny ; some of them expressed an opinion that they ' sparred like scientific boxers '.

The red bird got the first cut in, knocking Sam's bird over, out of wind, but with no serious hurt. Time was given, and W——y saw that his pet had the benefit of every second. He tenderly stroked and ' comforted ' the bird. Then he stood him down, the cock merrily crowing defiance.

' All right, old sonny,' said Sam ; ' save that till you've won.' The Breydonian onlookers made sundry appreciative remarks, but Sam demanded silence. ' Don't take Jacob off his job,' he said.

Jacob was extremely deliberate, as if he knew his work, and was in no hurry to attack ; it was evident he did not intend to strike until he saw a fair opening. Then, as the other was about to strike, Sam's bird was at him with a lightning stroke, getting his spur well in front, tearing the other bird down almost from throat to breast, and the fight was at an end. The red cock died in a very few minutes.

The doctor shook Sam's hand, and placing in the palm of one a five pound note, remarked, 'I wouldn't have lost that match for five hundred pound.'

A short time after this episode Sam's gallant cock was entered for exhibition at a local show; but some evil-minded person, who had an interest in a rival bird, managed to get at it the night previous, and pulled out all the tail feathers, leaving them strewn around in the fowl-run. Sam gathered them up, and just before the judges reached the pen in which his famous bird was being exhibited placed them in with it. Explanations followed, when the judges, to their credit, and greatly to the chagrin of all rival competitors, awarded Sam first prize.

A less scientific contest took place some time after this between a well-bred cock and one of Jacob's half-bred sons, for ten shillings a side. The first round ended in favour of the smarter bird, which had been trimmed in the orthodox style; this seized its untrimmed opponent by the comb, and made a big ado in trying to get the spur into its rival. They had to be separated, the combed bird bleeding profusely. After a bit of washing and doctoring the birds again faced each other, but Jacob the second's dander was up; and giving the other bird a smashing blow, sent it clean into an open hamper lying in the way, and there it remained, acknowledging defeat, and determined not to accept another round.

Enough has been written in this chapter to bear out my contention that the Breydon men, on holiday occurrences, enjoyed a robust, and on occasion a barbarous, interlude of sport, and indulged in fun that was diverting, if it was not always ridiculous.

A rather queer story, bearing upon this point, which I have heard repeated until one is somewhat inclined to accept its authenticity, was told of one Jumbo Clay, a man of colour and a pedlar, whom I often met trudging from house to house, public and otherwise, with his basket of swag hanging by a strap from his shoulder. He had come to this country at the close of the War of Emancipation in the States. With him was, contemporary, a lean, nerve-broken, light-coloured African, of very gentle manners, who had been injured by leopards in one of the menageries. With both I was passing friendly.

A certain amateur taxidermist (so the story ran) had obtained an ancient and dead pelican from a travelling show, where it had resided for something like twoscore years, being its oldest inhabitant. The skin was ‘ set up ’, the carcase, with true Breydonian pleasantry, had been dressed up to resemble a Christmas turkey, and was kept wrapped in a white cloth, to await Jumbo's accustomed call at his favourite pub. In came the negro, and was proffered his usual measure, and a pair or two of leather laces were sold to the jokers sitting at a game of cards.

‘ Jumbo,’ said the landlord, ‘ I've got a nice fat turkey for you and the old girl (producing the bird) ; it'll make a nice Christmas joint for you two.’ The jokers concurred on seeing the bird laid upon the counter.

‘ T'anks, mass'r—a hundred tanks ; de Lord bress yer, Mass'r Beckett ! If dat an't de powerfullest tukkey I eber see.’ And off he strode home with it, to hand in to ‘ de l'il ole yeller gal dat fowl ’.

How the dinner progressed Beckett did not get to know until several days after, for Jumbo religiously had kept away from the house. When they met again Beckett asked Jumbo how things had got on at Christmastide.

‘ Wal,’ said the negro, ‘ dat yer tukkey was trash ! Dat mus' ha' bin de grandfadder ob all de 'lil tukkeys as eber was. Him mus' hab come out ob de Noes Ark. De missis, she bake dat tukkey, but it was dat dam tough she couldn't get de knife

in tut ; she stabbed an' chopped it ; den she biled, and par-biled it—still no dam use. So we put de debil on de fire for a Christmas chump.'

Beckett, who had had an old cormorant hanging for some days at the back, which some one had shot, was prompted to ask Jumbo if he would like another turkey :

'Tukkey, Mass'r Beckett !' said Jumbo, shaking his head. 'No, t'anks, mass'r. I'se don't kyer to hab no mo' tukkeys ob dat sort—unless you lemme see dat yer tukkey wid de feet, de hid, an' de tail on !'

INDEX